BLOODY RED TABS

BLOODY RED TABS

General Officer Casualties of the
Great War 1914–1918

Frank Davies & Graham Maddocks

Pen & Sword
MILITARY

First published in Great Britain in 1995 by
LEO COOPER

Reprinted in this format in 2014 by
Pen & Sword Military
an imprint of
Pen & Sword Books Ltd
47 Church Street
Barnsley
South Yorkshire   S70 2AS

ISBN 978 1 78346 237 7

Printed and bound in England
by CPI Group (UK) Ltd, Croydon, CR0 4YY

Pen & Sword Books Ltd incorporates the imprints of
Pen & Sword Aviation, Pen & Sword Family History, Pen & Sword Maritime,
Pen & Sword Military, Pen & Sword Discovery, Wharncliffe Local History,
Wharncliffe True Crime, Wharncliffe Transport, Pen & Sword Select,
Pen & Sword Military Classics, Leo Cooper, Remember When,
The Praetorian Press, Seaforth Publishing and Frontline Publishing

For a complete list of Pen & Sword titles please contact
PEN & SWORD BOOKS LIMITED
47 Church Street, Barnsley, South Yorkshire, S70 2AS, England
E-mail: enquiries@pen-and-sword.co.uk
Website: www.pen-and-sword.co.uk

Dedicated to the memory of
Flight Lieutenant William George Davies
158 Squadron Royal Air Force
Killed in action, Normandy, 18 July, 1944.

As a child he believed that his father,
Sergeant John Davies, K.S.L.I.,
was a General in the Great War.

CONTENTS

ACKNOWLEDGEMENTS

The authors wish to acknowledge the help received from the following in the compilation of this work:

Tom McDonough for his many years of support and research at the Picton Library, Liverpool.

Gerald Gliddon, Peter Kinnear, Peter Liddle, Alf Peacock, Graham Roberts and Derek Sheard for their assistance.

Colonel H. J. Lowles, C.B.E., The Worcestershire & Sherwood Foresters Regiment, for permission to use a photograph of Gilbert Holiday's drawing of Brigadier-General Grogan, V.C.

Mr Timothy Vickers, Librarian, Prince Consort's Army Library, Aldershot, for permission to use the library for research and for the help received from him and his staff.

The Trustees of the Liddell Hart Centre for Military Archives, King's College, University of London, for permission to quote from the Liddell Hart papers.

The staff of the Public Record Office, Kew. Crown copyright material in the Public Record Office is reproduced by permission of the Controller of Her Majesty's Stationery Office.

The Public Record Office is now named: The National Archives. All extracts identified as PRO should now be referred to as TNA.

Every attempt has been made to trace the copyright of several illustrations in this book. Where it has not been established the author can only hope that anyone who can prove that they do hold such a copyright should get in touch with the publishers.

PREFACE

The idea for this book first came about on the Somme in 1989. Although we had travelled together on the Western Front many times by then, it was on a visit to Warloy-Baillon Communal Cemetery and Extension that we first thought about it seriously. We were standing by the grave of 'Inky Bill' – Major-General Ingouville Williams, C.B., D.S.O., who had been Frank's father's brigade commander in 1914, when he had served with the 1st Battalion The King's Shropshire Light Infantry. As we looked at the headstone, a thought crossed Frank's mind which he soon put into words: 'I wonder how many generals were killed and wounded in the Great War?'

This led to discussion on the topic and we had to admit that we just did not know the answer to the question, nor did we know of any published work which dealt with it. On our return home we searched in vain for anything that would give us what we sought, but the only books which dealt with generals directly were those which attacked either their competence or the 'fact' that they were never close enough to the front line to put themselves in danger. We already knew that this latter was untrue as by then we had seen enough generals' graves, purely by chance, on the Western Front alone, to know that more than a few of them *were* killed serving in the front line. However, we were also aware that the public's perception of Great War generals was that they were always far behind the lines in the safety and comfort of their châteaux.

As a result, we first embarked on a programme of research which would discover exactly how many generals were killed, wounded or taken prisoner during the course of the Great War. To emphasize our point, we disregarded those who had died from causes other than from enemy action or whilst not on active service near or in the front line. As the numbers began to grow, so did our incredulity and we began to wonder why anyone could ever have thought that the generals were not there.

This made us wonder just how such an ill-conceived myth had ever occurred and, even more so, how it had manged to endure for the best part of 75 years. It was not long before we decided that our findings were so dramatic that they had to be written down for all to see, – not *just* to

xi

'put the record straight', but to restore justice to the memory of senior officers who could not 'fight back' after so many years. At the same time, we decided that it would not be our brief to decide whether or not the British generals of the 1914–1918 War were more or less competent than those of our allies or their enemies. Although we had already formed our own opinions on this subject, many more knowledgeable and erudite authors than ourselves had debated the issue over many years, with so many conflicting views and conclusions.

The facts are indisputable, however, and are not confined to any one battle or period of the war. The number of casualties amongst general officers, which includes those who were killed, died of wounds, died during front-line service, were wounded (including gassed) or were taken prisoner, should impress all but the extremely bigoted or those with totally closed minds. There were 10 casualties in 1914, (the conflict did not begin until Austust), 47 in 1915, 48 in 1916, 51 in 1917 and 76 in 1918. The total of 232 casualties includes eight generals who were wounded twice.

The biographies of them all are set out in this book and show unstinting service to Crown and Empire and unbelievable bravery in the face of the enemy in many foreign campaigns, skirmishes and wars. It is our belief that we have discovered all those who became casualties, but in such a work, entailing such a vast amount of study in an area which has never been fully researched before, it is possible that we have missed some. If this is the case, we would be grateful for their details.

It is our earnest wish that three-quarters of a century after the end of the Great War the record *will* be put straight at last and it is our most earnest hope that from now onwards, when the poppy petals fall at the Service of Remembrance in the Albert Hall each November, people will realize that some of them fall for generals.

Frank Davies and Graham Maddocks
August 1994

CHAPTER 1

Châteaux Generals – The Enduring Myth, And Its Origins

The Myth

In 1990 a Hull teacher, Barrie Barnes, published a book, *This Righteous War*, about the 'Hull Pals' – the 10th to 13th Battalions of The East Yorkshire Regiment and their record in the Great War. In its preface the Member of Parliament for Hull East and now Deputy-Leader of the Labour Party, John Prescott, stated:

> 'Senior officers well behind the enemy lines (sic) seldom felt the conditions of horror, or the bitter consequences of their own orders, ignored the growing list of casualties and enforced a barbaric discipline which saw the shooting of shell-shocked soldiers.'[1]

Even if one allows for the fact that Mr Prescott presumably meant 'Senior officers well behind *our own* lines', it is inconceivable that, so recently as 1990, such a well placed person should still continue to propagate such untruths.

Mr Prescott's opinion was hardly published in isolation, however, nor was his bland statement ever challenged for its lack of accuracy, probably as it largely agreed with the popular perception, or more correctly misconception, in the minds of the general public, of the conduct of senior British officers in the Great War.

In similar vein, in an edition of the Merseyside newspaper 'The Liverpool Echo', published to commemorate the 75th anniversary of the Battle of Passchendaele, journalist Peter Grant stated quite gratuitously and without real relevance to his subject matter:

> 'There was the extraordinary Christmas when in No Man's Land the war ceased among the ordinary soldiers for festivities. When Tommy exchanged a Christmas tree with Fritz – when beer was drunk and no one wanted to resume the fighting.
>
> 'Then the generals, miles away in the next town's hotel and

amid the clinking of glasses, ordered the troops to attack. Lions led by donkeys.

'When people like Commander Haig declared in his cosy room that they should continue "over the top – regardless of loss".'[2]

Apart from the appalling English, if one presumes that Mr Grant was referring to the 1914 Christmas Truce, he is also appallingly inaccurate. For a start, Haig was not the Commander of the British Army in December, 1914, and it is most unlikely that British soldiers exchanged Christmas trees with the Germans, even if they might have drunk beer with them! However, like John Prescott, it is in his judgement of all senior British officers of the war that Mr. Grant, in three short paragraphs has done his best to keep fuelling one of the greatest British myths of the twentieth century.

Unhappily there are many, many more such examples to choose from, although one might have expected that the authors of both the above extracts might have been in a position to check the true facts before committing their opinions to print. They were probably steered towards these conclusions, however, by the media in general, who have also done much to perpetuate the myth, both on the large and the small screen.

Who will not have seen the scurrilous 1960s film *Oh! What a Lovely War*, or the equally reprehensible and more recent B.B.C. production *Blackadder Goes Forth*? Both of these outrageously lampoon generals and Staff officers to a level that borders on the defamatory without any attempt whatsoever to present a balanced view or even a truthful one – all in the doubtful name of entertainment and comedy. Humour is one of the oldest and most long-lasting weapons in the media's armoury and it is unfortunate that many modern opinions of the Great War were first formed from these sources, in some cases no doubt, quite subliminally. Perhaps what is most amazing, however, is that more than 75 years after the signing of the Armistice, these opinions remain largely unchallenged although it would never have been too difficult to challenge them, for the true facts have always been available.

Thus, the popular perception of British general officers of the Great War is that they were all incompetent butchers, uncaringly consigning men to certain death from châteaux far from the front line, where they skulked in splendid luxury, with polished boots, eating caviare and drinking champagne and having neither conception nor care of the true conditions suffered by the men in the trenches.

This, then, is the myth and, whilst it is not the purpose or scope of this book to discuss in detail the *competence* or otherwise of the generals and their staffs, it might be worth noting, at this stage, the opinions of just two people who have had far more reason to pursue the truth than the sensationalist and often ignorant media.

The respected historian and author John Terraine in his book *The Smoke and the Fire* makes this point:

'It is a simple historical fact that the British Generals of the First World War, whatever their faults, did not fail in their duty.

'It was not a British delegation that crossed the lines with a white flag in November 1918.

'No German Army of Occupation was stationed on the Thames, the Humber or the Tees.

'No British Government was forced to sign a humiliating peace treaty.

'The British generals had done their duty. Their Army and their country were on the winning side. That is the only proper, the only sensible starting point for the examination of their quality.'[3]

A similar view was expressed by a former soldier, Sergeant W. Wilson of the 2nd Royal Welch Fusiliers, in the book *Cheerful Sacrifice* written about the Battle of Arras in 1917. He states:

'Let sleeping dogs lie. The generals are all dead now and it is noticeable how most critics waited until they were dead before tearing them to pieces. I believe that our generals were the best and did their job to the best of their ability. After all we did win the war, didn't we?'[4]

However, the whole focus of this book is to dispel the myth that the generals were never there and to do this it is first necessary to discuss where they *should* have been.

Should They Have Been in the Front Line?

During the Great War senior officer rank in the British Army, in descending order, was: field marshal, general, lieutenant-general, major-general and brigadier-general, although in simple terms all of them (except field marshals) might be referred to as 'general'. Although a major is a higher ranked officer than a lieutenant, a major-general ranked lower than a lieutenant-general because his rank was originally titled sergeant-major-general. A field marshal, who kept his rank and entitlements until his death, was virtually an honorary rank, given for long or distinguished service or as a diplomatic distinction to a foreign notable. For instance, Kaiser Wilhelm II was a field marshal in the British Army in 1914. Sir Douglas Haig, however, was promoted field marshal a year after becoming Commander in Chief of the Army on the Western Front.

Full general was usually the highest active rank in the Army, held by the Chief of the Imperial General Staff after December, 1915, and also by most army commanders. An army was essentially a command structure covering an identifiable area of military operations, usually containing three or more corps. A lieutenant-general commanded a corps, which was made up of three or more divisions which were serving in a particular area of the line. A major-general commanded an infantry or cavalry division which, after 1915, consisted of specific divisional troops (artillery, engineers, transport, medical services etc.,) and three brigades of infantry or four brigades of cavalry. The composition of both these types of brigades altered later in the war. The lowest rank of general officer, the brigadier-general, commanded a brigade of troops whose composition varied according to its type – i.e. cavalry, infantry, artillery etc.

Infantry brigades consisted of headquarters and four (three after February, 1918) battalions of infantry. In 1914 there were nine field marshals, 19 generals, 28 lieutenant-generals, 114 major-generals and 180 brigadier-generals, but by 1918 the massive expansion in the British Army had increased these numbers to eight field marshals, (by this time the Kaiser had been stripped of his rank) 29 generals, 47 lieutenant-generals, 219 major-generals and 600 brigadier-generals.

Thus, as we have seen, officers of general rank commanded units of brigade strength and above and, as such, their job was not to be in the front line at all; they were too valuable to waste. John Terraine, in *The Smoke and the Fire*, quotes Lieutenant-Colonel C.F. Jerram, G.S.O.1 of the 46th Division as stating:

> 'Why didn't you and I and our generals go up and take charge? – See for ourselves and give necessary orders? – What the hell use would we have been? The ONLY place where it was possible to know what was going on was at the end of a wire, with its antennae to Brigades and Artillery.'[5]

Nevertheless, senior officers, no doubt acting with the noblest of intentions, put themselves in harm's way when they had no need (or no right) to, and sometimes suffered the consequences. Even the Commander in Chief of the British Army, Sir John French, at the Battle of Loos, was not immune from such a course of action:

> 'Sir John left St Omer on 24 September, the eve of the battle, and drove to a forward command post near Lillers, less that 20 miles behind First Army's front. His ability to influence the battle from this point was decidedly limited. He was connected to Robertson's room at GHQ by telephone, but there was no direct phone link with First Army headquarters at Hinges. Moreover, Sir John took with him only a couple of his personal staff, leaving all the bustling apparatus of GHQ far behind him.'[6]

Later, on 25 September, at a critical stage of the battle, he was far from where he ought to have been, and, after touring the casualty clearing stations up at the front, described later what he saw:

> 'Dead, dying and badly wounded all mixed up together. Poor fellows they bear their pain gloriously and many of them gave me a smile of recognition.'[6]

At this stage of the battle no one could find him because he was so far forward and a critical decision which might have brought a great victory was delayed for three hours. Thus, there is no doubt that he would have been of much more value back at GHQ where he would have been better able to control what was left of the battle. In fact this episode finally finished French's career and six weeks later he was replaced by Sir Douglas Haig – proof positive that senior officers do not belong in the front line.

Some of his generals and Staff officers were not quite so fortunate, however. On the first day of the battle, 25 September, Brigadier-General Bruce was captured and his Brigade Major, Captain Buchan, was killed when the Germans overran his forward position. The next day Brigadier-General Nickalls was killed, and the following day Major-General Capper died of wounds received in an assault on the German positions, Major-General Thesiger and two Staff officers, Lieutenant Burney and Major Le Motée, were killed and Brigadier-General Pereira was wounded. On 1 October Brigadier-General Pollard was wounded, on 2 October Major-General Wing and his A.D.C., Lieutenant Tower, were killed by a shell near the front line and the following day Brigadier-General Wormald was killed near Vermelles whilst supervising the clearing of the late battlefield. Thus, in the space of nine days, eight generals were lost. It would certainly have been better for them had they carried out the popular myth and stayed in their châteaux.

> 'Three divisional generals killed – Capper, Wing and Thesiger – and one brigadier a prisoner![7] Such losses in the higher ranks are hardly to be matched in our history. To equal them one has to go back a hundred years to that supreme day when Picton, De Lancy, Ponsonby and so many others died in front of their troops upon the field of Waterloo![8]

It is not difficult to see what motivated them, however. The generals were all 'red-blooded' soldiers who had served their country for many years in many campaigns. They were not the 'skulkers' that popular myth would have us believe. Four of the Loos generals had been wounded in previous actions and certainly knew what life under fire was like. They were all in the front line because they believed that they could help the morale of the men by their presence and help press home the attacks to success. They and their Staff officers certainly paid the price for their actions and the British Army paid an even heavier price in terms of lost experience and

5

lost leadership. Nevertheless, they should not have been there – they *should* have been in their châteaux.

After Loos, and its losses, the issue of the châteaux generals should have been resolved for once and for all! Tim Travers in his book *The Killing Ground* quotes quite clearly from the papers of Lieutenant-General Sir Aylmer Haldane, who was G.O.C. 3rd Division at the time:

> 'The reasons that GHQ Staff did not visit the front in 1916 and 1917 seems to be partly because Haig had decreed in 1915, as GOC 1st Army, "that no staff officer was to go nearer to the trenches than a certain line." This was because of the danger involved for difficult-to-replace Staff officers. This order appears to have originated in October 1915 in GHQ under Sir John French who, after three of his divisional Generals had been killed, said that senior officers should not visit the front.'[9]

This is almost certainly the basis of a communication, a copy of which is in the Public Record Office, dated 3 October, 1915, and is quoted in 'Stand To!' No. 33:

> 'To: 1st Army
>   2nd Army
>   3rd Army
>   Cavalry Corps
>   Indian Corps
>
> Three divisional commander have been killed in action during the past week. These are losses which the Army can ill afford, and the Field Marshal/C in C desires to call attention to the necessity of guarding against a tendency by senior officers such as Corps and Division Commanders to take up positions too far forward when fighting is in progress.
>
> signed R Robertson, Lt. Gen
Chief Gen Staff
GHQ, 3 Oct 1915'[10]

Thus, after October, 1915, any general or staff officer who remained behind in his château was actually acting *under orders* and for the most part could have lived out the war in complete safety, immune from virtually every enemy attack apart from aircraft and extremely long range guns. The facts, however, would argue that this was not the case.

Wartime Attitude to Generals Within the Army

Staff officers, with their red tabs and their immaculate uniforms, came in for a lot of criticism from front-line soldiers of the Great War, even if a lot of this criticism was not actually justified. However, one can not blame the criticizing soldiers totally either, for they merely resented what they saw – they had no conception of the work carried out by the Staff and their actual rôle in the prosecution of the war. In fact it is probably true that few soldiers ever had any conception about the war in any other place than on their own immediate section of front and then probably only on a limited level. Many soldiers regarded the whole of the western front as 'France', and made no distinction between the French and Belgian battlefields. Furthermore, trench warfare tended to intensify their sense of isolation and engendered a spirit of comradeship that was very insular.

Infantrymen would identify with their own section, platoon and company and perhaps at the top end of their loyalty, with their own battalion within the regiment. Most would not identify beyond that and would not specifically see themselves as part of ***th Brigade or **st Division, hardly ever * Corps and never Army, although they would naturally know to which of these higher units they belonged. Apart from inspections in England or on the march on the western front, they would not normally come into contact with generals at all in their own immediate area of the front. As a result, although their lives were ultimately in the hands of the 'brass', they would have seen very little of them – they just knew that they were there. Their loyalties would be to their comrades and their units – for the most part made up of men from their home towns and areas and they would almost certainly resent anyone outside this structure – especially a senior officer.

British society was much more hierarchical in those days and based much more on the class system which prevailed at the time, and the Army echoed this system fairly closely. Regular soldiers would have accepted this without demur, but for soldiers of the Territorial Force and New Armies it must have been difficult to understand. Perhaps soldiers from regiments which recruited from predominantly rural areas would have been more used to the idea of a local landowner with unlimited power – someone who controlled their immediate lives but with whom they had little contact – and thus they would have had no problem in accepting a general in the same position. Men recruited from the industrial areas, however, would almost certainly have regarded senior officers in the same light as industrial bosses. There would have been definite respect for them as their hierarchy, but also the suspicion that exists between any group of people who depend upon each other, but do not come into regular contact.

This is not to say that there was necessarily any resentment in their attitudes, but merely that there was a distance between them which could never be breached. The difference in life style between soldiers and ordinary officers was wide enough, in any case, and the Army did little to alter this situation. The fact that each officer, even of subaltern rank, had

7

his own servant or batman sought to keep the gulf as wide as possible. They would never have mixed in civilian life and it often came as a great shock to soldiers and officers alike to find out that they actually got on fairly well with each other in the trenches. They would certainly never have expected to.

Even among officers, however, there was a structure which shut out those considered to be unsuitable material – whatever their worth to the Army and the war. The old joke about wartime officers being referred to as 'Temporary Gentlemen' was not a joke at all; it was the way non-regulars were regarded. This was exemplified by the fact that, throughout the war, there were virtually no promotions to general rank from anything but the old Regular Army. Thus, of the worthy majors and lieutenant-colonels from the old Territorial Force of 1914, few ever made general rank no matter how good or successful they might have been, not even after four years' wartime experience.[11] These ranks were reserved almost exclusively for Regular Army officers and, by contrast, any Regular Army second lieutenant who served with the B.E.F. in 1914 and survived until 1918 had an excellent chance of becoming a brigadier-general at least – whatever his talents and military competence might have been. Despite the fact that many New Army officers, by dint of their successes in civilian life, were among the best educated and experienced junior officers in the Army, they were similarly virtually debarred from ever achieving senior rank.

There was bound to be some resentment of generals even among officers, which the generals themselves would have done nothing to alter. They probably also regarded themselves as an élite and were happy to maintain the distance between themselves and the rest. This is illustrated classically with just one episode just before the battle of Messines Ridge in June, 1917. On 4 June, Sir Douglas Haig, Sir Henry Rawlinson and 133 others from the Fourth Army held an Old Etonian dinner at Péronne. While the rest of the Army was existing on basic rations in the front line, their senior officers were dining in unbelievable if not insensitive luxury on such items as *Poulet de Mans Rôti, Salade Japonnais, Sorbet à la Norbonne and Gateau Etonian*, just a few miles away.[12]

Not that this was unusual of course. Senior officers in all previous wars had enjoyed such luxuries and then gone on to win great victories and not lost the confidence of their men.

> 'Drake in his tiny ship found room to take massive silver plate and even musicians when he set out to sail round the world. Marlborough campaigned 'in state' and was no worse a General for such a weakness. Nearly two centuries later Buller was living in the field in the greatest of comfort, yet popular belief in his competence was not shattered thereby.'[13]

It is probable that junior officers and other ranks alike felt no resentment towards their senior officers – just a distance, both physically and metaphorically. This made it easier at a later time, however, to propagate the myth that the generals were never among them.

This theory applies mainly to the Western Front, however, because in other theatres of war, such as Gallipoli, Palestine, Italy and Mesopotamia there were no châteaux for unworthy generals to skulk in anyway, even had they wished to. During the Gallipoli campaign, at least in the early phases, most senior officers had access to floating châteaux in the form of battleships of the Royal Navy, but these were certainly not immune from attack, and in any case the Gallipoli generals and Staff officers obviously did not rely on them, as the casualty lists prove. Further evidence that some at least shared a more rigorous existence alongside their troops on the Peninsula is provided by the famous set of photographs of Lieutenant-General W.R. Birdwood swimming in the sea off Anzac Cove.

Perhaps one accurate example of a château general exists from the Gallipoli campaign, however. There is no doubt that the Suvla Bay operation of August, 1915, did not succeed because of the failure of Lieutenant-General F. Stopford to act decisively and issue operational orders in its initial phase. His 'château' in this case was the sloop *H.M.S. Jonquil* and he certainly stayed on board when he should have been directing operations on shore.

Thus, we are able to see that there *was* a distance between senior officers and the rest of the Army and as a result, it would have been easy to understand if senior officers had been attacked for staying behind the lines in their châteaux, by those men who felt distanced. The facts are, however, that senior staff did *not* stay in their châteaux, skulking behind the lines and there is virtually *no* evidence of note written *at the time* that there ever was any criticism of them that they did. In contemporary evidence in the form of letters home, records, reports, diaries etc., which have survived the war, there is no significant anti-generals feeling at all, beyond the natural 'us and them' style grumbling always directed at those who have power by those who haven't, nor is there any great evidence at the time of the 'châteaux generals' allegation.

One obvious exception to this, however, is the poetry of the anti-war poet Siegfried Sassoon whose works have often been quoted by the 'general bashers' down the years. He was possessed of exceptional personal courage in the front line and even acquired the nickname 'Mad Jack' from his men because of his exploits, but he became increasingly bitter as the war progressed. One of his best known poems is *The General*, which exemplifies his view of those officers and the Staff:

> '"Good-morning; good-morning!" the General said
> When we met him last week on our way to the Line.

Now the soldiers he smiled at are most of 'em dead,
And we're cursing his staff for incompetent swine.
"He's a cheery old card," grunted Harry to Jack
As they slogged up to Arras with rifle and pack.

*

But he did for them both by his plan of attack.'

Perhaps it was Sassoon's skill and articulation of his subject matter that have allowed his views to assume the importance that they have done ever since, or perhaps it was the publicity he received at the time. Who does not know, for instance, about his dramatic and lone anti-war gesture of tearing the ribbon of his Military Cross from his service tunic and tossing it into the River Mersey? However, maybe it is significant that his criticism of generals and Staff officers in the above poem is for their incompetence and not for their absence from the line. Furthermore, there is no great groundswell of evidence to prove that his anti-generals views were widely supported at the time among his brother soldier poets. Their main thrust was against the war itself and all its obscenity and was certainly not focused on the 'red tabs'.

If the myth did not exist during the war among those who might have had good reason to have believed it, what was its origin and when did it date from?

Post-War Politics

The answer lies initially in the feeling of anti-climax, depression, sense of loss, futility and economic depression which follows any war. Returning soldiers were unprepared for the numbness and sadness that pervaded all walks of life in post-war Britain. They were probably as unaware of the war-weariness at home by 1918 as the civilian population were as ignorant of the true conditions they had endured at the front. Both soldiers and civilians alike tried to hide what they both knew to be true from each other. Soldiers on albeit brief leaves would never tell their loved ones the true horrors of the 20th Century mechanized mincing-machine war and spared them the details of what they endured. This is borne out even by letters of condolence written about fallen comrades. They were nearly always along the same lines: 'He was shot through the head and died instantaneously. He did not suffer at all and looked so peaceful as we buried him in a pretty little cemetery behind the lines.' The truth would nearly always be somewhat different and a lot more obscene, and as so many similar letters appeared in the newspapers, even the most idealistic of civilians could have worked out the truth for themselves, – but somehow they preferred not to. Similarly, civilians wanted to make the leaves of their loved ones as happy as possible and lived with them in a fantasy world of fun and jollity which concealed the horrors and fears which lurked within them, all the time their menfolk were away. Ironically, these fears were probably fuelled most of all by being kept in ignorance of the true course and progression of the war.

When the war was finally over, the euphoria of victory and the happiness of homecomings gradually began to give way to a terrible sense of loss and sorrow and the nation was numbed into a collective grief for those that had not returned and for a way of life that would never return. When the realization of the sheer numbers of dead gradually dawned on the population they began to ask what had happened and wanted to know why so many men had made 'the supreme sacrifice' to achieve victory and peace. The idealism that had made so many join the Colours in the first place gave way to disillusionment, especially when the 'Land Fit for Heroes' that they had been promised was for so many merely an empty shell. The natural recession which follows any war meant that for many the reward for their endeavours and horrific struggles was a decade and more of unemployment and the three and a half million war wounded were a ubiquitous and constant reminder of suffering, even to the most determined of those survivors and bereaved who wanted to forget. Many former soldiers just could not come to terms with post-war Britain and recalled the old days of happiness and mourned deeply for the comrades they had lost.

Gradually sadness and disillusionment gave way to anger and a determination to blame someone – anyone, for their lost youth, their lost opportunities and their lost comrades. Surely, they argued, someone must be to blame for what had happened and it certainly wasn't them. The most obvious target was those who had been in command – the generals. By the mid 1920s virtually all of the wartime generals were no longer in prominence and were not in a position to argue their case, but the politicians were still in powerful positions, were still ambitious and were still able to defend their own war records, in the most polished and articulate of ways. Some of them were more than happy to blame the generals for all the things that had gone wrong in the war who then suddenly became the scapegoats in the minds of the general public for a wide range of wartime tragedies from excessive losses to poor leadership and incompetent strategies. The public was happy to have someone to blame, and as the generals for the most part were not around any more to argue, they suddenly became the ogres of the war, not the heroes that they had traditionally been.

For many ex-servicemen it was an easy step to take, especially in the 1920s when socialism was growing fast and there was more than a hint of revolution in the air. Before 1914 few men had ever even left their villages or towns and many had a narrow and very insular outlook on a variety of topics and were mostly content with their traditional place in society. If the war had done nothing else, it had exploded their parochial views and expanded their minds and to many the spectre of revolution which had swept across Europe following the Russian Revolution of 1917 beckoned them with possibilities of power they could never have dreamed of before the war. New ideas widened the gulf between the social classes and lack of changes in their lot following the hope of the immediate post-war years fostered an even bigger 'us and them' attitude than had existed before.

They were more than happy to accept that the generals, whom they had never really understood anyway, were in actuality to blame for all those things about the war which made them feel at best uneasy, and at worst extremely angry. Certainly by the time of the general strike of 1926, maybe with more than just a hint of the politics of envy, and a deep-seated need to blame *someone*, the generals had become their scapegoats. But they must have been given a lead and a direction for this unease and anger by someone, and that someone is almost certainly that great political master of duplicity, David Lloyd George.

With that perspicacity for which he was justly famous, even before the war had ended, he began to dislodge any blame for the country's battle casualties from himself and the government, even though, in a democracy, the War Cabinet was ultimately responsible for any military strategy undertaken by its generals. He also realized that when a country is winning a war it will accept virtually any losses to 'get the job done', but after every victory comes the reckoning and he wanted to distance himself from the appalling figures which he knew would shock the nation when they slowly became aware of their enormity.

However, the real assassination job came in 1933 with the publication of his *War Memoirs*.[14] With an incredible attack on virtually all the senior staff (he excluded a few) which more than bordered on the defamatory, he actually stated that the generals were lacking in intellect and ability and it was only the politicians and the civilian population that had saved the country from defeat. These extracts from just one page illustrate the point:

'In the most crucial matters relating to their own profession our leading soldiers had to be helped out by the politicians. . . . They did not possess the necessary understanding of the probable character of the War to foresee that it would be a war which would consume a prodigious quantity of shot and shell. They preferred shrapnel to high explosive because the former was more useful in the Boer War. What they provided was on the assumption that the War would be conducted on the open field. When it developed into a war of deep digging they did not realise that in order to demolish those improvised ramparts it was essential to equip an army with thousands of guns of a calibre heavier that any yet trundled into the battlefield. . . . They did not realise that the machine-gun and the hand-grenade would practically take the place of the rifle.'[14]

Lloyd George fails to mention in the above extract that it was the politicians who ordered the Army to defend France and Belgium in 1914 and not give another inch of their soil away to the enemy. He also fails to mention that it was a political decision to defend Ypres, for instance, not a military one, but one nevertheless, that would consign a generation of Britain's best to the slaughterhouse of the dreaded Salient. No senior soldier – not even the most incompetent – of the type that Lloyd George vilifies would have defended Ypres, ringed as it was on three sides by high ridges, when the hills of the Flanders Plain lay just a few miles to the rear, but the politicians did. Lloyd George goes on to say:

'Politicians were the first to seize upon the real character of the problem in all these respects and it was they who insisted on the necessary measures being taken – and taken promptly – in order adequately to cope with it. It was politicians who initiated and organised these measures. In doing so, at each stage they had to overcome the rooted traditions, prejudices and practices of military staffs. It was politicians who insisted upon the importance of providing sufficient and suitable transport facilities behind the line on a great scale in order not only to bring up supplies, but to increase the mobility of the Army along the whole front. It was civilians, chosen by politicians who reorganised and developed these facilities. It was politicians who foresaw that any attempt to break through the immense fortifications thrown up by the enemy on the Western Front would involve enormous carnage and a prolongation of this destructive war. It was they who urged the finding of a way round on those vulnerable fronts. It was politicians who urged the importance of making the best use of the magnificent and almost inexhaustible fighting manpower in Russia and the Balkans by providing them with the necessary equipment to play their part in attacking the enemy on his Eastern and Southern Fronts. It was amateurs who were principally responsible for the tank, easily the most formidable of our weapons, and it was they who invented and urged the use of one of the most serviceable machines of the War, the Stokes mortar.

'Let anyone read the history of the War with care and then conjecture what would have happened if the ignorant and cold-shouldered civilian had not insisted on coming to the rescue of the military in the discharge of those functions which in peace and war constituted an essential part of the duties and responsibilities of the latter.'[14]

Most of what Lloyd George states is obvious nonsense, even to any casual student of the history of the Great War, but firmly gives the message to the general public – the war was won by politicians such as he – with the help of civilians of course, and the senior soldiers actually got in the way and made things worse. By the time this ignoble work was published, of course, most of the Great War senior officers, including Earl Haig, were dead, and could not answer back from the grave.

However, this work is not concerned, as already stated, with the competence or otherwise of the generals – there were occasions when poor generalship *did* let the side down, as there were in all armies of the Great War. It is concerned with the allegation that senior officers and their staffs were never at the front and Lloyd George is undoubtedly the architect of this allegation as well, while never wasting an opportunity to vilify his arch opponent Haig:

> 'There was no conspicuous officer in the Army who seemed to be better qualified for the Highest Command than Haig. That is to say, there was no outstanding General fit for so overwhelming a position as the command of a force five times as great as the largest army ever commanded by Napoleon, and many more times as great as the largest army ever led by Alexander, Hannibal or Caesar. I have no doubt that these great men would have risen to the occasion, but such highly gifted men as the British Army possessed were consigned to the mud by orders of men superior in rank but inferior in capacity, who themselves kept at a safe distance from the slime which they had chosen as the terrain where their plans were to operate.'[14]

So there it is in one sentence – the idea that gifted men were never allowed to come to the fore – and by putting it this way he avoids the obvious attacks that might have been levelled at him by relatives of the fallen, because stupid generals ('men superior in rank but inferior in capacity') kept themselves safe far behind the lines and let the rest make attacks over territory that they never saw. That is not all, however. Lloyd George continues in this vein of vilification:

> 'The solicitude with which most Generals in high places (there were honourable exceptions) avoided personal jeopardy is one of the debatable novelties of modern warfare. Generals can not any longer be expected to lead their men over the top with pointing sword. But this departure from the established methods of leadership by personal example has gone too far. Admirals of a rank corresponding to that held by the Army Commanders took exactly the same hazards in action as the humblest sailor in the fleet. Beatty was a man of dauntless intrepidity who sought

14

danger. His flagship was hit in the Dogger Bank fight and it was just as liable to be blown up at Jutland as the *Defence* and the *Invincible*. The Rear-Admirals commanding these battle cruisers were killed when their ships were sunk. Jellicoe was not altogether free from personal peril in the Jutland mists. When a naval battle is fought G.H.Q. moves into the battle zone.'[14]

Lloyd George's message here is clear – Admirals were obviously braver because they led their ships (and, incidentally, their men) into danger and when things went wrong, they died – unlike the generals who survived far behind the lines. This assumption is flawed in two obvious areas. Firstly, there was no other way an admiral could behave and no other place behind the lines to which he could escape – he had to be on board his ship – and in any case, throughout the whole war only three officers of comparative naval rank were killed in action. These were Rear-Admiral Sir Christopher Cradock in command of *H.M.S. Good Hope* at the Battle of Coronel on 1 November, 1914, and the two mentioned by Lloyd George – Rear-Admiral Sir Robert Arbuthnot in command of *H.M.S. Defence* and Rear-Admiral Horace Hood in command of *H.M.S. Invincible*, both of whom were killed at the Battle of Jutland on 31 May, 1916. Secondly, generals did die and in much greater proportions than those of their naval comrades. By making these odious comparisons, once more Lloyd George is attempting to vilify the Army Commanders in the most divisive of ways. He continues to make the comparison, however, even though he must have known (or at least was in the best possible position to check the true fact) that his information was false:

'When High Admirals are not immune from the jeopardy of war there is no reason why exalted Generals should be sacrosanct. It is a new thing in war for generals who never set eyes on a position to command their soldiers to attack it without the slightest intention of placing themselves in any peril by leading the attack themselves, or even in viewing the ground before action or coming near the battle whilst it is proceeding to its deadly end. It is certainly a novelty in war that military leaders swathed in comfort and security should doom hundreds of thousands of their bravest soldiers to lodge for weeks in slimy puddles with Death as their fellow lodger without even taking the precaution of finding out for themselves what the conditions are or are likely to become. In the olden days when commanders so directed a battle that it ended in a shambles for their own army, they ran the risk of being themselves numbered with the slain.'[14]

Apart from the fact that these views totally contradict his earlier statement, 'Generals can not any longer be expected to lead their men over the top with pointing sword,' they also make the erroneous point that, as the generals never came into the front areas, they had no knowledge of the ground to be fought over. This is another area of myth that we shall explore later.

To end his chapter, which has such page headings as 'Generals Who Avoided The Line' and 'They Should Have Seen For Themselves', Lloyd George emphasizes his opinion once more that the generals never put their own lives in peril, while he continues to make the comparison (for obvious reasons) that all those who did die as a result of these strategies were gallant and brave men.

> 'No amount of circumspection can prevent war leading to the death of multitudes of brave men, but now that Generals are not partaking in the personal hazards of a fight, they ought to take greater personal risks in satisfying themselves as to the feasibility of their plans and as to whether the objectives they wish to attain are worth the sacrifice entailed, and whether there is no better way of achieving the same result at less cost of gallant lives.'[14]

Thus did the former Minister of Munitions and Prime Minister state his case without giving any examples to back up his claims or even examining the true facts which would have refuted his scurrilous allegations. It is therefore at David Lloyd George that the finger of accusation for the true origin of the myth must point.

How the Myth Grew

The idea of absentee generals had already begun to gain some credence by the time Lloyd George's book appeared in 1933 and it is possible that he might have read the opinions of Lieutenant-Colonel C.O. Head who discussed the matter in his book *A Glance at Gallipoli* published two years earlier:

> 'War with impersonal leadership is a brutal soul-destroying business, provocative only of class animosity and bad workman-ship. Our senior officers must get back to sharing danger and sacrifice with their men, however exalted their rank, just as sailors have to do. That used to be the British way, but unfortunately, there was a serious lapse from it in the late war.'[15]

Once Lloyd George's memoirs were published, however, and were given their natural prominence in the press, the floodgates of condemnation were opened and generals became 'open season' for all those disgruntled people who had an axe to grind or simply needed someone to blame for their losses and suffering in the war. For many, after 1918, there was a psychological need to put the blame somewhere and now Lloyd George had offered them the perfect place.

In his memoirs Lloyd George had paid especial attention to the Battle of Passchendaele and he had used the chapter on this subject to show how much he thought the senior officers were responsible for the terrible loss of life on the Ypres Salient for such little gain. Haig came in for particularly scathing attention, as did the apparent ignorance of the atrocious battle-field conditions at G.H.Q. So bad were these attacks that the British Legion leapt to Haig's defence in the press, as did many other senior officers of the time. There were many other letters, however, which agreed with the former Prime Minister.

Amazingly, in later editions of his memoirs, he printed in a special appendix, which he entitled 'Corroborative Evidence', over forty letters which he claimed to have received from former soldiers from a lieutenant-colonel down to private soldiers which apparently endorsed his opinions on the matter:

> 'Since the publication of the foregoing chapters, I have received a very considerable number of letters from officers and men who took part in the Passchendaele Campaign, who actually fought in and through the mud, and witnessed the protracted horror, and who corroborate my testimony as to the terrain and confirm my opinion as to the utter stupidity of prolonging the struggle under such impossible conditions. Every one of these correspondents endorses fully my gravest allegations. I reprint below some extracts from their letters, in order to refute certain criticisms which have appeared from other quarters.
>
> 'I refrain from giving the names, but should the authenticity of the letters be doubted or challenged, I feel confident I can obtain the authority of any writer to submit his name and the original letter to any responsible person who can be trusted. I have not received a single letter from any one who took part in the actual fighting at Passchendaele which contradicts any of my statements, or suggests that the picture which I have endeavoured to paint is an exaggerated one.'[16]

Presumably all those persons who disagreed with him and wrote to the press to say so could not be bothered to write to him directly and it is equally amazing that no one considered writing to him (or the press) on the topic before his book was written, considering that everyone agreed with him once it was in print. Nearly all of these 'corroborative' letters agree with his criticism of the policy of attacking over an impossible battleground, but only a few deal with the 'absentee generals' theme. What a number of them do allude to, however, is the beginning of the propagation of the most enduring part of the myth – which states that no senior general had any idea of the true conditions which the men had fought over at Passchendaele, as they never came close to the front line during the battle and were horrified when they eventually discovered what conditions had been like.

Lloyd George did not invent this one himself, however. Although he uses it in *War Memoirs*, he took it from the work of Basil Liddell Hart who first related the story in *The Real War 1914–1918*, which was first published in 1930, and enlarged and revised in 1934 and retitled *History of the World War 1914–1918*:

> 'Perhaps the most damning comment on the plan which plunged the British Army in this bath of mud and blood is contained in an incidental revelation of the remorse of one who was largely responsible for it. This highly-placed officer from General Headquarters was on his first visit to the battle front – at the end of the four months' battle. Growing increasingly uneasy as the car approached the swamp-like edges of the battle area, he eventually burst into tears, crying, 'Good God, did we really send men to fight in that?' To which his companion replied that the ground was far worse ahead. If the exclamation was a credit to his heart it revealed on what a foundation of delusion and inexcusable ignorance his indomitable 'offensiveness' had been based.'[17]

This story has been repeated many times since it first appeared, and most people accept its veracity without demur, and yet it too is largely a myth. It presumes that generals and Staff officers were totally ignorant of the conditions at the front because they never went there, yet even Lloyd George published an account from Haig's despatches of 25 December, 1917, which later appeared in a supplement to the *London Gazette:*

> 'The low-lying, clayey soil, torn by shells and sodden with rain, turned to a succession of vast muddy pools. The valleys of the choked and overflowing streams were speedily transformed into long stretches of bog unpassable except for a few well-defined tracks, which became marks for the enemy's artillery.... To leave these tracks was to risk death by drowning, and in the course of the subsequent fighting on several occasions both men and pack animals were lost in this way. In these conditions operations of any magnitude became impossible.'[18]

Lloyd George, of course, uses the date of this despatch to show that it was only after the battle was over that the Staff officers discovered the true nature of the battleground, which of course fits in well with the 'Good God, did we really send men to fight in that?' story.

However, as early as 1936, Duff Cooper in his book *Haig* stated:

'That war is a ghastly business and that war waged against so powerful an enemy as Germany can only be won at the price of fearful sacrifice, hideous suffering and wholesale slaughter, were facts that had been present to the minds of all, and often before the eyes of many of the officers at G.H.Q. during the last three years. They were not ignorant of the conditions in which the men were fighting. Six young officers of brigade-major rank were deputed to visit regularly the front line and to report to the General Staff on the state of the ground as well as on other matters. In addition, the General Officer Commanding Royal Artillery, the Engineer-in-Chief and the Quarter-Master-General had each a liaison officer whose duty it was to keep his chief informed of the effects of the weather upon the operations of their various branches. They in turn informed the Commander-in-Chief. The legend of the staff officer who wept when he saw the mud of Passchendaele is either apocryphal or does little credit to the nerves of the man who could not bear to see conditions concerning which he had already received full information.'[19]

More information about the incident only came to light in 1958, however, when Liddell Hart was persuaded to name the 'highly placed officer from General Headquarters'. In a January, 1958, edition of *The Spectator*, he named him as Lieutenant-General Sir Launcelot Kiggell, Haig's Chief of Staff. Kiggell had died in 1954, so Liddell Hart felt there was no justification for not releasing his name four years later.[20] This disclosure by Liddell Hart was obviously taken up by others, for in the same year it appeared in Viscount Montgomery's memoirs:

'There is a story of Sir Douglas Haig's Chief of Staff who was to return to England after the heavy fighting during the winter of 1917–1918 on the Passchendaele front. Before leaving he said he would like to visit the Passchendaele Ridge and see the country. When he saw the mud and the ghastly conditions under which the soldiers had fought and died, he was horrified and said: 'Do you mean to tell me that the soldiers had to fight under such conditions?' And when he was told that it was so, he said: 'Why was I never told about this before?'

'The fact that the Chief of Staff of the British Armies in Europe had no idea of the conditions under which the troops had to live, fight and die will be sufficient to explain the uncertainties that were passing through my mind when the war ended.'[21]

If such a person as Viscount Montgomery of Alamein was prepared to believe the story, without checking its truth, it is no wonder that it has assumed such magnitude as a popular myth. The fact remains, however, that the incident did not quite happen as it has been reported down the years, nor was Kiggell the 'highly placed officer from General Headquarters', although he could well have been present at the time. The matter is further confused by the famous novelist and dabbler in the occult, Dennis Wheatley. In his book, *The Time Has Come*, published in 1978, he related a completely new version of the famous incident in which a brigadier-general and a general decided to settle a disagreement:

> 'A Rolls was sent for; they drove up through Ypres and as far as they could in the direction of St. Julien. When they could go no further Sir Archibald Murray stared appalled at the endless sea of mud. Then he exclaimed, 'Can we really have been sending men to attack across this! And he burst into tears.'[22]

In Wheatley's version, which he claimed to have taken from a well researched American book, Sir Archibald Murray is the famous 'highly placed officer from General Headquarters'.

However, the matter continued to interest historians and the general public alike and was the subject of correspondence between members of The Western Front Association in 1990 in their journal, Stand To!, and among the information published was some offered by its esteemed Honorary President, John Terraine. He quoted the highly respected historian Professor Brian Bond, who knew Liddell Hart well, as saying in 1988:

> 'This often repeated anecdote must be treated with caution. Sir James Edmonds, the official historian of the 1914–1918 war, told this story to Captain B.H. Liddell Hart (then military correspondent of the *Daily Telegraph*) in 1927, but Edmonds was a notorious and not always reliable gossip and it is improbable that he actually witnessed Kiggell's alleged outburst.'

Professor Bond adds:

> 'It seems unlikely to me that he would have been so completely ignorant of battlefield conditions even if he had not seen them for himself. This story illustrates the tendency whereby appropriate anecdotes are transformed into historical fact despite the flimsiness of the evidence on which they are based.'[20]

Further correspondence revealed that, in a post-Second World War interview, Brigadier-General John Davidson, head of operations staff at G.H.Q at the time of the Battle of Passchendaele, stated that the weeping staff officer was himself and not Kiggell and that he had held his hands to his face to show he was dumb to enquiries and not to hide tears.[23] He does not state whether or not Kiggell was present at the time, however.

The notes for this interview, which took place on 21 April, 1945, between Davidson and G.C. Wynne, of the Historical Section, Official War Histories, are still in existence and include the following passages:

> 'His only comment was that some hint might be given of the difficulties of a staff officer in his own position in the circumstances, knowing that the campaign had to be continued, but being unable to give any reason to the multitude of angry questions.
>
> 'The weeping staff officer story in Lloyd George's book was due to his holding his hands to his face to show that he was dumb to enquiries and not to hide tears. He agreed, however, that as he alone knew the reason it was difficult to put such an explanation in an official history, and better that he should take up this matter himself with the official account as a background. He agreed that it was really too trivial a matter to worry about.'[24]

The same officer also wrote a letter to Sir James Edmonds, the Official Historian, in July, 1938, in which he included the following information:

> 'There is just one point – D.H. is always supposed not to have known or to have been misinformed as to the conditions (physical) in front. This really is bunkum – as not only did he get reports from his own general staff, but he talked to numerous Regimental Officers and saw and discussed affairs regularly with Btn. Commanders, Brigade and Divisional Commanders as well as Corps and Army Commanders.'[25]

Thus is the most common myth about the châteaux generals dispelled, but despite the passage of time, it is still believed today and often quoted. In fact, the *Sunday Telegraph* of 20 May, 1990, repeated the 'Did we send men' part of the myth but actually attributed the words to Haig! There are more examples of the propagation of the myth in other books throughout the six decades since Lloyd George first gave it so much prominence, but perhaps this story is the most enduring.

In the 1960s the whole debate about the generals was brought up again with the publication of Alan Clark's *The Donkeys*[26], in which the generals came in for some fairly severe criticism, but it is significant that, although the book is about the campaigns on the Western Front in 1915, Clark mentions the deaths of only two of the ten generals who were killed there that year. Since that time the works of John Terraine have set the record straight in many ways and most modern historians steer a course of opinion somewhere between the views of Clark and Terraine. Nevertheless, the myth still persists among those who don't really know the truth or don't bother to seek it out.

The Facts

The obvious implication of the myth that generals and their staffs were never in the front line is that they didn't have the courage for front line service. The cemeteries and memorials of all the major battlefronts of the Great War dispel this myth immediately, as do the numbers they contain. Nor do these cemeteries and memorials only commemorate British generals and their Staff officers. Australians, Canadians, New Zealanders and South Africans also paid the ultimate price in the Empire's cause. Cemeteries and memorials do not show those who were wounded either, or those who made many visits to the front line and, returning safely, did not appear anywhere on any lists that would show where they had been.

Without doubt some red-tabbed officers were a positive nuisance in the front line:

> 'Last time we were in the trenches, our new Brigadier came round in a mackintosh and without any cap badges and Simmance thought he might be a spy. He refused at first to answer any of his questions but then he got angry and said he was the Brigadier, so Simmance thought it best to show him round – but telephoned the C.O. to find out if the Brigadier was about and he said he was. Afterwards the Brigadier complained to the C.O. who told him he couldn't expect anything else if he choos (sic) to walk about without a badge.'[27]

The lists of names contained in later chapters of this work are not one hundred per cent complete because much original source material does not exist after the passage of so much time, but the authors believe that they are the most comprehensive ever compiled and published. Corps Casualty Returns sometimes contain the names of commanders who were wounded but remained at duty, yet their unit war diaries made no reference to the incidents of their wounding at all. When this has been found to be the case and there is no corroborative evidence, the names of those officers have not been included.

Chapter 3 contains the names of seventy-eight generals who were killed in action, died of wounds or died as a result of active service, and Chapter 4 names another one hundred and forty-six who were wounded (which includes those who were gassed) or became prisoners of war.

Casualty figures for the Second World War make an interesting comparison. The rank of brigadier-general had been abolished by then and the rank changed to plain brigadier, but, even so, only fourteen brigadiers were killed in action and another three died of wounds, including one lieutenant-colonel who was acting as Brigade Commander.

It is also worth examining the known cause of death of general officers of the Great War, to see exactly how and where they died. There is some difficulty here because in certain cases no accurate cause of death was given, 'killed in action' or 'died of wounds' being the only records which have survived to the present day. In certain cases one can be fairly sure of exactly what caused the death of the general in question, even if it is not actually stated, but in the interest of historical accuracy, the actual cause of death has not been assumed.

A breakdown of the seventy-eight biographies of fatal casualties documented in this work shows that thirty-four were killed by shell fire or trench mortar rounds, twenty-two were killed by small arms fire, either rifle (including sniper) or machine-gun fire, three were drowned, one accidentally, one inadvertently poisoned himself, one died of cholera, one died as the result of a flying accident and one died from accidental injuries. Of the remaining fifteen, no direct cause of death is known, but it is most likely that the majority of them would have been killed by shell fire or small arms fire.

From a practical point of view, the *cause* of death of these men, is irrelevant, – they were still professional losses to the British Army and tragic losses to their families, but from the point of view of the châteaux generals myth the cause of death *is* important. If we examine the cause of death of the generals, the myth simply falls apart. Out of a total of seventy-eight fatalities, the deaths of thirty-four generals, or forty-three per cent of their number, were known to have been caused by shell fire. This is not too surprising in a war dominated by artillery, but is a low percentage for Great War casualties as a whole. Generals, like other troops, could have been killed far behind the lines – even in their châteaux – by shell fire, but none of them were, although two became casualties in their châteaux not far from the front line. In fact quite a few of them were killed by German artillery that could obviously see them. What *is* surprising is that twenty-two generals, or nearly twenty-eight per cent of their total casualties, were killed by small arms fire and at least twelve of these were killed by snipers. Unlike some artillery or trench mortar fire, which can be aimed indiscriminately and still find its target, small arms fire is virtually always deliberately aimed at soldiers who can be seen by the firer. Thus, soldiers killed by small arms fire must have been in the front line. As the myth makers were more than happy to recount, there were no châteaux in the front line.

Perhaps the most scurrilous aspect of the myth is that it implies that the generals *preferred* to stay well clear of the front line and ignorant of battle conditions, expecting others to carry out their orders. This would infer that they were cowards who lacked the physical courage to serve in the firing line themselves. This is not only defamatory, but is clearly untrue, as we have seen already, if tested against casualties alone. Nevertheless, there is another way of measuring the courage of the casualties – their prowess in previous battles. All the generals and a proportion of the Staff officers had fought in previous wars and a vast majority of those killed had been wounded in previous actions. None of them would have been unaware of what it was like to attack under fire and indeed, some of them had been promoted as a result of bravery in the field – sometimes being rewarded with a field promotion to brevet rank.[28] Many had seen their career prospects soar as a result of brave deeds performed throughout the Empire and certainly in Victorian times bravery was expected of a general, which is why so many of them were winners of the Victoria Cross, and certainly *not* the other way round.

If we examine bravery awards given to the casualties who are the subject of this book, who we *know* must have been in, or very near, the front line, it should give us more than a representative guideline to the bravery of all generals including the ones who survived unscathed.

If one discounts awards of chivalry or those given for loyal service, such as K.C.B., C.M.G. etc., out of the two hundred and twenty-four generals whose biographies appear in this book, ten were Victoria Cross winners, (three of them being awarded for deeds of valour during the Great War), one hundred and twenty-six were winners of the Distinguished Service Order, and of these, twenty won first Bars, two won second Bars and one won a third Bar. It is true that senior officers in the Great War *did* receive the Distinguished Service Order for military service, rather than for military merit, but the majority of awards were made for acts of gallantry, – especially Bars to an original award. Three were winners of the Military Cross, one was awarded the Albert Medal and one was a winner of the Distinguished Conduct Medal for service as a soldier during the South African War.

Even if we allow for the fact that not all D.S.O. awards were for 'services in the field', the proportion of bravery awards among all the men whose stories lie within these pages is still staggeringly high. The number of awards certainly points to the fact that the generals were well above average in terms of courage, in a war when courage was almost commonplace. It would seem inconceivable, therefore, that men who had proved themselves time and again on many battlefields in many wars would suddenly develop a desire for comfort and inactivity behind the lines.

Therefore it is our contention that the deeds and actions of the senior officers who paid the ultimate price for actually being where they shouldn't have been have finally and irrevocably dispelled the myth of the châteaux generals.

NOTES

1 B.S. Barnes, *This Righteous War*, preface.
2 *The Liverpool Echo*, 23 October, 1992.
3 John Terraine, *The Smoke and the Fire*, page 214.
4 Jonathan Nicholls, *Cheerful Sacrifice*, page 216.
5 John Terraine, *The Smoke and the Fire*, page 179.
6 Richard Holmes, *The Little Field Marshal*, pages 303 – 305.
7 Conan-Doyle missed out Brigadier-General Nickalls, killed on the 26th, and probably didn't count Brigadier-General Wormald, killed on 3 October, as he wasn't actually killed during the main course of the battle.
8 Doyle Sir A.C., *The British Campaigns in France and Flanders – 1915*, page 228.
9 T. Travers, *The Killing Ground*, pages 108–109.
10 Letter by Colonel F.G. Robson in *Stand To! – The Journal of the Western Front Association*, No. 33. page 34.
11 Exceptions to this unwritten rule whose biographies appear in this work were Brigadier-General A. B. Hubback, C.M.G., D.S.O., Brigadier-General R. H. Husey, D.S.O., M.C., Brigadier-General N. Lee, V.D., Brigadier-General F. G. Lewis, C.B., C.M.G., T.D. and Brigadier-General A. C. Lowe, C.M.G., D.S.O.
12 *Gun Fire* , issue 16, page 48.
13 H. de Watteville, *Journal of the Royal United Services Institute* article entitled *Generalship* February-November, 1933 issue, page 318.
14 Lloyd George D. *War Memoirs*, 1933.
15 Head C.O. Lt. Col., *A Glance at Gallipoli*.
16 Lloyd George D. *War Memoirs*.
17 Liddell Hart B.H. *The Real War 1914–1918*, page 367.
18 Supplement to *The London Gazette*, of 4 January, 1918, dated 8 January, 1918, page 116.
19 Cooper D. *Haig*, page 159.
20 John Terraine, *Stand To! – The Journal of the Western Front Association*, No. 29 page 36.
21 Montgomery B.L. *The Memoirs of Field Marshal The Viscount Montgomery*, page 35.
22 Wheatley D. *The Time Has Come*, page 155.
23 *Stand To!*, No. 30 page 3.
24 Public Record Office, CAB 45/114.
25 Public Record Office, CAB 45/133.
26 Clark A. *The Donkeys*.
27 The Liddle Collection Ref. 8 (GS), the diary of Captain P.R.F. Mason, 4th Bn. K.L.R. 20/12/1915.
28 A Brevet promotion was one where an officer was not promoted to a specific job, but was a recognition of service or bravery which would mean he would achieve the new rank when a suitable command became available. It was usually unpaid.

CHAPTER 2

'Honourable Exceptions' – The Reality

In his *War Memoirs*, set between two pages headed 'Generals Who Avoided The Line', and 'They Should Have Seen For Themselves', David Lloyd George, as we have already noted, quite gratuitously stated:

> 'The solicitude with which most Generals in high places (there were honourable exceptions) avoided personal jeopardy is one of the debatable novelties of modern warfare.'[1]

Although he does not name the 'honourable exceptions' he has in mind, his implication is still crystal clear; generals who did not avoid the line and who did go and see for themselves were a rarity.

Even if he genuinely believed that virtually all British Army generals were incompetent, he surely can not have believed that only a very small number of them ever put themselves in personal jeopardy or that they never went forward to see the true conditions of battle and the battlefields for themselves. Apart from the obvious casualty figures amongst senior officers that must have been available to him and which he surely must have known about, the popular press of the war years often contained stories of the exploits of generals who were in the thick of the fighting, and he must have known about these as well. Some of these were no doubt largely based on jingoistic patriotism, but they nevertheless reflected the popular views and beliefs of 1914 – 1918 and not the later 'myth', dispelled in Chapter 1.

As early as the winter of 1914 the famous weekly magazine *The War Illustrated* published a stirring if not most unlikely painting of a battle scene under the title 'General French in the Thin Khaki Line'. Sir John is shown, wearing his gold braid, spurred boots and sword, catching a wounded soldier whose rifle and cap are flying as he is about to fall to the ground. The text to the picture echoes perfectly the mood of the time:

> 'During the great battle of Ypres, when Britain's little Army was
> a line slender but of indomitable courage – strained almost to

breaking point, battling desperately against overwhelming numerical superiority, but nevertheless a band of steel resistance to all the efforts to break a way through – it was in those days that Sir John French, Commander-in-Chief of the British Forces in the Field, revealed a greatness of heart and spirit that made him a hero to all his men. It is worthy of note that he was in the field – not on a hill in the distance.

'With utter disregard for his own safety, he motored from point to point of the line of conflict, encouraging the soldiers by his presence, heartening them when the hordes of the enemy seemed inexhaustible and the struggle unavailing, partaking in their dangers and risking his life as they risked theirs.

'At one point, during a particularly fierce engagement, he left his car and ran on foot to a wood where his men were being forced to withdraw, step by step. As he hurried towards the fight, a man staggered, wounded, right in his path. Sir John caught him in his arms as he was falling, laid him down gently, and then continued rallying his soldiers, talking to them, cheering them, and so inspiring them with his own unfailing courage and dauntless spirit that they held on, and kept the position, despite the persistent hacking of the tremendous opposing forces.'[2]

We already know that Sir John French was a 'soldiers' soldier' and he *was* in the habit of visiting the front line, but even so the story is a hard one to believe. However, this is not the point. Modern readers are sceptical about *most* press reports, especially those involving wars, and with the history of the wars of the 20th Century to study and the example of Dr Goebbels' Propaganda Ministry never far from mind, they are justified in their scepticism. The readers of 1914 were not in this fortunate position, however, and the article and picture reflect exactly the public perception of a general in 1914. The fact that the editor of the magazine, J.A. Hammerton, makes the point 'It is worthy of note that he was in the field – not on a hill at a safe distance' shows that, even as early as the first winter of the war, it would seem that generals were not *expected* to go into combat areas, – at least by editors of popular magazines, who presumably, even by then, had measured the correct temperature of public opinion. That is a lesson which Britain's wartime Prime Minister had obviously not learned, even by 1933, when he made his outrageous assertions, or if he had done, it was one which he had curiously chosen to ignore.

As we have already seen, all senior officers in the Great War were the products of the reign of Queen Victoria, the British public school system and the British Empire itself. The whole basis of all their training and learning was service and loyalty to the Crown, the Army and the Empire and it is inconceivable that they would *not* have wanted to be in the thick

27

of any fighting that was taking place. This was not *merely* for reasons of personal bravery or the offensive spirit. Like any army of any era, officers who had been in action – particularly those who had distinguished themselves – had a far better chance of promotion than others who had seen little or no fighting. This is one reason why, as we have also noted, there was a much higher proportion of bravery awards among senior officers – they had reached their positions in the Victorian and Edwardian Army *because* of the action they had seen and the courage they had shown, not *despite* it. Therefore, to suggest that they would avoid the line during the Great War or not go forward to see battle conditions for themselves, is not only inconceivable, but downright scurrilous.

In truth, senior officers did play an active part in the prosecution of the Great War both from front line observation and participation, although for the most part, they were far too valuable in terms of experience and leadership to have been risked in such a way. As most of them survived these experiences unscathed, few records now remain of what they did and where they did it – and this is one probable reason why the 'myth' has been able to take such a hold on popular misconception. What follows are just a few examples of generals who were quite definitely at the forefront of the fighting.

The Unsafe Châteaux

At the end of October, 1914, the course of the war was not going very well for the British. After the retreat from Mons and the fighting on the Marne and the Aisne, both the Germans and the British had begun what was to be called the *race to the sea*. Both sides were trying to establish their forces on the Channel coast to deny the use of its ports to the other. On the line of advance of the German Army across the Flanders Plain lay the ancient cloth-producing town of Ypres and in between Ypres and the Germans stood the British Army. It was decided that Ypres had to be held at all costs and what became known as the First Battle of Ypres began in earnest on 21 October, 1914, when the two sides first clashed.

By the morning of the 31st the position was critical as the Germans in vastly superior numbers began to assault the village of Gheluvelt, which straddles the Menin Road – the main road which joins Menin to Ypres. The mediaeval walled town of Ypres itself is only four miles to the west. If Gheluvelt fell, then the way to Ypres would be wide open. Kaiser Wilhelm himself was known to be in the area and the German Army was desperate to give him the town of Ypres as a present. The British were equally determined to deny him his prize.

They were vastly outnumbered, but time after time repulsed the German attacks, their numbers being seriously reduced with each fresh assault, but still they held on. The defenders of Gheluvelt and the Menin Road were mainly from the 1st and 2nd Divisions of the old Regular Army. Only by the utmost bravery and professionalism did these men of the British Expeditionary Force time and again hold back the field-grey tide, but eventually and almost inevitably, just before midday, the Germans broke through the 1st Division's positions and took Gheluvelt.

Just two miles behind this blood-letting, just off the main road, was Hooge Château. A peacetime palace owned by the de Vinck family, it was now the meeting place of the commanders of the two divisions, Lieutenant-General S. H. Lomax who commanded the 1st Division and Major-General C. C. Monro who commanded the 2nd. Before the attack had begun, the Commander of I Corps, Sir Douglas Haig, had pulled back his own headquarters from there to another château a little to the rear, known as The White Château, so that Lomax could establish his own headquarters at Hooge in a degree of comfort.

But by lunchtime on 31 October no one was feeling very comfortable. It was obvious that the line had been broken and the signs of retreat showed that the situation was critical. Monro had arrived at the château at 12.45 to discuss the situation and the lunch that had been prepared lay unserved and uneaten as the two generals and their Staff officers pondered over their next move and awaited orders from the rear. The guns on both sides were active, for apart from support fire given by both sides to the battle at Gheluvelt all morning, British heavy guns had been pounding the châteaux in the German rear, hoping to hit the Kaiser or his Staff with a lucky shot. The German heavy guns had replied with desultory retaliatory fire, but soon they had a more obvious target.

They already commanded the ridges to the east and had a perfect view of the battlefield below and the ridge at Hooge as it sloped back towards Ypres. As a consequence, they could not fail to notice the large concentration of cars on the approach to the château which was an obvious advertisement to its use. It was not long before a German spotter aircraft flew low over the château and, amazingly, despite the fact that this was obviously noticed, it did not occur to anyone, presumably because they were so preoccupied with the critical situation, that they would soon become a target. Thus, they worked on, in a little room whose french windows opened onto the garden.

At about 1.30 p.m. the first shell, a 5.9 (some reports say it was an 11 inch), probably fired from a battery of three guns, screamed up the Menin Road and exploded in the château garden with a huge report. Most of the occupants of the room, including Lomax, rushed to the window to see where the shell had landed. Even then they did not think of taking cover. Monro, however, taking the opportunity of a break in the proceedings, took his Chief of Staff, Colonel R. Wigham, into the inner doorway, to seek his advice on whether or not they should return to their own

29

headquarters or move further forward. Just at that moment a second shell burst right in the window opening.

As the jagged metal from its explosion tore into the room, Lomax was mortally wounded, as it transpired, and five Staff officers from the two divisions were killed and one fatally wounded. Fortuitously, Monro and Wigham escaped relatively unscathed, although Monro was severely concussed by the explosion. Seconds later a third shell landed and struck the corner of the château, filling the scene of devastation with dust and falling plaster, but wreaking no more carnage.

Lomax was evacuated to a casualty clearing station and from there to England, where he died of his wounds nearly six months later. His body was cremated at Golders Green Crematorium. The German gunners who fired that second shell certainly achieved excellent results for their efforts. The owner of the château, Baron de Vinck, only escaped injury or death through sheer good fortune, because he had left the building minutes before the shelling began.

Sir Arthur Conan Doyle, writing about the whole incident after the war, stated that: 'It was a brain injury to the Army and a desperately serious one'[3] and there is no doubt that this was true, for such was the accumulated experience and talent that was wiped out on that October afternoon by that one shell.

Lomax, alone of those hit, would have had the satisfaction, at least, of knowing that the critical situation was saved later in the afternoon, when the 2nd Battalion of the Worcestershire Regiment, virtually the last reserve of the British Army at Ypres, counter-attacked and retook Gheluvelt at the point of the bayonet. They were ordered forward and spurred on by Brigadier-General C. FitzClarence, V.C., of the 1st Guards Brigade, another general who did not avoid the line, and was later to be killed in action at the forefront of his troops at Polygon Wood. Although the Germans later retook Gheluvelt and held it for almost all of the rest of the war, the Worcesters' action halted the impetus of the German attack, thus saving Ypres, the Flanders Plain and the Channel ports. No doubt Lomax was satisfied with the outcome of the battle, before he eventually succumbed to his wounds. Here at least was a perfect example of a general and his staff who were far from safe in a château.

The Generals of Loos

The Battle of Loos was a battle that no one in the British Army wanted to fight – at least not at first. Early in 1915 members of the French and British war cabinets had met to formulate and co-ordinate plans for the prosecution of the war that year. What they came up with was an autumn attack in the Champagne region, which was designed to eliminate the salient that existed opposite Compiègne, where the Germans were still quite close to Paris. At the same time an Anglo-French attack was to be mounted in Artois across the coalfields of Lens. Once these attacks had succeeded, it was hoped that a full-scale offensive would be possible, to break out into open country and perhaps end the war victoriously.

The planned date of this joint attack was to be 25 September and it soon became obvious that the attack in Artois would have to be a mainly British affair, which would allow the British Army to prove exactly what its capabilities were. After the British engagements of the spring, which were really no more than exploratory assaults, the coming battle would be fought with six infantry divisions, including some of 'Kitchener's Army' – 1914 volunteers who had heeded Lord Kitchener's call to volunteer to serve in the Army for the duration of the war. The main objective of the September attack would be to capture and hold the mining town of Loos.

Early reconnoitring of the ground to be fought over horrified Haig, whose First Army would bear the main brunt of the attack and Sir John French was no more hopeful of its success. The attack area was open and bare except for a vast coalfield whose slag heaps and machinery would give ample cover to the defending Germans but little to the attacking British. Kitchener, also, was not too sanguine about the chances of success at Loos – at least at first, but he eventually fell into line with French enthusiasm, as he became more and more despondent about a victorious outcome for the Dardanelles campaign and saw the need for an Anglo-French success.

Eventually it was planned that the battle would proceed as agreed, along a front of about seven miles, roughly between the towns of La Bassée and Loos which also included a position to the south-east of the town known as Hill 70. The attack was to be preceded by four days of incessant bombardment and, despite this, it was hoped that an element of surprise might be achieved on the morning of the attack by the use of 5,000 cylinders of chlorine gas.

On the morning of 25 September, as the French were preparing to make their attack further south, the gas was duly released and about an hour later the attack commenced, but not before the wind had changed and sent tons of chlorine drifting back towards the British lines. This catastrophe was really an omen for the rest of the battle. The next two days, especially, saw the fiercest of fighting and spectacular successes were matched by catastrophic losses before the main impetus of the attack broke down on 13 October and the battle really sank to its weary conclusion on 4 November.

By this time, although Loos itself had been captured and the British line had been pushed forward about two miles on a front of about four miles, the casualties were very high at over 50,000 sustained during the three main weeks of the fighting. Thus the battle, classed as a victory by the

British high command, was certainly a Pyrrhic one. The German losses were about one third of those of the British. Perhaps the worst thing about the whole shambles, however, was the fact that even the ground gained was of no vital military importance and the French attack in Champagne was no more successful either. Furthermore, most of the losses among the British, both Regular and New Army, were virtually pointless, apart from perhaps in teaching the lessons of full-scale battle. However, among those who would never profit from the experience were six officers of general rank.

The first senior casualty of the battle was Brigadier-General C. D. Bruce, who commanded the 27th Brigade of the 9th (Scottish) Division. The 9th Division had been ordered originally to capture the village of Haisnes, which lay between La Bassée and Hulluch, the 26th and 28th Brigades in attack and Bruce's 27th Division in support. In between them and Haisnes was a most formidable obstacle, the Hohenzollern Redoubt, a defensive position which jutted forward from the main German line and was virtually impregnable. As the attacking troops of the 28th Brigade moved forward against this position, they were caught in the wire which fronted it and mown down by the most relentless machine-gun and small-arms fire. The 26th Brigade on their left, however, was able to find a way around the side of the Redoubt and, when finally halted, was in touch with Haisnes itself. Bruce's 27th Brigade followed closely behind and its forward troops reached and took a position known as Fosse Alley, to the left of the Lens – Hulluch Road.

By nightfall Bruce and his Brigade-Major, Captain E. N. Buchan, had moved forward to the new front line in Fosse Alley, but as the forward troops in Haisnes, unsupported and with their flanks turned, began to filter back under relentless German attack, Brigade headquarters was transferred to a position to the right of the Hohenzollern Redoubt known as The Quarries. This was actually in the sector held by the 7th Division, who had been forced to retire there after an unsuccessful attack on Hulluch. During the night, however, the Germans were able to break through the gap between the 7th and 9th Division and attack the Quarries from the rear.

Hearing the attack and suddenly finding themselves out of touch with the rest of the brigade, Bruce and Buchan went underground into a deep dug-out to look for a field telephone. They were still underground when the Germans captured the position and Buchan was killed and his General was captured – the first British general of the war to go into captivity. It would be almost four years before Bruce would see England again. On the following day two more of his fellow generals would pay the penalty for being so far forward and not avoiding the line.

The loss of The Quarries during the night of the 25th/26th was a serious blow to the British on the front of the 9th and the 7th Divisions and one which was felt keenly by the enigmatic commander of the 7th Division, Sir Thompson Capper. This veteran of many colonial campaigns had already been wounded by an accidental explosion, before returning to command his division – one with an exceptionally fine fighting record – in July. He would have felt the loss of the position keenly and on the morning of the 26th an attack by the Norfolks to retake it failed dismally with a heavy loss of life. However, it was vital that The Quarries be recaptured and another attempt was made, this time preceded by a heavy bombardment. The troops used were pulled in from the 2nd Division and included the 2nd Worcesters of Gheluvelt fame. Although the British were able to establish themselves on the south-western edge of The Quarries, they were pinned down and found it almost impossible to move forward. The position – the former German front line – was very deep and very wide and was overlooked by houses which gave cover and a perfect line of fire to the Germans. As a result small parties of Worcesters were forced to break from cover and attempt to drive forward into the open, being encouraged all the time by their officers.

Suddenly, the figure of Major-General Capper was spotted running forward with the troops, joining in the assault and organizing the troops as he ran. What happened next is unclear, but he was next seen returning back down a shallow communication trench when he was hit by a bullet and fell. He was found and brought back by his A.D.C., who had to crawl a considerable distance with the General on his back until he could get him under cover. Unhappily, his efforts were in vain for Capper died of his wounds the following day in No. 6 Casualty Clearing Station at Lillers. He is buried in Lillers Communal Cemetery. There is no doubt that he had no need and probably no right to be so far forward as to present himself as such a prime target to some unknown German sniper and with his death the Army lost a most able soldier. No doubt he died trying to carry out one of his favourite maxims: 'We are here to do the impossible!'[3] He certainly could not have been accused of not wanting to see for himself.

On the same day Brigadier-General N.T. Nickalls, commanding the 63rd Brigade of the 21st Division, was killed near a position known as The Chalk Pit which was just forward of Loos to the left of the Loos - Hulluch road. It was the scene of bitter fighting as the British attempted to force their way across the road to a wood named Bois Hugo where the Germans held the high ground. The Germans made repeated counter-attacks against the men of the 63rd Brigade and these attacks were met with extremely accurate British rifle fire. Despite this, the Germans still surged forward and, in an attempt to rectify the situation, Nickalls, who should not have been so close to the front, walked calmly up to the firing line and ordered his men to charge. As he did so he was shot down. His body was never subsequently recovered and he is commemorated on the Loos Memorial to the Missing at Dud Corner Cemetery. He was the third general officer casualty of the Battle of Loos.

On the day that Major-General Capper died of his wounds Major-General G. H. Thesiger was also killed in action. It was he who had ordered the 9th Division to attack Haisnes and was thus responsible for the fierce fighting around the Hohenzollern Redoubt. To the left of the main redoubt was a position known as Fosse 8 which was basically a slag heap which gave a commanding view of the whole area. Although it was captured by the British in the initial assault on the first day of the battle, by the evening of that day the situation there had become critical. As a result, the 73rd Brigade from the 24th Division – a New Army Division – was detached to reinforce the 9th Division at Fosse 8. By the morning of 27 September the Germans retook Fosse 8 and the totally inexperienced 73rd Brigade, holding the line to the south-east, suddenly found itself cut off from the rest of the British and furiously attacked by the Germans. When Thesiger heard of its plight he insisted on going forward to see if he could help and whilst moving up the line past the Hohenzollern Redoubt he was caught in a fierce German bombardment and he and two of his Staff officers were killed. His body was never found and identified and he is commemorated on the Loos Memorial to the Missing. Even though they never knew of Thesiger's gesture, the gallant infantrymen of the 73rd Brigade managed to hold out until they were eventually relieved, despite the most desperate German attacks.

Even though the main fury of the battle had died down by the end of September two more generals were to die in the early days of October. Major-General F. D. V. Wing, commander of the 12th (Eastern) Division, a New Army Division, was killed by a shellburst, on the afternoon of 2 October, just after he had returned from the front line at Mazingarbe, where his troops were right next to the French. His A.D.C., Lieutenant C. C. Tower, was killed with him and they lie buried side by side in Noeux-les-Mines Communal Cemetery.

On the following day Brigadier-General F. Wormald, in command of the 5th Cavalry Brigade of the 2nd Cavalry Division, was killed by the bursting of a shrapnel shell in the trenches near Vermelles. The Brigade was engaged in clearing the battlefield and reconstructing trenches and there was surely no need for Wormald to have been there at all. He was certainly not avoiding the line. He is buried in Nedonchel Churchyard, not far from where he was killed. Brigadier-Generals Pereira, commanding the 85th Brigade of the 28th Division, and Pollard, commanding the 2nd Brigade of the 1st Division, were wounded during the battle.

Not since the Battle of Waterloo, fought almost exactly one hundred years earlier, had the British Army lost so many generals in one battle, and although Waterloo was fought over one day, and not over six weeks, the magnitude of the Loos battle and the number of its participants still make it a good comparison. What is perhaps more ironic, however, is that virtually no one knows that eight generals became casualties at Loos and fewer still have ever heard of their names, and yet the losses to senior officers in another battle fought exactly five hundred years earlier are well known to scholars the world over, through the words of William Shakespeare.

The immortal bard, in his play *Henry V*, while writing about English and Welsh losses sustained during the Battle of Agincourt, which was fought in October, 1415, stated:

> 'Where is the number of our English dead?
> [Herald presents another paper,]
> Edward the Duke of York, The Earl of Suffolk,
> Sir Richard Ketly, Davy Gam, esquire:
> None else of name; and of all other men
> But five-and-twenty.'

The eight generals who were casualties in the first major British offensive of the Great War on the Western Front deserve at least the same recognition. They certainly deserve better than to be ignored at best and slandered at worst by those who were in the best possible position to be able to honour their sacrifice.

Generals Who Sought the Line

Perhaps the main butt of the campaign of vilification against the generals in post Great War Britain was Douglas Haig himself. Over the years many books have been written about him and his conduct during the war and controversy still rages about his competence or otherwise. Many people, usually the most ill-informed, still see him as the epitome of the château generals and yet neither was he immune from the vagaries of war. His Director of Intelligence, Brigadier-General John Charteris in his book *At G.H.Q.* relates an incident that occurred in November, 1914:

> 'D.H. himself had rather a narrow escape a day or two ago. He was looking at a map opened on a table under a great glass candelabrum. A shell hit the house and down came the candelabrum on the map, very narrowly missing his head. A couple of signallers were killed at H.Q. at the same time.'[4]

It is inconceivable to think that this was a sole and isolated incident for any officer who served on the Western Front almost continuously throughout all the years of the war.

Major-General C. V. F. Townshend was one of the most enigmatic generals of the war. Although he is best known for his resolute defence of the besieged town of Kut-el-Amara and his less than helpful attitude to his own men in captivity once the town had fallen, there is no doubting his own personal bravery or his willingness to lead from the front. Fiercely ambitious and determined to achieve great status, he commanded the 6th Indian Division during the early campaigns in Mesopotamia and showed little regard for his own safety as he attempted to push his troops forward and take the most important Turkish city of Baghdad.

Before Townshend was forced to retire to Kut, he fought a number of actions against the Turks, notable among them being the Battle of Ctesiphon in November, 1915. Although some of his later decisions were certainly suspect and his conduct during Ctesiphon was certainly eccentric, he believed in setting a steady example to the men under his command in the old Victorian style and during this battle could never be accused of avoiding the line or not seeing the situation for himself. The Australian author Russell Braddon tells how Townshend had ridden up and down the line encouraging his men who were involved in desperate hand to hand combat with the enemy and then:

> 'Unperturbed either by the eleven Gurkhas lying dead around him or by their Turkish victims – each with his head split open, or cut off, by Gurkha kukris – Townshend watched the course of the battle. Binoculars to his eyes, he missed nothing: nor was he afraid to peer over the top of the trench to gain a panoramic view. He was cool, quiet and completely in control.
>
> 'Boggis!' (Townshend's servant)
>
> 'Sir?'
>
> 'A change of clothing.'
>
> '*Now,* Sir?'
>
> 'I always change at this time.'
>
> Frantically scurrying, Boggis made his way a mile to the rear to the river through the shot and shell of a violent battle: then made his way even more frantically back.
>
> 'Your clothes, sir.'
>
> 'Thank you Boggis.'
>
> Deliberately Townshend stripped and stood naked among his dead troops and his living officers: then slipped on a silk vest, silk underpants, a khaki shirt, his breeches, boots and sun-helmet, and, picking up his binoculars, eating a piece of plum cake passed to him by a junior staff officer, resumed his inspection of the battle.'[5]

Definitely eccentric, possibly even deranged, no one could accuse Townshend of not being there.

No less charismatic a figure than Townshend, though a great deal more important to the history of warfare, was Brigadier-General H. J. Elles who also led his troops from the front. As a young Lieutenant-Colonel of Royal

Engineers he had been charged, in late 1915, with investigating the military viability of the first tanks. Soon becoming a wholehearted champion of the cause of 'His Majesty's Landships' he went on to command the Tank Corps when it was formed in July, 1917. By this time tanks had been used with some immediate success at the battle of Flers-Courcellette during the Somme battle, although this success was not exploited at the time.

At the end of July, 1917, they were again used in force during the opening phase of the Third Battle of Ypres – the Battle of Passchendaele, but the atrocious weather conditions which prevailed there rendered them virtually useless and Elles feared that the many voices which called for their abolition as a force might be heard. However, during August, when they were used tactically, in a role for which they were ideally suited – clearing German blockhouses from the ridges – they redeemed themselves and cleared the way for their most triumphal action in the war, the Battle of Cambrai.

Planning for a mighty tank attack had begun after the Somme when Elles and others had realized that such an assault was possible if the element of surprise could be maintained, the area to be fought over was suitable and the proposed battlefield was not churned up by the usual lengthy preliminary bombardment. The area around Cambrai in France was chosen because it had all these necessary features, but it would mean assaulting the dreaded Hindenburg Line, a massive fortified defensive system where the trenches were sometimes 20 feet wide and the barbed wire fronting them was sometimes 150 feet deep.

In September, 1917, however, when it was obvious that the Passchendaele offensive was not going according to plan, Elles managed to convince Sir Julian Byng, the Third Army commander, that he could successfully break through the German lines at Cambrai by using his tanks, supported by six infantry divisions and cavalry and artillery. Elles proposed to use all the tanks available to him in France and those he could salvage from the Ypres area – some 400 in all – in one huge assault which would make or break the reputation and credibility of the Tank Corps. The plan was officially sanctioned on 20 October, 1917, and the attack was to take place exactly one month later.

On the eve of the battle Elles issued his now famous order, described in full by Lieutenant F. Mitchell, M.C. in 1933 in his book *Tank Warfare*. Mitchell not only took part in all the major tank actions of the war, but won his Military Cross in 1918 for his victorious encounter in the first tank-to-tank action in history.

'Special Order, No. 6

'1. To-morrow the Tank Corps will have the chance for which it has been waiting for many months, to operate on good going in the van of the battle.

37

2. All that hard work and ingenuity can achieve has been done in the way of preparation.

3. It remains for unit commanders and for tank crews to complete the work by judgement and pluck in the battle itself.

4. In the light of past experience I leave the good name of the corps with great confidence in your hands.

5. I propose leading the attack of the centre division.

(signed) Hugh Elles,
B.-G. Commanding Tank Corps
November 19, 1917.

The last paragraph filled everybody with astonishment and pride. The fleet was going into battle led by the commander in person in his flagship, the *Hilda*. Every crew felt that the eye of the chief would be watching them, and they swore not to betray his trust.

Throughout the whole of the war, on no matter what front, no general in command of any large body of troops ever led his troops into action. A general's place during a modern battle is well in the rear.'[6]

Although Mitchell is wrong, as this book proves, in thinking that *no* other general ever led his troops into action in the Great War, he does once more emphasize the belief amongst front line soldiers that 'A general's place during a modern battle is well in the rear.'

When the attack commenced at 4.30 a.m. on the morning of 20 November Elles went one better than to lead its centre, he also hoisted a brown, red and green flag – to symbolize mud, fire and green fields, from the top of his tank. This flag, which later gave the Tank Corps its colours, was deliberately flown so that all his men could see him and know where he was.

'By flying the flag the general would inevitably attract attention to his tank and be in the very forefront of danger, but when great issues are at stake, to take great risks is the prerogative of a great leader, and the brave flapping of that lonely flag was, that day, easily worth another hundred tanks to the enheartened Tank Corps.'[6]

Elles' tank continued to be in the forefront of the attack until it had reached its objective and then the General dismounted and returned on foot to his headquarters where he continued to direct the battle by field telephone and map in the more traditional way. History records that, although the tank attack during the Battle of Cambrai (often known as 'Cambria' to the troops) was a great success, that success was later thrown away and another great opportunity was lost. That, however, was not the fault of Brigadier-General Elles and his leadership from the front, and if he is not one of the 'Honourable Exceptions' that Lloyd George had in mind then he certainly deserves to be.

On 19 July, 1918, during the latter stages of the Battle of the Lys, the 9th (Scottish) Division under the command of Major-General H. H. Tudor recaptured the town of Meteren, not far from Bailleul, and took over 350 prisoners. There was nothing particularly unusual about this as the war in Flanders was turning inexorably against the Germans by this time. What was unusual, however, was that one of the 350 prisoners, an officer, was actually taken by General Tudor himself. Tudor found him in the newly captured town, in a ditch pretending to be dead, and brought him out at the point of his pistol. What was even more unusual was that this was not an isolated incident, because the General was in the habit of rushing forward once a position had been captured to see the ground for himself in order to consolidate the new position and prepare for any possible counter-attacks. On these occasions, apparently, he often took a prisoner himself.

The incident was described separately by two different officers, fourteen years apart. Lieutenant-Colonel W. D. Croft, C.M.G., D.S.O. first mentioned it in his book *Three years with the 9th Division*, published in 1919. Croft had served as brigade commander of the 27th (Lowland) Brigade, which was part of the 9th Division, from September, 1917, until the end of the war.

'Immediately the place was captured the divisional commander rushed off on his bike, taking me with him ... The divisional commander captured a prisoner as he usually did on these occasions. We were skulking along beside the knoll against which machine guns were becoming unpleasant, when, looking round, I saw him dart forward into a ditch with a funny little pistol, which I always told him would only annoy anyone if he fired it, and retrieve a Boche who was shamming dead.'[7]

The following account was written in a letter by Lieutenant-Colonel H. J. N. Davis, C.M.G., D.S.O. in 1933 in response to a request from the Official Historian for comments on the draft version of the capture of Meteren. Davis had commanded the 9th Machine Gun Battalion at the time of the capture. After receiving Davis' letter, the Official Historian made a note of the fact that no mention of the incident occurred in the 9th Division War Diary. Perhaps this was because of the modesty of its commander, or perhaps it was such a normal act for him that he didn't think it worthy of note.

'The only suggestion I submit is a reference to the capture of a German officer by our Divisional Commander (Gen Tudor) about an hour after the actual advance, and in the middle of Meteren 'village'. General Tudor made a point of going right up into the captured ground, to a view point, on these occasions during the well known lull whilst the German Arty. fire slowed down, owing to their shifting guns or because they were uncertain as to targets in the forward area.

'He told me he did this chiefly to see the ground beyond for himself so as to best meet counter attacks and to arrange his consolidation. No doubt also it had a cheering influence on the attacking infantry.

'I suggest that the knowledge that in the British Army (but probably in no other) a Divisional Commander went right forward behind his attacking troops and took a prisoner by the threat of his pistol may become of increasing historical value.'8

Thus, within sight of victory when it was not necessary to take chances, an experienced divisional commander had no qualms about reconnoitring captured ground himself and even managed to take prisoners as he rushed forward to newly captured positions. This is not the stuff of châteaux generals, nor those who avoided the line, nor was Tudor one of Lloyd George's 'notable exceptions'. He was merely a British general doing what he considered was his duty in the face of the enemy in the Great War.

For Valour – The Victoria Cross Generals

As we have already seen, bravery in action was a major stepping stone to promotion in the British Army before the Great War and throughout the course of the war many holders of the Victoria Cross served in senior positions. No fewer than ten generals who were holders of the supreme decoration for valour became casualties during the war and their biographies are chronicled elsewhere in this book.

We have already noted the part played by Brigadier-General C. Fitz-Clarence in the recapture of Gheluvelt and the fact that he was killed in action less than a fortnight later. He won his cross in the Boer War, as did Brigadier-General F. A. Maxwell, who also died in the Great War. Lieutenant-General W. N. Congreve, who was wounded at Vimy Ridge in June, 1917, also won his cross during the Boer War at the Battle of Colenso, a battle which resulted in the awards of two other Victoria Crosses – one of which was to Lieutenant F.H.S. Roberts, the son of Field Marshal Earl Roberts, V.C. who died of pneumonia at St Omer in northern France in November, 1914, whilst inspecting Indian troops in his capacity as Colonel-in-Chief of Overseas and Indian Forces in Europe. Lieutenant-General W. N. Congreve was the father of Brevet Major W. La T.

Congreve, V.C., who won his cross posthumously during the Somme battle of 1916.

Brigadier General J. E. Gough, who was fatally wounded by a sniper at Aubers Ridge in February, 1915, won his cross in Somaliland in 1904. Both Gough's father and uncle had won the V.C. during the Indian Mutiny. Brigadier-General P.A. Kenna was awarded his cross for rescuing a wounded officer at the Battle of Khartoum [Omdurman], in the Sudan in 1898 and he was subsequently killed at Suvla Bay during the Gallipoli campaign. Major-General Sir Charles Melliss won his decoration during the Ashanti War in 1900 and, before being captured after the surrender of Kut-el-Amara in April, 1916, he had beaten the Turks at the Battles of Shaiba and Nasariyeh.

The remaining V.C. casualty generals, Brigadier-General R. B. Bradford, Brigadier-General A. Carton de Wiart, Brigadier-General F. W. Lumsden and Brigadier-General B. C. Freyberg, all won their crosses during the Great War. Bradford and Lumsden were both killed in later actions. Bradford, whose brother also won the V.C. during the Zeebrugge Raid in 1918, was killed at Cambrai in November, 1917, and Lumsden was killed in June, 1918, a few days after being awarded the C.B.. He had already been awarded the D.S.O. and no less than three Bars. Two other brigadier-generals who were actually awarded V.C.s for deeds of valour during the Great War, but who did not become casualties, were Brigadier-General C. Coffin and Brigadier-General G. W. St. G. Grogan.

Clifford Coffin was born at Blackheath in 1870 and was commissioned into the Royal Engineers in 1888. He was appointed C.R.E. 21st Division in September, 1915, and held this post until January, 1917, when he was given command of the 25th Infantry Brigade of the 8th Division. At the same time he was awarded a D.S.O. 'For distinguished service in the field.' He was in command of the 25th Brigade on 31 July, 1917 – the opening day of the Battle of Passchendaele.

The 8th Division, which consisted of the 23rd, 24th and 25th Brigades, was ordered to attack across the Menin Road in a line from the old railway on the left of the road to Sanctuary Wood on the right. At zero hour, which was 3.50 a.m., the 23rd and 24th Brigades pushed forward with the 25th in support. At first everything went well and Bellewarde Ridge, Bellewarde Lake and Hooge, all sites of the 1914 fighting, fell on schedule, as the division advanced over half a mile. Once the men had dug in and begun to consolidate, Coffin's 25th Brigade moved through them and carried on until it was almost at the village of Westhoek. Then, suddenly, it came under intense machine-gun and rifle fire from Germans hidden in the remains of Glencourse Wood, and as its right flank was obviously in the air – the 30th Division on its right not having been able to get far forward enough to secure it – it was in danger of falling back and leaving a catastrophic gap in the line of advance.

It was at this stage that Coffin realized that the situation might become critical and determined to do something about it, although he should really have stayed behind at Brigade Headquarters. The citation for his Victoria Cross takes up the story:

'When his command was held up in attack owing to heavy machine-gun and rifle fire from front and right flank, and was establishing itself in a forward shell-hole line, he went forward and made an inspection of his front posts. Though under the heaviest fire from both machine-guns and rifles, and in full view of the enemy, he showed an utter disregard of personal danger, walking quietly from shell hole to shell hole, giving advice generally and cheering the men by his presence. His very gallant conduct had the greatest effect on all ranks, and it was largely owing to his personal courage and example that the shell-hole line was held in spite of the very heaviest of fire. Throughout the day his calm courage and cheerfulness exercised the greatest influence over all with whom he came into contact, and it is generally agreed that Brigadier-General Coffin's splendid example saved the situation, and had it not been for his action the line would certainly have been driven back.'[9]

On the following day the division was relieved and the situation saved, but only because of yet another general who sought the line and definitely went to see the situation for himself. Coffin was later awarded a Bar to his D.S.O. for his work in helping the 8th Division to withdraw under fire during the retreat following the German March offensive of 1918. He finished the war as a Major-General in command of the 36th (Ulster) Division.

George William St George Grogan, who was born at Plymouth in 1875, was commissioned in the West India Regiment in 1896. He then served in Sierra Leone, West Africa and Egypt before being transferred firstly to the King's Own Yorkshire Light Infantry and then the Worcestershire Regiment, with whom he went to France. It was while serving with this regiment that he won his first D.S.O. in 1917 for gallantry and devotion to duty while encouraging his men to consolidate captured German trenches and reporting valuable information back to brigade. This was the first official recognition that Grogan was an excellent leader of men and it showed that he always preferred to set an example himself and not leave matters to others. The morale among his men was always high because he was constantly among them in the front line, although this was not really where he should have been.

He was promoted to the temporary rank of brigadier-general in March, 1917, in command of the 23rd Infantry Brigade, which was part of the 8th Division and he must have been present when Brigadier-General Coffin won his V.C. at Westhoek on the opening day of the Battle of Passchendaele. It was some eleven months later, however, that Grogan was to emulate Coffin's example and win a cross of his own.

By May, 1918, the war had not yet turned completely in favour of the Allies following the great breakthrough made by the Germans after the Spring Offensive. After fierce fighting on the River Lys the 8th Division, with the other divisions of the Ninth Corps, was sent south to the region known as the Chemin des Dames north of the River Aisne and put in the line alongside the French. The 8th Divisional front was near Craonne, not far from where the British Army had fought in 1914. The intention was to give the divisions a chance to rest and re-equip, but it was just there that the German Army made its next and final hammer blow against the Allied lines on the early morning of 27 May.

Just as they did on 21 March, 1918, the Germans advanced under cover of thick mist but this time they also used tanks to aid their savage and devastating advance. For a while Grogan's 23rd Brigade near Gernicourt held off the advancing field-grey hordes but inevitably he had to fall back across the Aisne, south of the town of Pontavert where he was able to regroup with the remnants of the Division. The citation for his Victoria Cross best describes what followed:

'For most conspicuous bravery and leadership throughout three days of intense fighting, Brigadier-General Grogan was, except for a few hours, in command of the remnants of the infantry of a division and various attached troops. His actions during the whole battle can only be described as magnificent. The utter disregard for his personal safety, combined with sound practical ability which he displayed, materially helped to stay the onward thrust of the enemy masses. Throughout the third day of operations, a most critical day, he spent his time under heavy artillery, trench mortar, rifle and machine-gun fire, riding up and down the front line encouraging his troops, reorganising those who had fallen into disorder, leading back into battle those who were beginning to retire, and setting such a wonderful example that he inspired with enthusiasm not only his own men, but also the Allied troops that were alongside. As a result the line held and repeated enemy attacks were repulsed. He had one horse shot under him, but nevertheless continued on foot to encourage his men until another horse was brought. He displayed throughout the highest valour, power of command and leadership.'[10]

It was only after three days of almost continuous fighting that Grogan was relieved and the remnants of his command were stood down. In the same battle three other brigadier-generals had become casualties. Martin and Riddell were hit by the same shellburst, Martin being killed and Riddell

43

hideously wounded in the face and Rees was captured and was reputedly interrogated by Kaiser Wilhelm himself who was in the area to celebrate the hoped-for breakthrough. The stories of all four generals on the Aisne prove most emphatically that even within six months of the end of the war generals were not avoiding the line or letting others do their reconnoitring for them.

Grogan's V.C. was gazetted on 25 July, 1918, and the following day the *London Gazette* also published the citation for a Bar to his D.S.O. Once again it was for personal leadership and splendid example to his men in the face of the enemy. He continued to command the 23rd Brigade until the end of the war on the Western Front, and then served with the North Russia Relief Force until October, 1919.

Surely not even David Lloyd George would have ventured to suggest that any general who had won the V.C. was the type to avoid the line or perhaps the V.C. winners were his 'honourable exceptions'. Although winning the V.C. has always been the tangible recognition of bravery in the front line, every student of military history knows that, for every cross awarded, countless others were deserved but were never sanctioned or the deeds that might have earned them were never witnessed in the maelstrom of battle.

Equally so, many generals made many visits to the front line on a regular basis despite orders to the contrary and these were never recorded because they were seldom worthy of specific note. It is our contention, however, that the few examples shown here prove the point that generals in the Great War did not avoid the line and did go forward very often to see tactical situations for themselves. The reality was that they *did* put themselves in personal jeopardy on a regular basis and to have suggested that the vast majority of them acted otherwise than this, is the most *dishonourable* statement of all.

NOTES

1 Lloyd George D. *War Memoirs*
2 Hammerton J.A., (Editor), *The War Illustrated*
3 Doyle Sir A.C. *The British Campaigns in Europe*
4 Charteris J. *At G.H.Q.*
5 Braddon R. *The Siege*, Jonathan Cape, London 1969.
6 Mitchell F. *Tank Warfare*, Nelson, London, 1933.
7 Croft W.D. *Three years with the 9th Division*
8 P.R.O. CAB 45/128
9 *London Gazette* 14/09/1917.
10 *London Gazette* 25/07/1918.

CHAPTER THREE

The Fatal Casualties

Baldwin, A. H.   **Brigadier-General**
G.O.C. 38th Brigade   13th Division   Killed in action: 10 August, 1915

Anthony Hugh Baldwin was born in September, 1863, at Stratford-on-Avon. He was educated at Clitheroe Grammar School and Giggleswick. Baldwin was commissioned into the 1st Battalion Manchester Regiment, from the Militia, in May, 1884. He served in India from 1888 to 1895 and saw his first active service in the Miranzi Expedition of 1891. He served in the South African War in 1902 as Adjutant to the 6th Battalion Manchester Regiment. In 1910 he returned to India and retired on half-pay in June, 1914. At the outbreak of the Great War he offered his services and was given command of the 38th Infantry Brigade, which he trained and took to Gallipoli in June, 1915. On 9 August, 1915, Baldwin led his brigade in an attack on Chunuk Bair. The war diary[1] of the 38th Brigade for 10 August reads: 'At 3 am. on this date we were heavily attacked by the enemy and subjected to severe rifle fire. This attack, however, was beaten back. At 5 am. the enemy delivered another attack and succeeded in driving our troops back on our right flank for a short distance. However, the position they took rendered it impossible for us to hold the hill above "The Farm" and we were forced to retire. Just before retiring Brigadier-General Baldwin was killed.' All his Staff fell with him and Brigadier-General Cooper (q.v.) of the 29th Infantry Brigade was severely wounded at the same time. Brigadier-General Baldwin has no known grave; his name is commemorated on the Helles Memorial, Gallipoli.

Officers Died In The Great War: Commands and Staff.
1 PRO WO 95/4302

Barker, R. B.   D.S.O.*   **Brigadier-General**
G.O.C. 99th Brigade   2nd Division   Killed in action: 24 March, 1918

Randle Barnett Barker was born in June, 1870, was commissioned into the Royal Welsh Fusiliers in January 1891, and retired from the Army in 1913.

At the outbreak of war he was re-employed and appointed second-in-command of the 22nd Battalion Royal Fusiliers and later commanded the battalion in France. He was awarded the D.S.O.[1] for gallantry on the Somme in 1916 and a Bar[2] to this order for gallantry at Arras in 1917. He was appointed to command the 99th Infantry Brigade on 24 January, 1918. An appendix to the H.Q. diary[3] of the 99th Infantry Brigade records on 24 March: 'Shells began to fall in and around Gueudecourt, and at 5.45 pm. Brigadier-General R. B. Barker, D.S.O., and Captain E.I. Bell, M.C., his Staff-Captain, were killed by a shell.' Their bodies were carried to Albert for burial. Captain Francis Horner, formerly G.S.O.3 of the 2nd Division, according to notes[4] made by the official historian, was at Destremont Farm, near Le Sars, [Sht.57C, S.W.1 M.21.a.], when at 'about 11 o'clock two N.C.O.'s of the 99th Brigade came to ask if I could possibly procure a limber for the dead body of General Barker, which they had carried from Morval, I believe. I was able to get through to Miraumont and a limber was sent.' Despite the efforts of his men to ensure him a proper resting place, subsequent shell fire destroyed the graves of the General (his name is listed as Barnett-Barker in the C.W.G.C. Register) and his Staff-Captain and they are commemorated today by two special memorials in the Albert Communal Cemetery Extension, France.

Officers Died In The Great War: The Royal Welsh Fusiliers
1 L.G. 20/10/16.   2 L.G. 26/7/17.   3 PRO WO 95/1370.   4 PRO CAB 45/185.

Bradford, R. B. V.C. M.C.   Brigadier-General
G.O.C. 186th Brigade 62nd Division   Killed in action: 30 November, 1917

Roland Boys Bradford was born in February, 1892. He was one of the three sons of Mr & Mrs George Bradford of Darlington who gave their lives in the Great War[1] . The first to die was Lieutenant James Bradford, M.C., 18th Battalion Durham Light Infantry, who died of wounds on 14 May, 1917. The next to be killed was Brigadier-General Roland Bradford, V.C. M.C., aged 25, the youngest general officer in the British Army. Finally, Lieutenant Commander George Bradford, V.C., Royal Navy, was killed in action at Zeebrugge on 23 April, 1918. Roland Bradford entered the Army from the Territorial Force in 1912, obtaining his commission in the Durham Light Infantry. As Lieutenant-Colonel commanding the 9th Battalion Durham Light Infantry, he won the Victoria Cross on the Somme on 1 October, 1916. The *London Gazette* dated 25 November, 1916, records the following:

'For most conspicuous bravery and good leadership in attack, whereby he saved the situation on the right flank of his Brigade and of the Division. Lieutenant-Colonel Bradford's Battalion was in support. A leading Battalion having suffered very severe casualties, and the Commander wounded, its flank became dangerously exposed at close quarters to the enemy. Raked by machine-gun fire, the situation of the Battalion was critical. At the request of the wounded Commander, Lieutenant-Colonel Bradford asked permission to command the exposed Battalion in addition to his own. Permission granted, he at once proceeded to the foremost lines. By his fearless energy under fire of all descriptions, and his skilful leadership of the two Battalions, regardless of all danger, he succeeded in rallying the attack, captured and defended the objective, and so secured the flank.'

The A. & Q.M.G. diary[2] of the 50th Division records that on 5 November, 1917, Lieutenant-Colonel R. B. Bradford was wounded, but he stayed at duty; this was the second time that he had been wounded. A few days later, on 10 November, he was appointed to command the 186th Infantry Brigade. On 30 November the war diary[3] of the 186th Brigade records that Brigadier-General Bradford was killed by a shell near his brigade headquarters at K4d4.5 [1 mile S.W. of Graincourt]. Unaccompanied, he had left his headquarters dugout during a heavy bombardment at about 10 am., and his body had been found later in the day. He had been hit by a shell splinter and must have died instantly. Brigadier-General Bradford is buried in Hermies British Cemetery, France.

Officers Died In The Great War: The Durham Light Infantry
1 *Army Quarterly Vol. XVII*   2 PRO WO 95/2813.   3 PRO WO 95/3084.

Bridges, Sir William T. K.C.B. C.M.G.   **Major-General**
G.O.C. 1st Australian Division   **Died of wounds: 18 May, 1915**

William Throsby Bridges was born in February, 1861, at Greenock, Scotland. He was educated at Trinity College School, Port Hope, Canada, and the R.C.M.C., Kingston, Canada. He moved to Australia and entered the Army in the New South Wales Artillery, and served in the South African War from 1899 to 1900 as a Major of Artillery, attached to the Cavalry Division, but was invalided with typhoid fever. In 1902 he was A. & Q.M.G. H.Q. Commonwealth Military Forces; in 1909 he was Chief of the General Staff and from 1910 to 1914 he was Commandant of the Royal Military College of Australia. It was he who gave the Australians the title 'Australian Imperial Force'. He commanded the 1st Australian Division in Egypt and in the landings at Gallipoli in April, 1915. On 15 May he was on his way through Monash Valley when he stopped near 'Steele's Post'. As he went to continue on his way he ducked around the next traverse and fell, hit in the groin by a sniper's bullet. He was taken on board the hospital ship *Gascon* where General Birdwood went to see him and tried to cheer him, but Bridges, who had lost a great deal of blood, knew that there was little hope for him. He said that he would die content that he had commanded the first Australian Division to take the field. Shortly before his death he was told that the King had honoured him with the K.C.B.[1] The General Staff diary[2] has the following entry: '19th May. Anzac Cove. 9.5 pm. General W. T. Bridges died as a result of a wound in the thigh en route to Alexandria.' In the A. & Q.M.G. diary[3] of the 1st Australian Division there is a report from Egypt by Lieutenant-Colonel Patterson, the division's A.A. & Q.M.G., who had been sent back to Alexandria to arrange the return of animals and transport to Egypt. He wrote: '21st [May]. All work had to stop today because storemen taken for duty at funerals including General Bridges. Arch Deacon Ward and the Rev. Mr. Hordern conducted the service at the grave.' And a further entry: 'To funeral of General Bridges. Present: Generals Maxwell, Stanton, Ford and MacGregor, French Officers and Lt. Col. Earl of Dudley, Lt. Cols. Patterson, Johnson, ----- , and Appleton. The Rev. Mr. Horden conducted the service at the grave.' *The Times* for 3 September, 1915, reports his 'State Funeral in Melbourne.' Major-General Bridges was the only Australian soldier in two world wars to be brought home for burial. He is buried in the grounds of Duntroon Military College, Australia, the College that he had founded. The memorial stone erected on his grave was unveiled by General Birdwood.

---

1 Birdwood. *Khaki and Gown.*   2 PRO WO 95/4326.   3 PRO WO 95/4333.

Broadwood, R. G.   C.B.
G.O.C. 57th Division

Lieutenant-General

Died of wounds: 21 June, 1917

Robert George Broadwood was born in March, 1862, and commissioned into the 12th Lancers in 1881. In 1896 he served in the Dongola Expeditionary Force and in the following year he was present at the action at Abu Hamed and the subsequent occupation of Berber. He accompanied the Nile Expeditions of 1897 and 1898, when Douglas Haig (later Field Marshal Sir Douglas Haig, C. in C. B.E.F.) joined him and was given command of a Squadron of Cavalry in the Brigade of the 16th Lancers commanded by Colonel Broadwood. He was present at the Battles of Atbara and Khartoum. In the South African War, in which he served from 1899 to 1902, he was Brigadier-General Commanding the 2nd Cavalry Brigade when, on 30/31 March, 1900, he suffered a near disaster at Sannah's Post. The brigade, which was at Thabanchu, consisted of Household Cavalry, the 10th Hussars, mounted infantry and 'Q' and 'U' Batteries of the R.H.A. Broadwood was informed that a large force of Boers was moving rapidly on the town. He decided to move his force to Sannah's Post, a water-pumping station on the west bank of the Modder River. At daybreak on 31 March heavy shell fire from east of the Modder River fell on his bivouacs. His force attempted to retreat across the Korn Spruit towards Bloemfontein, but met with disaster when they encountered another Boer force. He suffered heavy casualties: the loss of seven 12 pounder guns, the personnel of an entire battery of R.H.A., and his convoy of baggage and supplies. Lieutenant-General Colvile was sent to his assistance, but did nothing to improve the situation. He sent Captain Ruggles-Brise to tell Broadwood to report to him, but Broadwood refused as he was in the middle of the action. In his report to the Secretary of State for War, Lord Roberts supported Broadwood's action, and stated that Colvile would have done better if, on his arrival with the 9th Division, he had proceeded at once to the scene of the engagement. In a letter[1] to General Sir Neville Chamberlain, dated 7 June, 1900, Broadwood admits that his report on the incident 'was about as elaborate an apology as one could write without inculpating subordinates'. He further said: 'Someone has to bear the blame and I don't feel that I can put it on anyone else's shoulders.' He became a C.B. in 1900. From 1904 to 1906 he was Brigadier-General Commanding the Orange River Colony District, and in 1906 he commanded troops in South China. In December, 1913, he retired as a Lieutenant-General on half pay. In October, 1916, he was appointed to command the 57th Infantry Brigade, which went to France in February, 1917, and joined the IInd Anzac Corps. Liddell Hart's notes[2] of a conversation that he had in August, 1937, with Colonel Allason [who had been G.S.O.1 of the 57th Division] records that Allason told him that 'General Godley, the corps commander, had reported Broadwood for "lack of fighting spirit" when he declined to launch his troops to attacks that had no chance of success, and protested that to carry out certain raids would sacrifice the lives of some of the best officers who would be needed if a real emergency arose. Broadwood felt these reproaches deeply. When the division was transferred to Haking's [XI] Corps, Haking made similar remarks, showing that the word had passed on. Broadwood was a man who had never taken care of his own life of [sic] that of his staff, while trying to preserve those of his men when sacrifice was unprofitable, and now seemed determined to get killed.' The A. & Q.M.G. diary[3] of the 57th Division reads: 'Croix du Bac. 21/6/17. Lt.-Gen. R.G. Broadwood, C.B., G.O.C. 57th Division, died of wounds received in action. He was struck by a shell while crossing the railway bridge over the River Lys at Houplines at 10.15 am. He died in the 54th Casualty Clearing Station at Estaires.' He had been going along with his G.S.O.2 and A.D.C. to see his Artillery Group. The Group Commander told him that the enemy were shelling a particular battery and that it was most unwise to cross the railway bridge, which was the only way to get there, as it was quite certain that the Boche had it under observation and on seeing him get on at one end of the bridge they would have time to fire a shell and to catch him before he got off at the other end. Broadwood, however, insisted on going on, but left behind his staff. As foretold by the Group Commander, the Boche put a shell on

49

to the bridge and knocked out the Group Commander and the Battery Commander, besides Broadwood himself. Both Broadwood's legs were blown to bits, and he died that afternoon in the ambulance.[4] The Liddell Hart notes[2] further record that, when Broadwood was mortally wounded, he said that he was glad to go after being told that he had no fighting spirit, and that his wish was to be buried between a soldier and a subaltern. Lieutenant-General Broadwood is buried in Anzac Cemetery, Sailly-sur-la-Lys, France, and, as he wished, on one side of his grave is the grave of a soldier, 2031 Gunner Robert Burnside, 14th Brigade Australian Field Artillery, and on the other side is the grave of a subaltern, Second Lieutenant Herbert Gittins, 5th Loyal North Lancs. Regiment.

Officers Died In The Great War: Commands and Staff.
1 PRO WO 105/7.   2 The Liddell Hart Centre for Military Archives (11/1937/69), King's College, London University.   3 PRO WO 95/2967.   4 Bond. *Staff Officer, The Diaries of Lord Moyne*

Brown, C. H. J. D.S.O.   Brigadier-General
G.O.C. 1st New Zealand Brigade New Zealand Division   Killed in action: 8 June, 1917

As Major Charles Henry Jeffries Brown he was awarded the D.S.O.[1] when he served with the Canterbury Battalion in Gallipoli in 1915, and as Lieutenant-Colonel he led the 2nd Auckland Battalion in France. He was appointed to command the 1st New Zealand Infantry Brigade, vice Brigadier-General Johnston (q.v.), on 15 February, 1917. He was killed in action during the Battle of Messines, as the diary[2] of the 1st New Zealand Infantry Brigade records: 'Battle of Messines. A Day – 8th June 1917. At about 11.40 am. the Brigade Commander, Brig. Gen. C. H. J. Brown, was killed by a shell whilst talking to the Divisional Commander [Major-General Russell] near the Moulin de l'Hospice.' *The Times* reported his funeral on 7 July, 1917: 'Beside the grave stood the late General's two sons. It is not often that one could be witness of such a scene on the battlefields of Flanders. Here were these two young New Zealanders, who had come so many thousands of miles from the Antipodes, burying their father within sound of the guns in the battle in which all three had fought.' Brigadier-General Brown is buried in Bailleul Communal Cemetery Extension, France.

L.G. 8/11/15.   2 PRO WO 95/3685

Bulkeley-Johnson, C. B. C.B.   Brigadier-General
G.O.C. 8th Cavalry Brigade 3rd Cavalry Division   Killed in action: 11 April, 1917

Charles Bulkeley Bulkeley-Johnson was born in 1867 and was educated at Harrow and the R.M.C., Sandhurst. He obtained his commission in the

Royal Scots Greys in 1887 and in 1899 he took part in the Nile Expedition, being present at the operations which led up to the defeat of the Khalifa. He had a good reputation as a sportsman, a good rider, polo player, cricketer and big-game hunter. In November, 1914, he was appointed to command the 8th Cavalry Brigade. His death was described in the newspapers and memorials of the time with all the glorious words that the writers could muster. Conan Doyle described how he died at the head of his Cavalry Brigade as they charged Monchy le Preux; the Regimental History of the Royal Scots Greys describes how he fell at the head of his Brigade at Monchy le Preux; the Harrow Memorials of the Great War were closer to the truth when they recorded that he was shot dead when out, almost alone, on a personal reconnaissance which saved the lives of countless of his men. He was a brave man, a General who died in the front line. The manner of his death is described very vividly by Captain D. W. J. Cuddeford, 'B' Coy., 12th Battalion Highland Light Infantry, in his book *And All For What* and his story in *The Great War. I was There!* Vol. 3. The General wanted to know what the situation was. Captain Cuddeford informed him that the enemy in front had been strongly reinforced during the past twenty-four hours and that the enemy was concentrating around the village of Pelves, down by the river. The General thought that he would like to see something of the enemy dispositions for himself. Captain Cuddeford told him that if they were spotted by the German snipers it would be necessary to dodge them by sprinting diagonally from shell hole to shell hole. The General insisted on going on against the Captain's advice, and perhaps being rather old for that sort of active dodging or, as it seemed to Captain Cuddeford at the time, too dignified to get well down at the sound of a bullet, he would persist in walking straight on. They had not gone far when one skimmed past the Captain and struck the General full on the cheekbone. Cuddeford never forgot his piercing shriek as he tumbled down and rolled over on the ground. They succeeded in dragging the General to a shell hole, but he died as they were getting him there. Cuddeford returned to his company and the snow came on again. He went out with a party and brought the General's body to their support line. Brigadier-General Bulkeley-Johnson is buried in Gouy-en-Artois Communal Cemetery Extension, France.

Officers Died In The Great War: Commands and Staff.

Bull, G. D.S.O.   **Brigadier-General**
G.O.C. 8th Brigade   3rd Division   Died of wounds: 11 December, 1916

George Bull was born in May, 1877, the third son of the Resident Magistrate of Newry, Co. Down, Ireland. He served with the 5th Battalion Royal Irish Rifles in the South African War, from 1900 to 1902, and then, in 1903, he was commissioned from the Militia into the Royal Garrison Regiment, transferring to the Leinster Regiment in 1905. In February, 1907, he transferred to the Royal Irish Fusiliers, with whom he went to war in 1914, as a Captain in the 1st Battalion. In November, 1915, he was appointed Commanding Officer of the 12th Battalion Royal Irish Rifles. He was awarded the D.S.O.[1] for gallantry and devotion to duty in the field. On 3 December, 1916, he was appointed to the rank of Brigadier-General Commanding the 8th Infantry Brigade. Three days later the brigade's war diary[2] records that he went on a tour of the trenches: 'Courcelles. December 6th 1916: Brig.-Gen Commanding proceeded to Bus-lès-Artois and visited the 7th K.S.L.I. He afterwards proceeded on a tour of the trenches with the Brigade-Major. December 7th: Brig.-Gen. Bull, D.S.O., was wounded by a hostile sniper whilst on a tour of the Brigade Sector with the Brigade-Major and G.S.O.3, 3rd Division.' The *Belfast Newsletter* of 13 December, 1916, reported that he was wounded in the shoulder and loin. He died of his wounds at Varennes on 11 December. Brigadier-General George Bull is buried in Varennes Military Cemetery, France.

Officers Died In The Great War: Royal Irish Fusiliers.
1 L.G. 3/6/16.   2 PRO WO 95/1416.

Cape, G. A. S. C.M.G.	Brigadier-General
C.R.A. Acting G.O.C. 39th Division	Killed in action: 18 March, 1918

George Augustus Stewart Cape was born in March, 1867, and was commissioned into the Royal Artillery from the Militia in November, 1889. He served in Uganda from 1898 to 1900 and was a Special Service Officer in the South African War from 1899 to 1900. In 1901 he took part in the expedition up the Gambia. Prior to and in the early years of the Great War he served as a G.S.O. until he was appointed Brigadier-General Commanding the Royal Artillery of the 39th Division on 18 October, 1917. On 7 March, 1918, the G.O.C. of the Division, Major-General Feetham (q.v.), went on leave to the U.K. and Brigadier-General Cape assumed command in his place. The General Staff diary[1] of the 39th Division records: '18th March. A Tactical Exercise (without troops), involving a counter attack on Ronssoy, was carried out by the Staff and Battalion Commanders of the 116th Infantry Brigade under the direction of Brigadier-General G. A. S. Cape, who was commanding the division during the absence on leave of Major-General E. Feetham. During this Exercise a salvo of 75 mm. shells killed General Cape (just south of Ronssoy) and severely wounded Captain L. E. H. Whitby of the Machine Gun Corps. Brigadier-General Hornby assumed command.' Two of the pall bearers at Cape's funeral, Brigadier-General Hornby (q.v.) and

Brigadier-General Bellingham (q.v.), were themselves wounded shortly afterwards. Brigadier-General Cape is buried in Peronne Communal Cemetery Extension, France.

Officers Died In The Great War: Royal Regiment of Artillery (R.H.A. and R.F.A.).
1 PRO WO 95/2567

Capper, Sir Thompson. K.C.M.G. C.B. D.S.O.   Major-General
G.O.C. 7th Division   Died of wounds: 27 September, 1915

Thompson Capper was born in October, 1863, and was commissioned from the R.M.C., Sandhurst, into the East Lancashire Regiment in 1882. He saw service in India and Africa with the Chitral Relief Force in 1895 and in the Sudan in 1898. In the South African War, in which he served from 1899 to 1902, he was awarded the D.S.O.[1] for his services. From 1906 to 1911 he was Commandant of the Indian Staff College and was made a C.B. in 1910. In 1911 he was promoted to the rank of Brigadier-General Commanding the 13th Infantry Brigade, and Inspector of Infantry in 1914. As Major-General Commanding the 7th Division he took the division to Zeebrugge on 6 October, 1914, and subsequently to the First Battle of Ypres. He was created a K.C.M.G. in 1915. In April, 1915, he was obliged to relinquish his command of the 7th Division when he was wounded in the left shoulder by flying fragments during a jam-tin bomb demonstration, but when he had recovered he returned to resume command of the Division on 19 July, 1915. At the Battle of Loos, the attack on the Quarries, near Hulluch, failed to recapture them in spite of a concentrated bombardment. 'General Capper had gone forward to organise this attack and he was mortally wounded. The spot where he fell was exposed to a heavy rifle and machine-gun fire, and Humphrey Noble, his A.D.C., getting his wounded General onto his back, had to crawl a considerable distance on his hands and knees before he was able to bring him safely under cover.'[2] In a letter[3] written in February, 1920, Colonel G. H. Boileau, who had been C.R.E. of the 7th Division, describes the event: 'General Capper was not killed riding his charger and waving his sword as rumoured at the time. He was shot in the back returning from visiting the front line while going down a shallow straight communication trench in the captured German front system; this was commanded by houses and dangerous in daytime. I met the General being carried down, he was then unconscious and did not recover.' Captain E. P. Bennett, V.C. M.C., who was with the 2/Worcesters in 1915, also wrote a letter[3] in May, 1926, in which he describes the attack on the Quarries at the Battle of Loos: 'Suddenly we were faced with the German front line trench. Far too wide to get across, and we had to drop into it. Colonel Lambton [C.O. 2nd/Worcesters] then sorted us out into our companies and again gave the advance. Unfortunately, the trench was very deep and there were few places where we could get out. The result was the battalion streamed by as best it could. The rifle fire was hot and we were coming over, necessarily, in small numbers at a time. As I ran across I overtook General Capper running with our men. He was actually joining in the assault. He must have been shot almost immediately as I did not see him again. ------ I was just bracing myself up for the final assault when the order passed down "dig in", and on my left I saw a Staff officer in our line wearing a red hat, who had presumably given the order. I imagine he was one of General Capper's Staff who joined in the assault with him.' Major-General Capper was shot through the lungs and died in Number 6 C.C.S. the next day. He is buried in Lilliers Communal Cemetery, France.

Officers Died In The Great War: Commands and Staff.
1 L.G. 31/10/02   2 Gough. *The Fifth Army.*   3 PRO CAB 45/120.

Clifford, H. F. H.   D.S.O.   Brigadier-General
G.O.C. 149th Brigade   50th Division   Killed in action: 11 September, 1916

Henry Frederick Hugh Clifford was born in August, 1867, the second son of Major-General The Hon. Sir Henry Clifford, V.C. who, as a Major in the Rifle Brigade, won the V.C. 'for conspicuous courage at the Battle of Inkerman'. Henry Clifford entered the Army in February, 1888, was gazetted to the Suffolk Regiment and served in the South African War from 1899 to 1902. In February, 1915, he was awarded the D.S.O.[1] for services connected with operations in the field, and in May of the same year he was wounded when he was hit in the left arm by a sniper's bullet. He was appointed Brigadier-General Commanding the 149th Infantry Brigade in June, 1915, and in August, 1916, his division was moved to the Somme to take part in the attack of 15 September. The troops of the 149th Infantry Brigade were employed in the construction of assembly trenches which formed three sides of a big parallelogram, the trenches on each flank being designed as a means of access to the main assembly trench. Brigadier-General Clifford, with his Staff-Captain, Captain D. Hill, went up to inspect the work, a space of some 25 or 30 yards still remained to be evacuated. He was deeply impressed by the feeling that there was something unfair about the comparative immunity from danger enjoyed by officers of high rank, by the notion that this sentiment must be shared by the men under his command, and by the conviction that it was his duty to set a high example by declining to take any very special precautions for the preservation of his personal safety. When he reached the point where the construction work on the main assembly trench ended, instead of retracing his steps and inspecting the trench from the other side, which he might have done in perfect safety, he attempted to reach it by walking across the open space through which the trench had not been driven. When he was about half-way across he was shot through the heart by a sniper in High Wood.[2] Brigadier-General Clifford is buried in Albert Communal Cemetery Extension, France.

Officers Died In The Great War: The Suffolk Regiment.

1 L.G. 18/2/15. 2 *The History of the Suffolk Regiment*, and *Q.6. And Other Places*, by Francis Buckley, state that the sniper was in High Wood, but the C.W.G.C. register entry states that he was shot by a sniper in Delville Wood.

Cole, A. W. G. L.   C.B.   D.S.O.   Brigadier-General
G.O.C. 25th Brigade   8th Division   Died of wounds: 9 May, 1915

Arthur Willoughby George Lowry Cole was born in November, 1860. He entered the Army, as a Second-Lieutenant in the 23rd Regiment of Foot, in August, 1880, and became a Lieutenant in the Royal Welsh Fusiliers in 1881. He served in Burma from 1885 to 1887; West Africa from 1897 to 1898 and in Northern Nigeria in 1900, with the Kaduna Expedition, when he was severely wounded. In the South African War, from 1901 to 1902, he was in command of the 17th Mounted Infantry Mixed Column, and for his services was awarded the D.S.O.[1] In 1906 he returned to Nigeria in command of the Sokoto Expedition, and in 1907 he was made a C.B. He had retired from the Army, but in October, 1914, he returned first as Brigadier-General in charge of Administration, Northern Command, and later as Commander of the 25th Brigade. The operations order[2] for the 25th Infantry Brigade in May, 1915, said: 'The 8th Division is to break through the enemy's line in the neighbourhood of Rouges Bancs, and gain a position from our line on the left in the neighbourhood of La Cardonnerie Fm. through Fromelles – Le Clercq and back to our lines again. The 24th Infantry Brigade will attack on the right, the 25th Infantry Brigade on the left, dividing line Sailly – Fromelles road.' During the action an order to retire had been given by some unauthorized person and the movement spread rapidly among the troops immediately east of the Sailly – Fromelles road.[3] The official history[4] records that 'Brigadier-General Lowry Cole arrived at the breastwork [at 6.25 am.]. He found that all forward movement had ceased, and that no-man's-land was being swept by heavy fire. He directed the 2/Lincolnshire to get across by the mine craters. Shortly after he had given this order a number of men of the Rifle Brigade and Irish Rifles were seen streaming back over the German breastwork. Most strenuous efforts were made by the brigade staff to restore order, and Brigadier-General Lowry Cole, standing on the parapet in his endeavour to stop the retirement, was mortally wounded' [at 6.45 am.] Brigadier-General Cole, (his name is listed as

Lowry-Cole in the C.W.G.C. Register) is buried in Le Trou Aid Post Cemetery, Fleurbaix, France.

Officers Died In The Great War: Commands and Staff.
1 L.G. 31/10/02. 2 PRO WO 95/1724. 3 8th Division History. 4 Edmonds. *Military Operations France and Belgium, 1915.*

Cox, E. W. D.S.O.   **Brigadier-General**
B.G.G.S. (Intl) G.H.Q. France   **Drowned: 26 August, 1918**

Edgar William Cox was born in Islington, Middlesex, in May, 1882, and was educated at Christ's Hospital, of which he was subsequently appointed a governor. He was commissioned into the Royal Engineers in December, 1900. From 1902 to 1903 he was employed on the Sierra Leone and Liberia Boundary Commission, and from 1906 to 1909 he was on survey duty in the East African Protectorate. From 1912 to the outbreak of war he served in the War Office as a G.S.O.3. In August, 1914, he went to France to serve on Sir John French's Staff. During this period he was awarded the D.S.O.[1] for distinguished service in the field. He returned to the War Office in 1916 and served as a G.S.O.2 with the Director of Military Intelligence. In January, 1918, he succeeded Brigadier-General Charteris as Head of Intelligence on Sir Douglas Haig's Staff. Howard Spring, the novelist, was working as a clerk at G.H.Q. at the time of the German breakthrough in March, 1918, and he describes the effect that the pressures of that time had on Brigadier-General Cox and how he, 'chain-smoked cigarettes by day and night, allowing himself little time to eat and no time to rest, he wore his body to a shadow. The time came when the clouds lifted, the tension relaxed, the miracle of salvation intervened. General Cox said he would go for a bathe. His chauffeur drove him to Berck Plage, and the General went down to the sea alone. No one saw the manner of his end. His body was recovered from the sea some time later.'[2] Brigadier-General Cox is buried in Etaples Military Cemetery, France.

Officers Died In The Great War: Corps of Royal Engineers
1 L.G. 23/1/15. 2 Spring. *In the Meantime*

East, L. W. P. C.M.G. D.S.O.   **Brigadier-General**
C.H.A. XIII Corps   **Killed in action: 6 September, 1918**

Lionel William Pellew East was born in July, 1866, the son of Rear-Admiral J. W. East. He was educated at the R.M.A., Woolwich, and was commissioned into the Royal Artillery in September, 1885. During his service he took part in a number of frontier expeditions in India, including the Hazara Expedition of 1891, the second Miranzai expedition of the same year and the operations against Abor Tribes on the north-eastern frontier of Assam in 1894, where he was severely wounded and was awarded the D.S.O.[1] in recognition of services during the operations carried out in the Northern Chin Hills. He held the appointment of G.S.O.2 in the Welsh Division of the Western Command from September, 1909, to September, 1913. In 1915 he commanded a brigade of artillery at the Battle of Festubert and was wounded in the head during a bombing fight at Loos.[2] In 1916 he was promoted to Brigadier-General and was made C.M.G. in the same year. His appointment as C.H.A. was made in March, 1916, and he became B.G.R.A. XIII Corps in February, 1917. It was near Festubert, where he had been previously wounded, that he was killed. The Royal Artillery diary[3] of XIII Corps records: 'Ferfay. September 6th 1918. Brigadier-General East, Commanding Heavy Artillery, was killed during the afternoon by a machine gun, while reconnoitring for forward observation posts.' Brigadier-General East is buried in Lapugnoy Military Cemetery, France.

Officers Died in The Great War. Royal Regiment of Artillery (R.H.A. and R.F.A.)
1 L.G. 15/9/91. 2 *Royal Artillery War Commemoration Book.* 3 PRO WO 95/902

Ellershaw, W.   **Brigadier-General**
S.S.O. War Office   **Drowned as a result of enemy action: 5 June, 1916**

Wilfred Ellershaw was born in July, 1871, and commissioned into the Royal Artillery in April, 1892. From 1899 until 1906 he was employed almost continuously as an instructor at the Royal Military Academy, and afterwards as an Instructor at the School of Signalling. At the outbreak of war in 1914 he went to France with a Field Battery. Later he was, until his death, employed on special service at the War Office. On Sunday, 4 June, 1916, he joined Kitchener's ill-fated party on their journey to Scapa Flow, on their way to Russia. When H.M.S. *Hampshire* sank on 5 June, General Ellershaw was drowned. His grave is the sea off Marwick Head, Orkney. His name is commemorated on the Hollybrook Memorial, Shirley, Hampshire.

Officers Died in The Great War. Royal Regiment of Artillery (R.H.A. and R.F.A.)

Feetham, E. C.B. C.M.G.   **Major-General**
G.O.C 39th Division   **Killed in action: 29 March, 1918**

Edward Feetham was born in June, 1863, and was educated at Marlborough. He served in the Royal Monmouthshire Royal Engineers (Militia) before he was commissioned into the Royal Berkshire Regiment in 1883. In the Sudan Expedition of 1885 he served with the Camel Corps, and in 1886 he was with the Frontier Field Force. He served in the South African War from 1901 to 1902, in command of the 10th Battalion of Mounted Infantry. For his services in the Great War he was made C.B in 1915 and C.M.G. in 1917. On 20 August, 1917, he was appointed to command the 39th Division. In 1918, whilst he was on leave, Brigadier Cape (q.v.), who had taken temporary command, was killed and Brigadier-General Hornby (q.v.) assumed command. Major-General Feetham resumed command on 23 March and six days later he also was killed. The 39th Division's A. & Q.M.G. diary[1] records: 'Domport sur la Luce. March 29th, 11 am. Major-General Feetham killed by shell in Ignaucourt.' However, the General Staff diary[2] of the 39th Division has the following entry: 'March 29th. About 12 noon, the enemy commenced bombarding Demuin whilst the G.O.C. and G.S.O.1 were walking up the main street. One shell burst on the houses they were passing and a fragment struck Major-General Feetham in the neck. A medical officer attached to a battalion of the Gloucestershire Regiment assisted Lt.-Colonel Gosset to carry the G.O.C., who was unconscious, clear of the village, but from the first there was no hope. Scarcely a day passed since he assumed command of the Division without his going to the very foremost positions held by our troops, where, regardless of all dangers, he by his own personal example stimulated his men to maintain their position and defeat the enemy.' In eleven days the 39th Division had lost two commanders. Major-General Feetham was buried at the French Communal Cemetery at Guignemicourt in the afternoon of 1 April, but his body was later moved to Picquiny British Cemetery, France.

Officers Died In The Great War: Commands and Staff.
1 PRO WO 95/2569.   2 PRO WO 95/2567

Findlay, N. D.   C.B.   **Brigadier-General**
C.R.A. 1st Division   **Killed in action: 10 September, 1914**

Neil Douglas Findlay was born in May, 1859. He entered the R.M.A., Woolwich in January, 1877, and was commissioned into the Royal Artillery in December, 1878. He saw service with the Hazara Expedition of 1888 and served in the South African War from 1899 to 1900. In 1905 he was made a C.B. He held various Royal Artillery Staff appointments and in July, 1910, he commanded the Royal Artillery of the 1st Division, Aldershot Command. The C.R.A.'s diary[1] of the 1st Division records: '10th September 1914, Priez. Continued march at 6 am. Action at Courchamps-Priez-Nevill St. Front. Artillery in action against rearguard of German column of all arms, first holding ridge north of Preuil and Priez, and then north of Chouy. Action finished about 5 pm. Appendix A: About 12 noon a shell burst near the road and mortally wounded General Findlay.' Brigadier-General Charteris wrote:[2] 'He was selecting a position for his artillery, when, by pure chance, some of our infantry passed by near him and drew, on themselves and him, heavy German shell fire.' So died the first British General to be killed in action in the Great War. Brigadier-General Findlay was buried in Courchamps Churchyard, but his body was later moved to Vailly British Cemetery, France.

Officers Died In The Great War: Royal Regiment of Artillery (R.H.A. and R.F.A.).
1 PRO WO 95/1239. 2 Charteris. *At GHQ*

Fitton, H. G. C.B. D.S.O.   Brigadier-General
G.O.C. 101st Brigade 34th Division   Died of wounds: 20 January, 1916

Hugh Gregory Fitton was born at Gloucester Crescent, London, in November, 1863. He was educated at Eton and the R.A.M.C., Sandhurst, and was commissioned into the Royal Berkshire Regiment in February, 1884. He was attached to the Egyptian Army, his first campaign being the Sudan Expedition of 1885, and, as D.A.A.G, he was with the expedition to Dongola in 1896, where he was wounded and was awarded the D.S.O.[1] in recognition of services during operations in Sudan. In the Nile Expedition of 1897 he served as Staff officer to the G.O.C. Flying Columns and took part in the Battles of Atbara and Khartoum. In the South African War he was D.A.A.G to the 7th Division. In 1902 he transferred to the Royal Warwickshire Regiment and two years later to the Royal West Kent Regiment, and from 1905 to 1907 he commanded the Regiment in Hong Kong and Singapore. In 1910 he was made a C.B. At the beginning of the Great War he was Director of Recruiting at the War Office, but on 19 June, 1915, he was appointed to command the 101st Infantry Brigade of the 34th Division. The brigade arrived in France on 9 January, 1916. The history of the division[2] records: 'On the 19th January [1916] the Division suffered its first battle casualty. Brigadier-General Fitton, while on a visit of instruction to the 16th Infantry Brigade, near Ypres, in company with the G.O.C. of the Brigade [Brig-Gen. C. L. Nicholson] was in the front line at night. Owing to a communication trench having been blown in, the party had to cross a bit of open [ground], and the night being bright, they were spotted by a watchful sniper, who got the General [Fitton] through both thighs. Brigadier-General Nicholson, commanding the Brigade, and his Brigade-Major, Captain B. Tower, were the only ones present and they had a difficult job getting the wounded General, who was a very big man, down the trench, though some stretcher bearers of the K.S.L.I. came to their help.' [The 1st Battalion, K.S.L.I., of the 16th Infantry Brigade, was at this time in the front line near Forward Cottage, 1¾ miles N.E. of Yprcs.] Brigadier-General Fitton died at 1.20 pm. the next day at No. 10 C.C.S., the first man of the 101st Infantry Brigade to be killed in action. He is buried in Lijssenthoek Military Cemetery, Poperinghe, Belgium.

Officers Died In The Great War: Commands and Staff.
1 L.G. 17/11/96. 2 *The 34th Division.*

FitzClarence, C. V.C.   **Brigadier-General**
G.O.C. 1st Guards Brigade 1st Division   **Killed in action: 12 November, 1914**

Charles FitzClarence was born in May, 1865, at Bishop's Court, Co. Kildare, Ireland. He was educated at Eton and Wellington, and was gazetted Lieutenant from the Militia to the Royal Fusiliers in November 1886, and transferred to the Irish Guards in October, 1900. He served in the South African War from 1899 to 1900 and was twice wounded in the defence of Mafeking. The events for which he was decorated with the Victoria Cross for three specific acts of bravery were detailed in the *London Gazette* of 6 July, 1900: 'On 14 October, 1899, Captain Fitz-Clarence went with his squadron of the Protectorate Regiment, consisting of only partially trained men, who had never been in action, to the assistance of an armoured train which had gone out from Mafeking. The enemy were in greatly superior numbers, and the squadron was for a time surrounded, and it looked as though nothing could save them from being shot down. Captain FitzClarence, however, by his personal coolness and courage inspired the greatest confidence in his men, and by his bold and efficient handling of them not only succeeded in relieving the armoured train, but inflicted a heavy defeat on the Boers, who lost fifty killed and a large number wounded. The moral effects of this blow had a very important bearing on subsequent encounters with the Boers. On 27 October, 1899, Captain FitzClarence led his squadron from Mafeking across the open, and made a night attack with the bayonet on one of the enemy's trenches. A hand-to-hand fight took place in the trench, while a heavy fire was concentrated on it from the rear. The enemy was driven out with heavy loss. Captain FitzClarence was the first man into the position and accounted for four of the enemy with his sword. The British lost six killed and nine wounded. Captain FitzClarence was himself slightly wounded. On 26 December, 1899, during the action of Game Tree, near Mafeking, Captain Fitz-Clarence again distinguished himself by his coolness and courage, and was again wounded severely through both legs.' He was Lieutenant-Colonel commanding the Irish Guards from July, 1913, to August, 1914, and then, in September, 1914, went to France and took command of the 1st Guards Brigade of the 1st Division on the 26th of that month. He was killed in a night attack near Ypres which is described in the war diary[1] of the General Staff 1st Division, as follows: 'At 2.30 am. the two Guards Battalions (2/Grenadier & 1/Irish) and the 1/Munsters started from Brigade H.Q. to get into position on the west edge of Polygon Wood. Just as the heads of the column arrived about 200 yards from the Polygon Wood the Germans opened fire from the trenches near the south-west corner of the wood. November 12th, 4.25 am. General FitzClarence killed.' Brigadier-General FitzClarence, 'O.C. Menin Road', has no known grave.

He is commemorated on the Menin Gate Memorial to the Missing, Ypres, Belgium.

Officers Died In The Great War: Commands and Staff.
1 PRO WO 95/1227

Follett, G. B. S. D.S.O. M.V.O. — Brigadier-General
G.O.C. 3rd Guards Brigade Guards Division — Killed in action: 27 September, 1918

Gilbert Burrell Spencer Follett was born in July, 1878, and was educated at Eton and the R.M.C., Sandhurst. He was commissioned into the Coldstream Guards in 1899, and in the South African War he was wounded at Magersfontein. He was made a M.V.O. in 1907. In the early years of the Great War he commanded the 1st and 2nd Battalions of his Regiment until he took acting command of the 2nd Guards Brigade on 23 March, 1918. His promotion to Brigadier-General followed a few days later and he was transferred to command of the 3rd Guards Brigade in April, 1918. The H.Q. diary[1] of the 3rd Guards Brigade records the action in which he was mortally wounded: '27th September 1918. 3rd Guards Brigade H.Q. thereupon set out [from the sunken road in front of Dernicourt] for the next headquarters agreed upon, some 1300 yards north-east of Lock 7. When about 1000 yards east of the canal, Brigadier-General Follett was hit by machine-gun fire below the right shoulder; he became unconscious immediately and was carried back to the dressing station near the canal.' Major-General Ponsonby wrote in his diary[2] a few days later: 'I heard news about Gilley Follett, he was killed a few days ago by a machine-gun bullet. He was in command of 3rd Guards Brigade. He was a great friend of mine and I have known him for many years. He had been wounded three times already in this war.' Two of those wounds had been received when Follett was Lieutenant-Colonel commanding the 2nd Battalion Coldstream Guards in July and November, 1916. He was awarded the D.S.O.[3] when 'although wounded he inspected the front line trench under heavy fire.' Brigadier-General Follett is buried in Beaumetz Cross Roads Cemetery, Beaumetz-les-Cambrai, France.

Officers Died In The Great War: Coldstream Guards.
1 PRO WO 95/1222. 2 PRO WO 95/2594. 3 L.G. 10/1/17.

Forster, G. N. B. C.M.G. D.S.O. — Brigadier-General
G.O.C. 42nd Brigade 14th Division — Killed in action: 4 April, 1918

George Norman Bowes Forster was born in October, 1872, and was educated at The United Services College, Westward Ho!, and the R.M.C. Sandhurst. In 1893 he was commissioned into the Royal Warwickshire

Regiment. He served in the Nile Expedition of 1898, being present at the Battles of Atbara and Khartoum, and served in the South African War from 1899 to 1902. He was Adjutant of the 1st Battalion from 1902 to 1904, and from 1904 to 1908 he was Assistant Commandant of the Mounted Infantry School, India. He went to France with the 7th Battalion of his regiment and eventually commanded the battalion. He was wounded twice and was awarded the D.S.O.[1] for distinguished service in the field. In August, 1917, he was appointed to command the 42nd Infantry Brigade and on 4 April, 1918, when his brigade of the 14th (Light) Division was in action near Villers Bretonneux his headquarters was overrun, as is recorded in the division's A. & Q.M.G. diary:[2] 'Augbiny. 4th April 1918. German attack. 42nd Inf. Bde. HQ. captured. Brigade-Major (Captain Bonham-Carter) escaped. Brg. Gen. Forster reported missing.' A more detailed account appears in the Staff diary[3] of the 42nd Infantry Brigade: 'Hamel. 4th [April 1918] 8.30 [am.] onward. The shelling became intense on the whole forward system and the village of Hamel. All wires were cut by 10.30 am. and it was practically impossible to get messages by runners through. The 9th R.B. were attacked about 10.30 am. and from this hour onwards no very concise accounts can be collected. The 5th Ox & Bucks L.I. commenced to withdraw, their right having been turned, and the 9th R.B. conformed. 11 am. The enemy at this hour were heavily attacking and by 12 noon had captured the whole of the trench line and entered the village. Brigade Hqs. (only 500 yards behind the front line) was surrounded before any message was received and the B.-G.C. and the Staff-Capt. and Signalling Officer are missing together with 15 O.R. The Brigade-Major hid in a ditch about 200 yards from the late H.Q. and escaped through the enemy's outposts at night.' Brigadier-General Forster has no known grave; his name is commemorated on the Pozières Memorial to the Missing, France.

Officers Died In The Great War: The Royal Warwickshire Regiment
1 L.G. 1/1/17.   2 PRO WO 95/1880.   3 PRO WO 95/1889.

Fulton, H. T.   C.M.G.   D.S.O.   **Brigadier-General**
G.O.C. 3rd New Zealand Brigade   **Died of concussion: 29 March, 1918**
New Zealand Division

Harry Townsend Fulton was born in August, 1869. His first appointment, from local Militia forces in New Zealand in 1892, was as Second-Lieutenant in the Argyll and Sutherland Highlanders, but in the following year he transferred to the West Yorkshire Regiment. Two years later he joined the Indian Staff Corps and in 1897 was appointed to the 2nd Battalion Gurkha Rifles. He served on the north-west frontier of India in 1897 and 1898, and took part in the Malakand Mohmand Expeditions and the Tirah campaign. In the South African War, from 1899 to 1901, he served with the New Zealand Mounted Rifles. During the campaign he was severely wounded and was awarded the D.S.O.[1] in recognition of services during operations in South Africa. From August, 1914, he was employed with the New Zealand Expeditionary Force in Samoa, and in 1915 he went to Egypt and thence to France. He commanded the 3rd New Zealand Brigade from March to July, 1916. In 1917 he was made a C.M.G. and in December, 1917, he resumed command of the 3rd New Zealand Brigade. The events of 28 March, 1918, are recorded in the New Zealand Official History:[2] 'During the day [28th] there had also been a marked increase in enemy artillery as well as machine-gun fire. The 1st Canterbury's trenches had been pounded from close range. In the evening an unlucky 5.9 in. shell secured a direct hit on the cellar which was the [N.Z.] Rifle Brigade headquarters in Colincamps. The whole place was wrecked, and the occupants completely buried. Major Purdy was killed, and Captain Dailey, with the signals and intelligence officers, was wounded. General Fulton, who had arrived back on the 27th, succumbed later to the effects of concussion. General Fulton was the third and last [the others were Brown and Johnston] of the New Zealand brigadiers to fall in action.' The brigade diary[3] records the event: 'Colincamps. 28th March 1918. 9.15 pm. Brigade H.Q. wrecked by a 5.9 in. shell. General Fulton died of concussion. Major Purdy was killed almost instantly. Major Dailey evacuated wounded.' Brigadier-General Fulton is buried at Doullens Communal Cemetery, Extension No. 1, France. Major Purdy is buried close by.

Officers Died In The Great War: Indian Army.
1 L.G. 27/9/01.   2 Stewart. *Official History of New Zealand's Effort in the Great War* Vol.3.
3 PRO WO 95/3706

Glasfurd, D. J.   Brigadier-General
G.O.C. 12th Australian Brigade   4th Australian Division   Died of wounds: 12 November, 1916

Duncan John Glasfurd was born in India in November, 1873, and was educated in Edinburgh and at the R.M.C., Sandhurst. He obtained his commission in the Argyll and Sutherland Highlanders in 1893. In the South African War he served as Adjutant of his battalion and he was wounded twice. In 1901 he served in Jubaland against the Ogaden Somalis, and in Somaliland from 1902 to 1904, when he commanded the 4th Somali Camel Corps. He was Director of Military Training, Commonwealth Forces, in Australia, for four years before the Great War and at the outbreak of the war he accompanied the 1st Australian Division on the General Staff and was present during the whole of the operations in Gallipoli. From General Staff Officer he was promoted, in March, 1916, to command the 12th Australian Infantry Brigade. On 12 November, 1916,

General Glasfurd was inspecting the line into which his Brigade was about to move. He was in 'Cheese Road', a sunken lane forming the support line in front of Flers, when he was mortally wounded by a shell. [This lane is now part of the road into Gueudecourt from Le Sars.] The General Staff diary[1] of the 4th Australian Division records: 'November 12th 1916. Brigadier-General Glasfurd, commanding 12th Australian Brigade, was wounded by a piece of H.E. shell this morning, whilst going round the trenches near the Sunken Road north-west of Gueudecourt. The missile entered his back and is believed to be lodged in his kidneys. It took 10 hours [to get him] down to 38 Casualty Clearing Station at Heilly. November 12th, 10.30 pm. Brigadier-General Glasfurd died of wounds at No. 38 C.C.S.' His death occurred at a time when the carnage of the Somme was just ending, yet so popular was Glasfurd that the Divisional Commander, Major-General Sir H. V. Cox, made a formal announcement of his death in Routine Order No.206, dated 13 November: 'It is with great regret that the G.O.C. announces to the division that Brigadier-General D. Glasfurd died yesterday of wounds received in action in the Front Line. General Glasfurd was employed in Australia before the war, and was with the 1st Division throughout the fighting on ANZAC. He joined the 4th Division as brigade commander on its formation in Egypt and has served with it ever since.' Brigadier-General Glasfurd is buried in Heilly Station Cemetery, Méricourt-l'Abbé, France.

Officers Died In The Great War: Argyll and Sutherland Highlanders.
1 PRO WO 95/3443.

Gordon, A. F. C.M.G. D.S.O.   Brigadier-General
G.O.C. 153rd Brigade 51st Division   Died of wounds: 31 July, 1917

Alister Fraser Gordon was born in February, 1872, and was educated at The College, Inverness, and the R.M.C., Sandhurst. He was gazetted to the Royal Highlanders in October, 1890, but transferred to Gordon Highlanders in November of the same year. In 1895 he was with the Relief Force during operations in Chitral and, from 1897 to 1898, he served on the north-west frontier of India and took part in the Tirah Campaign. He was awarded the D.S.O.[1] for his services in the operations in Ashanti, West Africa. He proceeded to South Africa in 1901, where he was Railway Staff Officer for a time before taking part in the operations in the Transvaal until 1902. In the Great War he went to the front at the very beginning and he was wounded in the leg at the Battle of Festubert in May, 1915. After he recovered he was employed as a Brigadier-General on the Staff at the War Office, and was made a C.M.G. He took command of the 153rd Infantry Brigade in May, 1917. Two days before the opening of the Third Battle of Ypres General Gordon and his Brigade-Major,

Captain Hugh Lean, of the Highland Light Infantry, while walking round the trenches, were struck by the same shell, Lean being killed and General Gordon mortally wounded.[2] Brigadier-General Gordon died two days later and is buried in Lijssenthoek Military Cemetery, Poperinghe, Belgium.

Officers Died In The Great War: The Gordon Highlanders.
1 L.G. 26/4/01.   2 Brewsher. *History of the 51st (Highland) Division*

Gordon, C. W. E.   Brigadier-General
G.O.C. 123rd Brigade   41st Division   Killed in action: 23 July, 1917

Charles William Gordon was born in April, 1878, and was educated at Harrow. He was commissioned in the 3rd (Militia) Battalion Black Watch in 1897, and joined the 2nd Battalion in 1899. He served throughout the South African War and then accompanied his battalion to India for ten years. On his return to England he became Adjutant to the 6th Battalion South Staffordshire Regiment (T.F.), and went with the battalion to France in March, 1915. In the following June he rejoined the Black Watch and was severely wounded at the Battle of Loos. He commanded a battalion of his regiment at the Battle of the Somme in 1916 and was appointed a Brigadier-General in the same year. The war diary[1] of the 123rd Brigade records the following: 'Westoutre. 23rd July 1917. On the overland track between "Spoil Bank" and Voormezeele, General Gordon and Captain Pragnell [Brigade-Major] were killed by a direct hit by a shell. General Gordon was killed outright and Captain Pragnell died five minutes later.' Brigadier-General Gordon and Captain Pragnell are buried in Reninghelst New Military Cemetery, Belgium.

Officers Died In The Great War: The Black Watch.
1 PRO WO 95/2637

Gore, R. C. C.B. C.M.G.   Brigadier-General
G.O.C. 101st Brigade   34th Division   Killed in action: 13 April, 1918

Robert Clements Gore was born in February, 1867, and was educated at Haileybury and the R.M.C., Sandhurst, and was commissioned into the Argyll and Sutherland Highlanders in 1886. He served with distinction in the Great War and was made a C.B. and C.M.G. In January, 1916, he was appointed Brigadier-General Commanding the 101st Infantry Brigade of the 34th Division. In a letter[1] written to the Official Historian in June, 1931, Lt. Colonel Rt. Hon. W. Guinness, D.S.O. [who was Brigade-Major of the 74th Brigade, 25th Division, and who later became Lord Moyne] describes the events that led to the death of Brigadier-General Gore: 'The headquarters of both the 101st and the 74th Brigades were occupying the same cellar in the farm at S.21.b.6.2. on the Mont de Lille [S.E. of Bailleul], when it was blown in. The explosion killed General Gore and his Signalling Officer, [Captain F. G. Avery] and wounded Captain Gilbey, his Brigade-Major, and amongst other casualties were the Staff-Captain and the Signalling Officer of the 74th Brigade. Practically everyone in the cellar except General Craiggie-Halkett and myself were knocked out ---- the control of both brigades might very easily have been entirely blotted out.' There is some slight disparity between War Diaries, The Probate Register and *The Times* as to the date of death, but his headstone bears the date 13 April, 1918. Brigadier-General Gore is buried in Lijssenthoek Military Cemetery, Poperinghe, Belgium.

Officers Died In The Great War: Argyll and Sutherland Highlanders.
1 PRO CAB 45/123.

Gosling, C. C.M.G.	**Brigadier-General**
G.O.C. 7th Brigade 25th Division	**Wounded: 1 May, 1916**
G.O.C. 10th Brigade 4th Division	**Killed in action: 12 April, 1917**

Charles Gosling was born in June, 1868, and was educated at Eton. He entered the Royal Irish Rifles in August, 1888, and transferred to the King's Royal Rifle Corps in the following November. Gosling served nearly the whole of his service abroad, and was aboard the Royal Indian Marine Troopship, *Warren Hastings*, when it was wrecked off the island of Reunion on 14 January, 1896. He was awarded the Silver Medal of the Royal Humane Society for twice attempting to save a man who had been washed overboard. He saw active service in the South African War from 1899 to 1902 in the mounted infantry. In 1912 he took command of the 3rd K.R.R.C. in India, and in 1914 took the battalion to France and served with it until he was wounded in February, 1915, in an attack on St. Eloi. He returned to France in the following May and was given command of the 7th Infantry Brigade, which he commanded for twelve months until he was again severely wounded in May, 1916. In this year he was made a C.M.G. Once again he returned to France, in December, 1916, this time to command the 10th Infantry Brigade. On 12 April, 1917, near Arras, Captain Fellowes, his Brigade-Major, was shot by a sniper and Brigadier-General Gosling was killed by a shell. They are buried side by side in Hervin Farm British Cemetery, St. Laurent-Blagny, France.

Officers Died In The Great War: Commands and Staff.

Gough, J. E.   V.C.   K.C.B.   C.M.G.   **Brigadier-General**

C.O.S. 1st Army   **Died of wounds: 22 February, 1915**

John Edmond Gough was born in India, in October, 1871, the son of General Sir Charles Gough, V.C., G.C.B., and the nephew of General Sir Hugh Gough, V.C., G.C.B. He was educated at Eton and the R.M.C., Sandhurst, and was commissioned into the Rifle Brigade in March, 1892. He first saw active service in British Central Africa from 1896 to 1897 with the expeditions against the Chitsusi and Chilwa, and also served in the Nile Expedition of 1898, being present at the Battle of Khartoum. He served in the South African War from 1899 to 1902, including the defence of Ladysmith. In East Africa from 1902 to 1903, during operations in Somaliland he won the Victoria Cross, the third member of the Gough family to do so. The *London Gazette* of 15 January, 1904, carried the following account: 'During the action at Daratoleh, on the 22nd April 1903, Major Gough assisted Captains Walker and Rolland in carrying back the late Captain Bruce (who had been mortally wounded), and prevented that officer from falling into the hands of the enemy. Captains Walker and Rolland have already been awarded the Victoria Cross for their gallantry on this occasion, but Major Gough (who was in command of the column) made no mention of his own conduct, which has only recently been brought to notice.' From 1907 to 1909 he was Inspector-General of the King's African Rifles, and in June, 1910, he was made a C.M.G. In October 1913 he was appointed Brigadier-General General Staff to Sir Douglas Haig, Aldershot Command, and in this capacity he went to France with the 1st Army Corps. The accounts of his death vary from Conan Doyle's description: 'an accidental shot killed General Gough,' to his old regiment's history which records that: 'There was an eagle-eyed German sniper on the Aubers Ridge, twelve hundred yards away. There was the sudden hiss of a bullet, the distant snap of a rifle, and General Gough's plans and career were both at an end. They carried him to his old Company Mess to die.'[1] Gough was visiting his old battalion of the Rifle Brigade when he was hit. Haig attended his funeral and Colonel Stephens, commanding the battalion, told him that it was a chance shot which had ricochetted off the Fauquissart high road.[2] Brigadier-General Charteris describes the events: 'Poor Gough has been killed, just when he was getting the dream of his ambition, the command of a division. D.H. sent me off to get him back. Moynihan [Sir Berkeley Moynihan], who had operated on Gough last year, was ordered to await him. All we knew was that he had been seriously wounded – shot through the stomach. I reached him in the early afternoon, but it was impossible to get an ambulance to him until after dark. He was quite conscious in the ambulance. His C.B. had just appeared in the 'Gazette,' his only comment when I told him was, "I would get that now, anyhow, even without a war". Moynihan operated, and thought there was some hope he might pull through; his heart failed at 5 am.'[3] His brother, General Hubert Gough, who was only twenty miles away and rushed to Estaires to see him, wrote: 'I found him stretched on a table, awaiting examination, perfectly calm. At first it was thought that the bullet had not taken a dangerous course, but by next morning bad symptoms had set in.'[4] The A. & Q.M.G. diary[5] of the 1st Army records: 'Monday, February 22nd. Funeral of General Gough. With Mrs. Gough's approval General Gough was buried at 4 pm. in the cemetery at Estaires' [Communal Cemetery and Extension, France]. The firing party at his funeral was provided by 'A' Coy. of the 2nd Battalion The Rifle Brigade, his old company. On 20 April, 1915, the posthumous honour of a K.C.B. was conferred on him by the King.

Officers Died In The Great War: Commands and Staff.
1 Berkley. *The Rifle Brigade 1914–18.* 2 Duff Cooper. *Haig.* 3 Charteris. *At GHQ.* 4 Gough. *The Fifth Army.* 5 PRO WO 95/181

Granet, E. J. C.B.   Brigadier-General
C.R.A. 11th Division   Died of wounds: 22 October, 1918

Edward John Granet was born in August, 1858, and was educated at Eton. He entered the Royal Artillery in 1878. During the the South Africa War, in 1901 and 1902, he served as D.A.A.G. and was at the Headquarters of the Army from 1902 to 1905. He was Assistant Director Remounts from 1906 to 1910 and then he became a military attaché at Rome and Berne from 1911 to January, 1915. He was made a C.B. in 1911. In March, 1915, he was appointed C.R.A. of the 11th Division and he was wounded at Suvla Bay in August of that year. The following entry appears in the C.R.A's diary:[1] 'August 13th, 1915. Nibrunesi Point. In the morning the enemy shelled Lala Baba hill with a big gun. One shell fell in the trench and wounded Brigadier-General Granet, Commanding R.A. 11th Division, and his servant.' In a letter[2] to the official historian, Lieutenant-Colonel W. J. K. Rettie, D.S.O., who commanded the 59th Brigade R.F.A. of the 11th Division, described the event as follows: 'On the morning of the 13th a gun, somewhere up Sari Bair way, opened on the fleet, and to judge from the sound of the projectile the line of fire was right over our heads, as we sat on the hill top observing the fire. Suddenly, whether by intention or by disgraceful shooting on the part of the enemy, the song of an approaching shell instead of dying away as it passed over became a shriek and a roar and it burst among us. I was hit with a shower of gravel, luckily in the back and received no damage, but the C.R.A. who was a little way off was badly wounded in the face and hands by the stones.' The Army List for January, 1919, lists his name as having died, but the Common-wealth War Graves Register for Berne (Schosshalde) Cemetery, Switzerland, where he is buried, states that he 'Died 22nd October 1918, as a result of wounds received at Suvla Bay, Gallipoli.'

Officers Died In The Great War: Royal Regiment of Artillery (R.H.A. and R.F.A.).
1 PRO WO 95/4298.   2 PRO CAB 45/244.

Hamilton, H. I. W.   C.V.O.   C.B.   D.S.O.   Major-General
G.O.C. 3rd Division   Killed in action: 14 October, 1914

Hubert Ion Wetherall Hamilton was born in June, 1861, and commissioned into the Queen's Regiment in 1880. He served in the Burmese Expedition from 1886 to 1888, and in the Egyptian Campaigns from 1897 to 1899, including the Battles of Atbara and Khartoum, and was awarded the D.S.O.[1] in recognition of his services in Egypt and the Sudan. He served in the South African War from 1899 to 1902 as D.A.A.G and A.A.G. Army Headquarters, and as Military Secretary to General Lord Kitchener. From 1902–1905 he was Kitchener's Military Secretary in India. He was made a C.B. in 1906 and given command of the 7th Infantry Brigade. His appointment as Major-General, General Staff, Mediterranean Command was made in 1908 and in 1909 he was made a C.V.O. When the Great War broke out he was commanding the 3rd Division at Bulford. He narrowly escaped death early in the war when, as General Smith-Dorrien's diary[2] records: '26th September 1914. Two days ago General Hamilton, General Lindsay and Lord Loch were talking together when one [anti-aircraft pom-pom shell] landed on the ground in the middle of the three of them, luckily without doing any damage.' He was not to be so lucky a month later as Major Billy Congreve[3], who was an A.D.C. to General Hamilton, described: 'October 14th. La Couture. Hammy is dead, and we lose a splendid soldier and I a very good friend. He and Thorpe [Captain Thorpe, another A.D.C.] were out to the north of Vieille Chapelle; he had gone to see personally why our left was hung up. They were dismounted and standing on the road, when a salvo of shrapnel burst right over them. One bullet hit him in the forehead, and he died almost immediately. He never spoke or opened his eyes.' There were several other officers besides Thorpe, yet nobody else was hit. Congreve describes how his body was brought back and how he had to remove the General's spurs before they could get his body in the coffin they had made for him. They had dug his grave against the walls of La Couture church and he was buried there that night. Congreve describes the scene: 'At 8.30 pm. we all assembled, there was a representative from each unit, and Sir Horace Smith-Dorrien turned up also. The rifle and machine-gun fire was very heavy and it sounded but a few yards away, so loud was it and so still the night. Stray bullets now and then knocked up against the church and gravestones, but somehow nobody bothered about them. Just before the Chaplain arrived the firing ceased, but while the short service was being read it commenced again louder and nearer than ever, so loud indeed that the Chaplain's voice could hardly be heard. The scene was the strangest and most beautiful I have ever seen. The poor old church battered by shells, the rough wood coffin with a pewter plate nailed to the lid on which we had stamped his name, a rough cross of flowers made by the men, the small guard with fixed bayonets and the group of twenty or thirty bareheaded officers and men. Above all the incessant noise, so close, sometimes dying down only to seem to redouble itself a few minutes later. A ghastly sort of light was given by a couple of acetylene lamps from a car. Sir Horace, in that rather wonderful voice of his said: "Indeed, a true soldier's grave. God rest his soul." Nobody else spoke.' The next day a French inhabitant of the village offered his own cross which he kept by him in his house ready for his own grave. The ornate affair of wood was erected on the General's grave. General Hamilton did not lie in France for long. On 21 October, *The Times* reported: 'The funeral of Major-General Hubert Ion Hamilton, who was killed in action in France, took place yesterday in Cheriton, Folkestone.' The grave is on the right of the gateway to St. Martin's Churchyard, Cheriton, Kent, England. The stone bears no reference to a military life, no reference to rank, decorations or cause of death, just: 'Hubert Hamilton 1861 – 1914' and a verse from a poem, *Ye Wearie Wayfarer*, by the Australian poet, Adam Lindsay Gordon:

> Question not but live and labour
> Till your goal be won.
> Helping every feeble neighbour,
> Seeking help from none.

In the chancel of St. Peter's Church, Marchington, Uttoxeter, is a brass plaque on which is engraved: 'To the Glory of God, and in Sacred Memory of Hubert I. W. Hamilton, Major-General, C.V.O. C.B. D.S.O., who fell in the service of his country October 14th 1914, at Le Couture. I have fought the good fight. I have finished my course. I have kept faith.' No one now living in the village knows why the plaque was placed there.

Officers Died In The Great War: Commands and Staff.
1 L.G. 15/11/98. 2 PRO CAB 45/2063. 3 Thornton & Fraser. *The Congreves, Father and Son.*

Harvey, W. J. St. J.   Brigadier-General
G.O.C. 19th Brigade   7th Indian Division   Died of wounds: 1 February, 1916

William James St. John Harvey was born in September, 1872, and was educated at Eton and the R.M.C., Sandhurst, and was commissioned into the Black Watch in November, 1892. He served in the South African War from 1899 to 1902, and was severely wounded at Magersfontein, during the advance on Kimberley. He was employed with the Egyptian Army from 1906 to October, 1914, during which time he took part in the operations in Blue Nile Province in 1908, and operations in the Atwot region in 1910. In October, 1914, he was recalled from Egypt to command the 2nd Battalion Black Watch in France. In September, 1915, he was promoted to Brigadier-General and appointed to command the 19th (Dehra Dun) Brigade of the 7th Indian Division, in Mesopotamia. On 20 January, 1916, in the attack on Hanna on the River Tigris, he was wounded. Brigadier-General Harvey died of his wounds at Amara and is buried in the Amara War Cemetery, Iraq.

Officers Died In The Great War: The Black Watch.

Hasler, J.   **Brigadier-General**
G.O.C 11th Brigade   4th Division   **Killed in action: 27 April, 1915**

Julian Hasler was born in October, 1868, and commissioned into the East Kent Regiment in September, 1889. He saw service with the Chitral Relief Force in 1895 and two years later he took part in in the operations on the north-west frontier of India, in Bajaur, in the Mamuad Country, and in the attack and capture of the Tanga Pass. He served in the South African War from 1899 to 1902, and was severely wounded. In 1903 he served in the Kanosokoto Campaign in Northern Nigeria and again served in that country two years later. In February, 1915, he was appointed to command the 11th Infantry Brigade, and two months later was killed in action. On the night of the 27 April he was killed by a shell in St Jean. General Bulfin wrote a letter[1] in October, 1925, in which he refers to the death of General Hasler: 'I saw poor Julian Hasler at St Jean on the 27 April, the place was being heavily shelled – I sent him up Grogan and Le Preu, my G.S.O.2 and 3, to help him, and some signallers but all lines were constantly cut so I ordered him to get out of it as soon as it was dark. He was killed about 9 pm. that night – he could have got away at 6 pm. but delayed.' Brigadier-General Hasler is buried in White House Cemetery, St Jean-lès-Ypres (now St Jan), Belgium.

Officers Died In The Great War: The Buffs (East Kent Regiment).
1 PRO WO CAB 45/140.

Hepburn-Stuart-Forbes-Trefusis, The Hon. J. F. D.S.O.   **Brigadier-General**
G.O.C. 20th Brigade   7th Division   **Killed in action: 24 October, 1915**

The Hon. John Frederick Hepburn-Stuart-Forbes-Trefusis was born in January, 1878, the son of Lord and Lady Clinton, and was educated at

Eton. In the South African War he served as a Trooper in the Imperial Yeomanry, but in 1901 he was gazetted as a 2nd Lieutenant in the Irish Guards. He was known as 'Jack Tre' in the Brigade of Guards. In January, 1914, he was appointed Adjutant of the R. M. C., Sandhurst, and in the following September he was Adjutant of the 1st Battalion Irish Guards, B.E.F., and in December of the same year was gazetted Temporary Lieutenant-Colonel in the Irish Guards. In February, 1915, he was awarded the D.S.O.[1] for services in connection with operations in the field. His appointment as Brigadier-General Commanding the 20th Infantry Brigade was made in August, 1915. He was killed on the Givenchy front: 'The Germans acquired a distinct superiority in sniping before the 7th Division took over the line [from Quinque Rue to Givenchy]. This the Division could not allow and special measures were taken to suppress the hostile snipers, who took only too heavy a toll before they were mastered. Their most notable victim was General Trefusis, killed on October 24th when going round his trenches with General Berners just before the 21st Brigade relieved the 20th at Givenchy.'[2] The war diary[3] of the 20th Brigade records: 'He was shot through the forehead by a sniper and died almost immediately.' Brigadier-General Hepburn-Stuart-Forbes-Trefusis is buried in the Guards' Cemetery, Windy Corner, Cuinchy, France.

Officers Died In The Great War: Irish Guards.
1 L.G. 18/2/15.   2 Atkinson. *The Seventh Division 1914–1918.*   3 PRO WO 95/1652

Heyworth, F. J.   C.B.   D.S.O.   Brigadier-General
G.O.C. 3rd Guards Brigade   Guards Division   Killed in action: 9 May, 1916

Frederic James Heyworth was born in March, 1863, and was educated at Eton. In December, 1883, he was gazetted Lieutenant in the Scots Guards from the Militia. He served in the Sudan in 1885 and in the South African War from 1899 to 1902, and was awarded the D.S.O.[1] in recognition of services during operations in South Africa. He was Officer Commanding the Scots Guards and Regimental District when the Great War broke out and was appointed to command the 20th Brigade when Brigadier-General Ruggles-Brise (q.v.) was wounded in November, 1914. He was made a C.B. in 1915 and in August of that year he took command of the 3rd Guards Brigade and in the following May he was killed in action. The diary[2] of the Guards Division records the events leading to his death: 'May 9th. Brigadier-General F. J. Heyworth, Commanding 3rd Guards Brigade, killed by a sniper at long range. Otherwise a quiet day.'

Summary of Operations – 14 May, 1916: 'At 4 am. on May 9th the enemy sprang a mine opposite H.16 [Bellewaarde Sector]. Brigadier-General Heyworth was killed by a sniper in "Muddy Lane" when going up to the front line about 7 am. on May 9th to inspect the new crater.' [Muddy

Lane was a communication trench which was located just north of Birr Cross-Road and Outpost Farm on the Menin Road.] Brigadier-General Heyworth is buried in Brandhoek Military Cemetery, Vlamertinghe, Belgium.

Officers Died In The Great War: Commands and Staff.
1 L.G. 27/10/01.   2 PRO WO 95/1190.

Hodson, G. B. C.B. D.S.O.   **Brigadier-General**
G.O.C. 33rd Indian Brigade   11th Division   **Died of wounds: 25 January, 1916**

George Benjamin Hodson was born in October, 1863, and commissioned, in May, 1882, into the South Staffordshire Regiment, transferring, in February, 1884, to the Oxfordshire Light Infantry, and in September of the same year transferring again to the Indian Staff Corps. He served in the Burmese Expedition from 1885 to 1887; the Hazara Expedition of 1891, and served on the north-west frontier of India in 1897 and 1898. He took part in the Aro Expedition in Southern Nigeria in 1902, and was awarded the D.S.O.[1] for services during the Aro Expedition. He was made a C.B. in 1911, and was A. & Q.M.G. Indian Army from 1912 to September, 1914. In October, 1915, he was appointed to command the 33rd Indian Brigade which was part of the 11th Division. Brigadier-General Hodson was wounded at Suvla, Gallipoli, on 14 December, 1915. The brigade diary[2] said that he was wounded in the head by a sniper, while looking over a parapet, and the General Staff diary[3] of the 11th Division said that the wound was a serious one, but the case was not considered hopeless. Unfortunately, his condition was hopeless and he died of his wounds at Tigne Hospital, Malta, on 25 January, 1916. He is buried in the Pieta Military Cemetery, Malta.

Officers Died In The Great War: Indian Army.
1 L.G.12/9/02.   2 PRO WO 95/4299.   3 PRO WO 95/ 4297.

Hoghton, F. A.   **Brigadier-General**
G.O.C. 17th Brigade   6th Indian Division   **Poisoned: 12 April, 1916**

Frederick Aubrey Hoghton was born in March, 1864, and commissioned into the East Yorkshire Regiment in March, 1883, but transferred to the Indian Army in March, 1887. He served with the Mohmand Field Force in 1897, as D.A.Q.M.G. (Intelligence), and held Staff appointments at H.Q. India until December, 1914. He was appointed a Brigade Commander in 1915 and commanded the 17th Brigade of the 6th Indian Division in Mesopotamia. He was 52 years of age when he suffered the privations of the siege of Kut, and his end is described by F. J. Moberley[1] : 'On the night of the 11/12th April, Brigadier-General F.A. Hoghton, Commanding the 17th Infantry Brigade, who had been in poor health for some time, was taken suddenly ill from poisoning by herbs locally gathered, and died. In their craving for vegetable food, many men gathered grass and other vegetation growing locally and this was the cause of many cases of poisoning more or less severe.' They buried the General that afternoon in the little cemetery at the north end of Kut.[2]

Officers Died In The Great War: Indian Army. (Hoghten)
1 Moberley. *The Siege of Kut.* 2 Sanders. *In Kut and Captivity*

Holmes, W. C.M.G. D.S.O. V.D.
G.O.C. 4th Australian Division

Major-General
Died of wounds: 2 July, 1917

William Holmes was born in Sydney, Australia, in September, 1862, and was commissioned into the 1st New South Wales Infantry Regiment in 1886. In the South African War he served with his Regiment from 1899 to 1900, and was wounded at Diamond Hill. Invalided home in 1900, he was awarded the D.S.O.[1] in recognition of his services during operations in South Africa. From 1904 to 1911 he was A.D.C. to the Governor-General of Australia and was awarded the Volunteer Decoration in 1905. In the Great War he commanded the Australian Naval and Military Force in the New Guinea Expedition and became the first Governor of German New Guinea after its capture. He commanded the 5th Infantry Brigade in Gallipoli and during the evacuation. General Holmes then went to France where, in January, 1917, he was appointed to command the 4th Australian Division and was made a C.M.G. The events which led to his death are described in a footnote to the Official History[2] : 'A chance salvo fired at a usually safe track behind Hill 63 mortally wounded one of the most eminent of Australian citizen soldiers, the commander of the 4th Division, Major-General W. Holmes. He was taking the Premier of New South Wales, the Hon. W. A. Holman, to survey the battlefield of Messines. In his own visits, Holmes used to take the straightest route, however dangerous, but on this occasion he had left the car at the "White Gates" to avoid a dangerous corner farther on. As the party started on foot, the salvo burst. Holmes was hit through chest and lung. He was hurried by his A.D.C., Captain D. S. Maxwell, to the nearest assistance at "Kandahar Farm", but he died while being carried to the dressing station.' Major-General Holmes was buried at 3 pm. the next day in Trois-Arbres Cemetery, Steenwerck, France.

Officers Died In The Great War: Commands and Staff.
1 L.G. 19/4/01.   2 *Official History of Australia in the War of 1914–1918*, Vol. 4.

Howell, P. C.M.G.
B.G.G.S. II Corps

Brigadier-General
Killed in action: 7 October, 1916

Philip Howell was born in December, 1877, and entered the Indian Army, in the Queen's Own Corps of Guides, in 1897. On more than one occasion he acted as Special Correspondent of *The Times*, including the Macedonian Rebellions of 1903 and the Turkish Revolution of 1908. In 1913 he was gazetted Major in the 4th Hussars. He held several Staff appointments in India, and from 1909 to 1911 he was a General Staff Officer at the War Office. He saw active service on the north-west frontier of India in 1908. From 1912 to 1913 he was a General Staff Officer at the Staff College. In 1915 he was made a C.M.G. and appointed a B.G.G.S., becoming B.G.G.S. of II Corps in June, 1916. His death is recorded briefly in the General Staff diary[1] of II Corps: [the date contradicts other documents which give his date of death as 7 October] 'October 6th 1916. Brigadier-General P. Howell, B.-G.G.S. II Corps, was killed today in Authille. October 7th 1916. Brigadier-General Howell was buried today in Varennes Cemetery,' France.

Officers Died In The Great War: 4th (Queen's Own) Hussars.
1 PRO WO 95/639

Husey, R. H. D.S.O.* M.C.
G.O.C. 25th Brigade 8th Division

Brigadier-General
Died of wounds whilst P.O.W.: 30 May, 1918

Ralph Hamer Husey was born in 1882, and was educated at Marlborough. He joined the Herts. Yeomanry as a Trooper and subsequently was commissioned into the London Rifle Brigade. On the declaration of war he volunteered for foreign service and proceeded to France with his regiment in November, 1914, as a Captain, and in 1915 he was awarded the M.C. In July, 1916, he was appointed to command his battalion. He was awarded the D.S.O.[1] in January, 1918, and a Bar[2] to this order for his conduct at Arras on 27–28 March when the German advance was held up. His actions, which led to the award, were described in the *Gazette* as follows: 'During an enemy attack, when the enemy approached close to his Battalion Headquarters, he held up the forward end of a communication trench with the personnel of his headquarters and a few other men, and largely assisted in breaking up the enemy attack. He used a rifle himself at close range and inflicted many casualties on the enemy. He then conducted an obstinate withdrawal to the next line of defence, where the enemy was finally held up. He set a magnificent example of courage and determination.' In May, 1918, he was appointed a Brigadier-General and given command of the 25th Infantry Brigade. He had been wounded four times already in the war and he did not retain his command for very long before he was mortally wounded. The brigade diary[3] records the events of 27 May, 1918: 'Cesar. At 1 am. a very heavy barrage came down on our trench system, and back areas were also shelled with H.E. and gas. This continued until 4.5 am. when S.O.S rockets were sent up from the front line and the infantry attack commenced, supported by tanks and using smoke. Within the hour the Redoubt Line was penetrated and brigade headquarters was involved in the fighting. The Brigade Commander at this stage moved back to Gernicourt in order to organise the defences along the river bank. The Gernicourt line was already held by two companies of the 22nd D.L.I. Pioneers and on arrival of two reserve companies of the 2nd East Lancs. Regt. they were placed in this line, with a few oddments of other units. Touch was obtained with the 24th Infantry Brigade on our left and the line was held until midday, when the enemy pushing forward on the flanks made the position untenable. The next line taken up was from the left of Gernicourt Wood towards Bouffignereux village, towards which the Germans were rapidly advancing. By this time practically all the Divisional Artillery and the French Batteries were out of action or had been captured. The 75th Brigade, 25th Division, arrived and took up a line from Bouffignereux Hill to the left, and the remnants of the 25th Brigade were absorbed in this formation. At the close of the day the Brigadier, Brigade-Major, Signals Officer and Captain Lowe (attached) were casualties, the two former missing, the two latter wounded, and the personnel of brigade headquarters suffered badly. The Brigade-Major [Captain Pascoe] was killed, whilst later in the day Brigadier-General Husey was badly wounded and died three days afterwards in German hands.' Brigadier-General Husey is buried in Vendresse British Cemetery, France.

Officers Died In The Great War: 5th (City of London) Battalion The London Regiment (London Rifle Brigade).
1 L.G. 1/1/18. 2 L.G. 22/6/18. 3 PRO WO 95/1728.

Ingouville-Williams, E. C. C.B. D.S.O.
G.O.C. 34th Division

Major-General
Killed in action: 22 July, 1916

Edward Charles Ingouville-Williams was born in December, 1861, and commissioned into the East Kent Regiment from the Militia in 1881. He saw active service with the Sudan Expedition in 1884 and 1885, and with the Nile Expedition in 1898 and 1899, when he was employed as Special Service Officer with the Egyptian Army and was present at the Battles of Atbara and Khartoum. In the South African War, from 1899 to 1902, he served on Sir Charles Warren's Staff as Provost Marshal and later commanded a mobile column, and for his services he was awarded the D.S.O.[1] In 1903 he transferred to the Worcestershire Regiment, and from 1904 to 1908 he commanded the 2nd Battalion. In 1910 he was made a C.B. and was appointed Commandant of the School of Mounted Infantry, Longmoor, until, in 1912, he became Brigade Commander of the 16th Infantry Brigade, Irish Command. He was appointed Major-General Commanding the 34th Division in July, 1915. In a letter[2] written in September, 1930, Colonel Steward describes an incident for which General Ingouville-Williams' gallantry deserves mention. 'Before the attack [1 July, 1916, on the Somme], three waggons of T. M. shells had been ordered by him to Becourt Château, and were exposed to shell fire on the crest of the road from Albert. Two got over, but the driver of the third got whizzbanged and hid in the C. Trench alongside. General Williams got up out of the C. T. and drove the waggon down himself.' The divisional history[3] records the events that led to his death: 'On the 22nd the Divisional Commander, Major-General Ingouville-Williams, C.B., D.S.O., was killed while reconnoitring ground in the vicinity of Mametz. He went out soon after lunch, accompanied by his A.D.C., Lieutenant Grainger Stewart, 16th Royal Scots, and about 8 pm. a telephone message was received that the G.O.C. had been killed by shell-fire whilst walking back from Contalmaison, round the south end of Mametz [Wood], to meet his car which was at Montauban. Exact spot was square X.30.a.3.7., on top of the bank. Extract from War Diary 34th Division. So died the first commander and maker of the 34th Division – an absolutely fearless man; a stern disciplinarian, but with a tender heart.' Guy Chapman, who served with the 13th Battalion Royal Fusiliers, 111th Infantry Brigade, one of the two brigades transferred to the 34th Division to replace the 102nd and 103rd Brigades, describes how the news was received by some of the other ranks:[4] 'On the 30th we moved up to Albert once more. A few drafts had come to us, but except for officers, we were still woefully under strength. We were also fed up with being away from our own division. The 34th, to which we had been loaned, now only possessed one of its own brigades, its eight washed-out battalions of Tynesiders having been sent up north to our own division. Some hooted with derision when the divisional commander was killed near Mametz Wood; it was reported that he was souvenir hunting. And why not hoot? What was this Hecuba to them?' Despite this attitude among his temporary brigades, his own men buried 'Inky Bill' at Warloy-Baillon Communal Cemetery Extension with due respect, as is recorded in the divisional war diary:[5] '23 July, 1916. Major-General Ingouville-Williams buried at Warloy Cemetery 4 pm., Rev. W. K. Griffin officiated. Gun-carriage supplied by A/152. Firing party, escort and pall bearers by 101st Infantry Brigade. R. E. made coffin and dug grave. A.A. & Q.M.G. to 101st Infantry Brigade and Warloy to make arrangements. D.A.A. & Q.M.G. to Iranvilles and to Amiens for wreath. A. & Q. officers to funeral of G.O.C.' Major-General

Ingouville-Williams is buried in Warloy-Baillon Communal Cemetery and Extension, France.

Officers Died In The Great War: Commands and Staff
1 L.G. 19/4/01. 2 PRO CAB 45/137. 3 *The 34th Division 1915 – 1919.* 4 Chapman. *A Passionate Prodigality.* 5 PRO WO 95/2438

Johnston, F. E. C.B.   **Brigadier-General**
G.O.C. 3rd New Zealand Brigade   New Zealand Division   Killed in action: 7 August, 1917

Francis Earl Johnston, was born in October, 1871, the eldest son of the Hon. Charles Johnston, Speaker of the Legislative Council of New Zealand. He was commissioned into the North Staffordshire Regiment in December, 1891. He served in the expedition to Dongola in 1896 and saw service in the South African War from 1900 to 1902. He was Inspector of Artillery, Coastal Defences and Ammunition, New Zealand Military Forces, and then commanded the 1st New Zealand Brigade at Gallipoli and was made a C.B. in 1915. In July, 1917, he became commander of the 3rd N.Z (Rifle) Brigade. The New Zealand Official History[1] describes how he died, when his brigade was in trenches near La Basseville, east of Ploegsteert Wood: 'The front-line posts themselves lay in converted shell holes on high ground about an isolated windmill on the road from Warneton to Gapard, and formed a marked salient with the enemy on three sides. These posts and the rear trenches generally were alike, waist deep in mud. Whilst visiting these outposts in the early morning of 7th August, General Earl Johnston was killed instantly by a sniper's bullet.' He is buried in Bailleul Communal Cemetery and Extension, France.

Officers Died In The Great War: North Staffordshire Regiment.
1 Stewart. *Official History of New Zealand's Effort in the Great War*, Vol. 2.

Kay, Sir William A. I. 6th Bart.   C.M.G.   D.S.O.   **Brigadier-General**
G.O.C. 2nd Brigade   1st Division   **Wounded: 17 March, 1918**
G.O.C. 3rd Brigade   1st Division   **Killed in action: 4 October, 1918**

William Algernon Ireland Kay was born in March, 1876, the son of Lieutenant-Colonel Sir William Kay, 5th Baronet, and Lady Kay. He was educated at Harrow and was commissioned into the King's Royal Rifle Corps in July, 1896. He served in Sierra Leone from 1898 to 1899, and in the South African War from 1899 to 1902. He went to France with the Expeditionary Force on Sir John French's Staff, and was badly wounded in October, 1914. He was awarded the D.S.O.[1] , one of the first D.S.O.'s gazetted during the Great War, when, as a Major of the 2/K.R.R.C., he made a reconnaissance of great value on 1 October, reaching a point within 100 yards of the enemy's outposts. He succeeded his father as the 6th Baronet in October, 1914. On recovering from his wound he served as G.S.O.1 of the 24th Division in 1916. In March, 1918, he took command of the 2nd Infantry Brigade when its commander, Brigadier-General Kemp (q.v.), was wounded. Twelve days later, as the war diary[2] of the 2nd Brigade records: '17th March 1918. Gen. Kay wounded in the face by a machine-gun bullet whilst visiting the forward posts of the Royal Sussex Regiment.' He was made a C.M.G. in 1918, and returned to France in April to take command of the 3rd Infantry Brigade when its commander, Brigadier-General Morant (q.v.), was wounded. He was killed in October, 1918, as the war diary[3] of the 3rd Infantry Brigade records: 'Magny-la-Fosse. 4th October 1918. Brigadier-General Sir W. A. I. Kay, Bart. C.M.G. D.S.O., and Captain W. F. Somervail, D.S.O. M.C. [Brigade-Major] were killed whilst reconnoitring new area.' The King's Royal Rifle Corps Chronicles for 1918 say that 'he was killed instantaneously by a gas shell near St. Quentin.' Brigadier-General Sir W. A. I. Kay is buried at Vadencourt British Cemetery, Maissemy, France. Captain Somervail lies in the next grave.

Officers Died In The Great War: The King's Royal Rifle Corps.
1 L.G. 9/11/14. 2 PRO WO 95/1268. 3 PRO WO 95/1277.

Kenna, P. A. V.C. D.S.O.
G.O.C. 3rd Mntd. Brigade   2nd Mntd. Division

Brigadier-General
Died of wounds: 30 August, 1915

Paul Aloysius Kenna was born in August, 1862, and was educated at Stonyhurst College. After two years as a Lieutenant with the Militia he entered the R.M.C., Sandhurst, from where he was commissioned into the West India Regiment, and subsequently served in the West Indies and in West Africa. In 1889 he transferred to the 21st Hussars, later to be known as the 21st Lancers, and served with this regiment in India from 1890 to 1895. In 1895, whilst at home in Ireland, he rescued a man from drowning in the River Liffey, in Dublin. For this he received the 'Vellum Testimonial' of the Royal Humane Society. He went with the 21st Lancers to Egypt in 1896 and took part in the Nile Expedition of 1898 and was awarded the Victoria Cross. The *London Gazette* of 15 November, 1898, records his gallantry: 'At the Battle of Khartoum, on 2nd September 1898, Captain P. A. Kenna assisted Major Crole Wyndham, of the same regiment [21st Lancers], by taking him on his horse, behind the saddle (Major Wyndham's horse having been killed in the charge), thus enabling him to reach a place of safety; and after the charge of the 21st Lancers, Captain Kenna returned to assist Lieutenant de Montmorency, who was endeavouring to recover the body of second Lieutenant R. G. Grenfell.' He served in the South African War from 1899 to 1902 and was for part of that time in command of a cavalry column, and for his services he was awarded the D.S.O.[1] From 1902 to 1904 he was with the Somaliland Field Force and took part in the action at Jidballi. In 1905 he was appointed Brigade-Major to the 1st Cavalry Brigade at Aldershot, and held that appointment until gazetted to command the 21st Lancers in September, 1906. He was appointed to command the Notts. and Derby (Yeomanry) Mounted Brigade in April, 1911, and was promoted to Brigadier-General in August, 1914. In the spring of 1915 he took his mounted brigade to Egypt and later to Suvla Bay, Gallipoli. At 'Chocolate Hill' on 29 August, 1915, whilst inspecting his lines, he 'was hit, the bullet striking [his] left arm and entering [his] abdomen. He was carried out with great difficulty to the 31st Field Ambulance. Surgeon Captain Rowe rendered first aid with the greatest promptitude and care', as the diary[2] of the 3rd Mounted Brigade records. Brigadier-General Kenna died of his wounds the next day. He is buried in Lala Baba Cemetery, Suvla, Gallipoli.

Officers Died In The Great War: Commands and Staff.
1 L.G. 26/6/02.   2 PRO WO 95/4293.

Kitchener, Rt. Hon. H. H., Earl, of Khartoum   Field Marshal
K.G. K.P. P.C. G.C.B. O.M. G.C.S.I. G.C.M.G. G.C.I.E.
Secretary of State for War   Drowned as a result of enemy action: 5 June, 1916

Horatio Herbert Kitchener was born in June, 1850, at Crotter House, Ballylongford, County Kerry, Ireland, and was educated at a French school in Switzerland. In 1886 he passed into the R.M.A., Woolwich, and qualified for a commission in the Royal Engineers in December, 1870. He offered his services to the French Army of the Loire and served for a short time, but fell ill. He received his commission in the Royal Engineers in 1871, and from 1874 to 1878 went on a survey of Palestine. From 1878 to 1882 he was sent on a survey of Cyprus. He commanded Egyptian Cavalry from 1882 to 1884 and the Nile Expedition of 1884 and 1885. In 1886 he was appointed Governor General of the Eastern Sudan, and was wounded in the jaw in a raid on the local leader of the Dervishes in January, 1888. In 1892 he became Sirdar, and was created a K.C.M.G. in 1894. In 1896 the River War was inaugurated by an advance on Dongola and Kitchener was promoted to Major-General. In 1898 he fought the Battles of Atbara and Khartoum, and was created a G.C.B. He became Chief-of-Staff to Lord Roberts in the South African War in 1899 and was made a Viscount and Commander-in-Chief in India in 1902. When he left India in 1909 he was created a G.C.I.E. and promoted Field Marshal. In 1914 he was created the 1st Earl Kitchener of Khartoum, and on 3 August of that year he became Secretary-of State for War. He immediately made provision for the expansion of the six regular divisions and fourteen territorial divisions to seventy divisions. In 1915 he was the target of the press for the lack of shells, and for the failure of the landings in Gallipoli. He went to Gallipoli in November to see the situation for himself and made personal inspection of the positions at Helles, Suvla and Anzac; at times he was only twenty yards from the enemy's trenches. His suggestion that there should be a partial withdrawal was rejected and the peninsula was evacuated. In the same year he was invested with the Order of the Garter. In June, 1916, he was to go to Russia to confer with the Tsar on the military situation. On the afternoon of 4 June, 1916, he motored from his house at Broome Park, near Canterbury, to London to take the night train to Thurso, on his way to Scapa Flow. His party consisted of Lieutenant-Colonel O. A. G. Fitzgerald, his Personal Military Secretary; Sir Frederick Donaldson, Technical Adviser to the Ministry of Munitions; L. S. Robertson, Sir Frederick's adviser; H. J. O'Beirne, Counsellor at the British Embassy in Petrograd; Brigadier-General W. Ellershaw (q.v.); Second-Lieutenant R. D. MacPhearson, 8th Cameron Highlanders; a cipher clerk; three servants and Kitchener's personal detective, Detective M'Laughlin, of Scotland Yard. When they reached Thurso they were taken to Scapa Flow where they boarded H.M.S. *Hampshire*, in which they were to complete their journey. *Hampshire* was a fast armoured cruiser which had just returned from the Battle of Jutland with the rest of the Grand Fleet. The ship left Scapa Flow on the afternoon of 5 June, taking a route up the west coast of Orkney. Just a few hours later the *Hampshire* hit a mine and sank in a raging storm off the Orkneys. Only 12 members of the crew survived, all Lord Kitchener's party were drowned and of his party only Lieutenant-Colonel Fitzgerald's body was washed ashore. Field Marshal Lord Kitchener's grave is the sea off Marwick Head, Orkney. The islanders erected a tower in his memory on the cliffs near to the spot where H.M.S *Hampshire* went down. His name is officially commemorated on the Hollybrook Memorial, Shirley, Hampshire.

Officers Died In The Great War: Commands and Staff.

Lee, N. V.D.   **Brigadier-General**
G.O.C. 127th Brigade 42nd Division   **Died of wounds: 22 June, 1915**

Noel Lee was the son of Sir Joseph Cocksey Lee of Tilford in Surrey and was educated at Eton. He had commanded his Territorial Brigade since 1911. In his memoirs[1], Lieutenant-General Sir William Marshall recalls that in the battles of June 1915, 'the retirement and partial destruction of the Naval Brigade left the right flank of the Manchesters "in the air" upon a very advanced position. Their Brigadier-General, Noel Lee, an excellent leader of men and in civil life a partner in a well-known Lancashire shipping and cotton firm, was wounded; many of their officers killed.' The diary[2] of the 127th Brigade records that brigade headquarters was in the third line trench on the east side of Krithia Nulla, and that on '4th June at 12 noon Brigadier-General Noel Lee had been wounded.' He had received a shell wound in the throat from which he died in hospital, in Malta, from haemorrhage due to the reopening of the wound. Brigadier-General Lee is buried in Pieta Military Cemetery, Malta. His eldest son, Captain Noel Esmond Lee, King's Royal Rifle Corps, was killed in action on 24 August, 1917.

Officers Died In The Great War: The Manchester Regiment. 6th Battalion (Territorial). 1 Marshall. *Memories of Four Fronts.* 2 PRO WO 95/4316.

Lipsett, L. J. C.B. C.M.G.
G.O.C. 4th Division

Major-General
Killed in action: 14 October, 1918

Louis James Lipsett was born in June, 1874, and was commissioned into the Royal Irish Regiment in October 1894. In 1897 and 1898 he took part in operations on the north-west frontier of India. He held Staff appointments in South Africa from 1904 to 1907 and then became A.D.C. to Major-Generals commanding the 6th Division, Eastern Command and the 2nd Division, Aldershot Command from 1907 to 1908. In 1911 he was G.S.O.2 with the Canadian Forces, and in September, 1915, he was appointed Brigadier-General Commanding the 2nd Infantry Brigade of the 1st Canadian Division. When Major-General Mercer (q.v.) was killed, Lipsett took command of the 3rd Canadian Division in June, 1916, and commanded this division until September, 1918, when he took command of the British 4th Division. He was made a C.M.G in 1915 and a C.B. in 1918. In October, 1918, Major-General Lipsett became the last British General to be killed in the Great War when he was mortally wounded in front of his own front line, as is described in the diary[1] of the General Staff, 4th Division: 'Escaudoeuvres [near Cambrai]. 14/10/18. At 15.15 a telephone message was received from Brigadier-General Green, Commanding 10th Infantry Brigade, to say that the Divisional Commander, Major-General Lipsett, had been killed while engaged on a reconnaissance. This constitutes a very deplorable loss to the Division. The facts appear to be as follows: General Lipsett had gone up with General Macnaughten, of 12 Brigade, and an officer of 49th Division to reconnoitre the 49th Divisional front which this division expects to take over. His particular object was to gain a view of the crossing of the river Selle between Haspres and Sauloir. He was crawling down the slope E. of the wood in P.25.a., in front of our own posts which ran along the E. edge of the wood W. of Sauloir, when he was hit in the face, probably by a machine-gun bullet. He managed to stagger back to the wood, but died almost immediately. 15/10/18. The funeral of Major-General Lipsett, C.B.

C.M.G. took place at Quéant at 15.00, arrangements being made by the 3rd Canadian Division which he had commanded for 2½ years. Among those present were the G.O.C.'s First Army, Canadian Corps and XXII Corps, representatives of the 4th Division, Canadian Corps and 3rd Canadian Division and Major H.R.H. The Prince of Wales.' Major-General Lipsett is buried in Quéant Communal Cemetery British Extension, France.

Officers Died In The Great War: The Royal Irish Regiment.
1 PRO WO 95/1448.

Lomax, S. H.
G.O.C. 1st Division

Lieutenant-General
Died of wounds: 10 April, 1915

Samuel Holt Lomax was born in August, 1855, and entered the Army, in the 90th Foot, in June, 1874. He fought in the Kaffir and Zulu campaigns of 1877 and 1878, being present at the Battles of Kambula and Ulundi. He was a Captain in the Scottish Rifles by 1880, a Brigade Commander in 1904 and in 1910 had become the General Officer Commanding the 1st Division. Brigadier-General Charteris, writing[1] of the days of mobilization in 1914, said that: 'On July 29th the precautionary orders reached Aldershot and on 4 August came the declaration of war. General Lomax (Commanding the 1st Division) had just been told officially that he had not been selected for further employment. The reason given was that he had little or no war experience. He took his division to France and, until mortally wounded in the Salient, he was perhaps the best Divisional General of those early days of the war.' The *London Gazette* dated 19 October, 1914, announced his promotion to the rank of Lieutenant-General for distinguished service in the field. The war diary[2] of the A. & Q.M.G. of the 1st Division on 27 October, 1914, records that: '1st Echelon Div. H.Q. moved back in the evening to the Château Hooge.' As Duff Cooper records[3]: 'Haig had moved his reporting centre back to White Château in order that Lomax might make himself more comfortable in Hooge Château. Major-General Sir Ernest Swinton, who as a Lieutenant-Colonel in 1914, had been sent to write articles about the British Army, as no correspondents were allowed at the front, wrote[4] of Hooge Château: 'As I drove away, I turned round to look back at the Château of Hooge standing a little to the north of the road. The approach was packed with cars – a splendid advertisement to catch the eye of any chance enemy airman who happened to wander above and proclaim that here was a British headquarters.' The events at the château on the afternoon of 31 October, 1914, are described in Chapter 2. The shell which fell that day left a heavy casualty list of the Staff officers who were asssembled there. General Lomax was dangerously wounded and died later [six months

83

later]. Colonel F. W. Kerr, Lt.-Col. A. J. Percival, Major G. Paley, Captain R. Ommaney and Captain F. M. Chenevix-Trench were killed on the spot. Lt. H. M. Robertson, Major I. W. Forsett and Lt.-Col. Boys, C.R.E. of the 2nd Division, were wounded. Two other officer casualties were: Captain G. P. Shedden, 35th Heavy Battery, R.A., who was killed, and Captain R. Giffard, General Lomax's A.D.C., who was mortally wounded. Major-General Munro escaped with concussion and soon recovered. Nearly six months later *The Times* reported the death of Lieutenant-General Lomax in a London nursing home on 10 April, 1915. His funeral service took place at All Saints', Norfolk Square, and he was cremated at Golders Green Crematorium. No mention was made of him dying of wounds received in action, and his name does not appear in the C.W.G.C. Register at Golders Green. He is buried with his wife under a personal private memorial in Plot AH of Aldershot Military Cemetery, Hampshire.

Officers Died In The Great War: Commands and Staff.
1 Charteris. *At G.H.Q.* 2 PRO WO 95/1235. 3 Cooper. *Haig.* 4 Swinton. *Eyewitness*

Long, W. C.M.G. D.S.O.   Brigadier-General
G.O.C. 56th Brigade 19th Division   Killed in action: 28 January, 1917

Walter Long was born in July, 1879, the son of Mr Walter Long, M.P., who at the time of his son's death was Secretary of State for the Colonies. He was educated at Harrow from 1893 to 1898 and a year later he was gazetted to the Royal Scots Greys from the Militia. He was a Champion Light-Weight boxer at Harrow and twice won the Middle-Weight Boxing Championship of the British Army. He served with his Regiment in the South African War and was with Sir John French's cavalry in their ride to the relief of Kimberley, and then was badly wounded at Dronfield. In recognition of his services he was awarded the D.S.O.[1] Between the wars he served as A.D.C. to the the Governor General of the Dominion of Canada. In August, 1914, he went to France as a Captain in charge of a Squadron of his Regiment. Later he commanded the 6th Battalion Wiltshire Regiment, and was made a C.M.G. His appointment to Brigadier-General commanding the 56th Infantry Brigade came in November, 1916. The History of the 19th Division[2] records how he was killed: 'A great loss was sustained by the Division on the 28th by the death of Brigadier-General W. Long who was killed in the trenches near the junction of "Yankee Street" and the "Red Line" in front of Hébuterne village. This gallant officer knew no fear and it was while inspecting the front-line trenches that he met his death.' General Carton de Wiart remembered the event[3]: 'We went into the line at Hébuterne. The division had the great misfortune in losing one of its brigade commanders – the only officer to be killed in that tour of the trenches. He was Toby Long of

84

the Scots Greys, a fine soldier and a great sportsman.' The A. & Q.M.G. diary[4] of the 19th Division recorded: 'Couin. 28th January 1917. Bt. Lt.-Col. (T/Brg-Gen.) W. Long, C.M.G. D.S.O., 2nd Dragoon Guards, Commanding 56 Infantry Brigade, was killed today by a hostile shell.' The Commanders of the Fifth Army and Vth Corps were present when they buried Brigadier-General Long at Couin British Cemetery, France.

Officers Died In The Great War: 2nd Dragoons (Royal Scots Greys).
1 L.G. 31/10/02.   2 Wyrall. *History of the 19th Division 1914–18.*   3 Carton de Wiart. *Happy Odyssey.*   4 PRO WO 95/2058

Longford, 5th Earl of   K.P.   M.V.O.   Brigadier-General
G.O.C. 2nd Mounted Brigade   2nd Mounted Division   Killed in action: 21 August, 1915

Thomas Pakenham was born in Dublin in October, 1864, the son of General the 4th Earl of Longford, and was educated at Winchester and Christ Church, Oxford, (M.A.). In 1887 he succeeded his father as the 5th Earl, and he entered the Army as a Second-Lieutenant in the Life Guards. He served in the South African War from 1899 to 1900 and in 1902, and was at Lindley as a Captain with the 45th Imperial Yeomanry on 31 May, 1900, when he was wounded and captured, but was left behind when the Boers retired. He was created a K.P. and M.V.O in 1901. In 1912 he was given command of the 2nd South Midlands Mounted Brigade and in August, 1914, was promoted Brigadier-General. At Gallipoli on 21 August, 1915, his brigade was ordered forward from Lala Baba to attack Scimitar Hill. The attack failed and among the many who fell that day was Brigadier-General Lord Longford. His body was never recovered; his name is commemorated on a special memorial at Green Hill Cemetery, Suvla, Gallipoli.

Officers Died In The Great War: Commands and Staff

Lowe, A. C.   C.M.G.   D.S.O.   Brigadier-General
C.R.A. 66th Division   Killed in action: 24 November, 1917

Arthur Cecil Lowe was born at Walton-on-Thames in 1868. He was admitted to the Honourable Artillery Company in 1891. He served in the South African War with a Field Battery of the City of London Imperial Volunteers and was awarded the D.S.O.[1] for his services. He subsequently became a Major in the Honourable Artillery Company and then a Lieutenant-Colonel of the Territorial Forces Association. He was appointed C.R.A. of the 66th Division when Brigadier-General Stewart (q.v.) was wounded in August, 1917. Three months later the C.R.A.'s diary[2] of the 66th Division records that he was killed in action near Ypres at 8 am. on 24 November. Brigadier-General Lowe is buried in Ypres Reservoir Cemetery, Belgium.

Officers Died In The Great War: Royal Horse and Field Artillery (Territorial Force).
1 L.G. 27/9/01.   2 PRO WO 95/3123.

Lumsden, A. F. D.S.O.   Brigadier-General
G.O.C. 46th Brigade 15th Division   Killed in action: 24 June, 1918

Alfred Forbes Lumsden was born in June, 1877, and commissioned from the Militia into the Royal Scots in April, 1900. He served in the South African War, and from February, 1908, to May, 1912, was employed with the West African Frontier Force. In the Great War he was wounded at Ypres, as a Captain in the 9th Battalion of his Regiment in February, 1915, but returned to command the 2nd Battalion and was awarded the D.S.O.[1] in recognition of his services in the prosecution of the war. He was appointed to command the 46th Brigade in February, 1918, and in June of that year 'was killed by shell fire in Battery Valley [south-west of Feuchy, near Arras] whilst accompanying General Reed [G.O.C. 15th Div.] on a tour round the trenches.'[2] Brigadier-General Lumsden is buried in Duisans British Cemetery, Etrun, France.

Officers Died In The Great War: The Royal Scots.
1 L.G. 4/6/17.   2 Stewart and Buchan. *The Fifteenth (Scottish) Division 1914–1919*

Lumsden, F. W. V.C. C.B. D.S.O.***   Brigadier-General
G.O.C. 14th Brigade 32nd Division   Wounded: 2 August, 1917
                                                     Killed in action: 4 June, 1918

Frederick William Lumsden was born at Frizabad, India, in 1872, and was educated at Bristol Grammar School. He was commissioned into the Royal Marine Artillery in September, 1890, and graduated from the Staff College in 1907. In 1910 he was appointed a G.S.O.2 in the Straits Settlements, an appointment that he held in Singapore for four years, returning home just at the outbreak of the Great War. He served with the Royal Marine Artillery howitzers until July, 1915, when he left to take up his appointment as a G.S.O.3 on the Staff of the 1st Army, where he was chief assistant to Brigadier-General Charteris. In November of that year he became a Staff officer of Canadian Corps troops, and in 1916 he became G.S.O.2 of the 32nd Division. He was awarded the D.S.O.[1] for distinguished service in the field, and then, a few months later, he achieved an unusual distinction when he was awarded two Bars[2] to his D.S.O. in the same issue of the *Gazette*. The first Bar was awarded for reconnoitring the enemy's position under very heavy fire and bringing back most valuable information, and the second for leading a reconnaissance party which carried out its task with conspicuous success. In order to qualify for the command of an infantry brigade he gave up his Staff post, and was appointed to command the 17th Battalion Highland Light Infantry on 6 April, 1917. He only held the command for six days when he was appointed to command the 14th Infantry Brigade of the 32nd Division, but in that period he had gained the honour most coveted by all soldiers, the award of the Victoria Cross, for his action in recovering enemy guns at Francilly-Selency, near St Dentin.[3]

The *London Gazette* of 8 June, 1917, records the following: 'For most conspicuous bravery, determination and devotion to duty. Six enemy field guns having been captured, it was necessary to leave them in dug-in positions, 300 yards in advance of the position held by our troops. The enemy kept the captured guns under heavy fire. Major Lumsden undertook the duty of bringing the guns into our lines. In order to effect this, he personally led four artillery teams and a party of infantry through the hostile barrage. As one of these teams sustained casualties, he left the remaining teams in a covered position, and through very heavy rifle, machine gun and shrapnel fire, led the infantry to the guns. By force of example and inspiring energy he succeeded in sending back two teams with guns, going through the hostile barrage with the teams of the third gun. He then returned to the guns to await further teams, and these he succeeded in attaching to two of the remaining guns, despite rifle fire, which had become intense at short range, and removed the guns to safety. By this time the enemy, in considerable strength, had driven through the infantry covering points, and blown up the breach of the remaining gun. Major Lumsden then returned, drove off the enemy, attached the gun to a team and got it away.'

While in command of the 14th Infantry Brigade, he was wounded on 2 August, 1917, but very soon returned to duty. In the *Gazette* of 22 April, 1918, he was awarded a third Bar to his D.S.O.[4] The action which won him this third Bar occurred when his brigade formed the left of an attack in a raid on the enemy's lines. He first of all superintended the assembly in advanced trenches, and then to each successive object, encouraging his men. At the final objective, where there was some slight hesitation owing to the heavy machine-gun and rifle fire, adding to the exhaustion of the troops, he led the assault on a group of seven 'pill boxes' and after their capture made a valuable reconnaissance of the enemy's position. He then supervised the withdrawal, forming the covering party, with which he himself withdrew, being the last to leave the position. Not all his deeds earned the approval of his fellow officers. Lieutenant-Colonel H. M. Davson, who commanded a R.A. Brigade of the 32nd Division, refers to how 'He spent his time dancing about in No Man's Land.'[5] On 1 June, just a few days before he was killed, he was made a C.B. On the night of 3

June, 1918, he was near his front line when there was an alarm of an attack. He went to see for himself what the trouble was and he was, as *The Times* stated, 'shot through the head by a rifle bullet', although the A. & Q.M.G. diary[6] of the 32nd Division records: 'Brigadier-Lumsden, V.C. C.B. D.S.O., killed by splinter of shell near front line about 1 am.' The 14th Brigade's diary[7], in the Summary of Operations for June, records that the brigade headquarters was at Ransart when, 'On the night of the 3/4 June the S.O.S. was sent up on the left of the right battalion. The G.O.C. while moving along the parados to ascertain the situation was hit by a bullet (in the head) and instantaneously killed.' Command of his brigade passed to another Brigadier-General with the V.C. and D.S.O., Brigadier-General L. P. Evans. Brigadier-General Lumsden is buried at Berles New Military Cemetery, Berles-au-Bois, France.

---

1 L.G. 1/1/17.   2 L.G. 11/5/17.   3 Blumberg. *Britain's Sea Soldiers.*   4 L.G. 22/4/18.
5 Davson. *Memoirs of the Great War.*   6 PRO WO 95/2374.   7 PRO WO 95/2391.

MacInnes, D. S. C.M.G. D.S.O.   **Brigadier-General**
Inspector of Mines. G.H.Q. France.   **Died of accidental injuries : 23 May, 1918**

Duncan Sayre MacInnes was born in Hamilton, Ontario, Canada, in July, 1870, the younger son of Donald MacInnes, a member of the Senate. He entered the R.M.C., Kingston, Canada, and passed out with the Sword of Honour and the Gold Medal, and obtained a commission in the Corps of Royal Engineers in July, 1894. From 1895 to 1896 he was with the Ashanti Expedition and served in the South African War from 1899 to 1902, and for his services he was awarded the D.S.O.[1] He was with the South African Constabulary from 1902 to 1904 and then went to Canada to serve on the Staff from 1905 to 1908. When he returned he became a G.S.O.3 serving on the Royal Flying Corps Committee. He went to France as a Major commanding the 54th Field Company, R.E., of the 7th Division and was wounded on 26 November, 1914. After duties at the War Office he returned to France in 1917 as C.R.E. of the 42nd Division. Nine months later he was appointed Inspector of Mines at G.H.Q. France with the rank of Brigadier-General and he was made a C.M.G. On 23 May, 1918, he was killed. In St Paul's Church, Camberley, Surrey, is a bronze memorial plaque to 'Brigadier-General Duncan Sayre MacInnes, C.M.G. D.S.O., Royal Engineers. Wounded November 1914 when with the 9th (sic) Division. Killed in action 23rd May, 1918. Age 47. Buried at Etaples.' *The Times* for the 25 May, 1918, reported that he had been killed in action, but the *C. W. G. C. Register* states that he died of accidental injuries.

Officers Died In The Great War: Corps of Royal Engineers.
1 L.G. 19/4/01.

Maclachlan, R. C. D.S.O.   **Brigadier-General**
G.O.C. 112th Brigade   37th Division   **Killed in action: 11 August, 1917**

Ronald Campbell Maclachlan was born in July, 1872, and was educated at Cheam, Eton and the R.M.C., Sandhurst. In July, 1893, he was gazetted to the Rifle Brigade and served with the 3rd Battalion of his Regiment in India, and with the 2nd Battalion in the South African War from 1899 to 1900, where he took part in the Defence of Ladysmith, being severely wounded at Wagon Hill on 6 January, 1900. He returned to the 3rd Battalion in India and took part in the Tibet Expedition of 1903 and 1904. In 1908 he was made Adjutant of the Officers Training Corps at Oxford and held that post until September, 1911. On the termination of this appointment, the Honorary Degree of M.A. was conferred upon him by the University of Oxford for services rendered to the university. He assisted in the raising and the training of the 8th (Service) Battalion Rifle Brigade in 1914, and took the battalion to France in May, 1915. At Ypres in December, 1915, he was severely wounded. He was awarded the D.S.O.[1] in 1916 for distinguished service in the field, and in November of that year he returned to France. In January, 1917, he was appointed Brigadier-General Commanding the 112th Infantry Brigade. The brigade diary[2] records: 'Oostaverne Sector. 11 Aug. General R. C. Maclachlan, D.S.O., killed by a sniper about 7 am. while going round the line with Lt.-Col. Dill, G.S.O.1.' Brigadier-General Maclachlan is buried in Locre (now Loker) Hospice Cemetery, Belgium.

Officers Died In The Great War: The Rifle Brigade.
1 L.G. 3/6/16.   2 PRO WO 95/2536.

Martin, C. T. D.S.O.*   **Brigadier-General**
G.O.C. 151st Brigade   50th Division   **Killed in action: 27 May, 1918**

Cuthbert Thomas Martin was born in December, 1877, the third son of Sir Acquin and Lady Martin. He was educated at Beaumont College and was commissioned into the Highland Light Infantry from the Militia in September, 1897, and served in the South African War from 1899 to 1902. In August, 1914, he went to France with his regiment and took part in the retreat from Mons and was severely wounded in action on the River Aisne. In 1916 he returned to France as second-in-command of a service battalion of the Highland Light Infantry, and almost immediately was given command of his old regular battalion. He was awarded the D.S.O.[1] for distinguished service in the field. In October, 1917, he was appointed to command the 151st Brigade and in the following April he received a Bar[2] to his D.S.O. 'for conspicuous gallantry and devotion to duty. This officer commanded his brigade with great energy and ability through four days of fighting against vastly superior numbers of the enemy on a very extended front, largely by his personal example and the fighting value of the Brigade when they had very heavy casualties and were very tired.' The history[3] of his division records his final moments: 'At 7 am. he [Brigadier-General Riddell] was at 151st Brigade Headquarters with Brigadier-General Martin, of the latter Brigade, when the enemy was reported close at hand. As the two Brigadiers hurriedly left the dug-out they found themselves almost surrounded. As they began to fight their way through, the Germans were scattered by a salvo of their own shells, but one, however, unfortunately burst overhead and General Martin was instantly killed and General Riddell wounded.' In a letter[4] written nearly seventeen years later, Mr. A. L. B. Childe, who had served with the 5th Battalion Durham Light Infantry, which was a battalion of the 151st Infantry Brigade, writing of the Battle of the Aisne in 1918, said: 'Lieutenant Williams went with the Sergeant Major to reconnoitre the wood to our rear (i.e. between the sunken road where we were and the road running East-West meeting the road due south through Chaudardes, about 150 yards away). When retiring to the sunken road we were surprised to find our Brigadier lying dead.' Brigadier-General Martin has no known grave; his name is commemorated on the Soissons Memorial to the Missing, France.

Officers Died In The Great War: The Highland Light Infantry.
1 L.G. 4/6/17. 2 L.G. 16/9/18. 3 Wyrall. *The History of the 50th Division.* 4 *PRO CAB 45/114.*

Matthews, G. E. C.B. C.M.G.   Brigadier-General
G.O.C. 198th Brigade 66th Division   Died of wounds: 13 April, 1917

Godfrey Estcourt Matthews was born in June, 1866. He was commissioned into the Royal Marines in September, 1884, and in January, 1897, was seconded for service with the Egyptian Army. Apart from a break of a few months he served in Egypt for 16 years. He served in the Nile Expeditions of 1897, 1898 and 1899 and was present at the Battles of Atbara and Khartoum. He became Governor of the Province of Upper Nile, and was subsequently appointed Commandant of the troops in the Khartoum District. Before leaving Egypt in 1913 he was made a C.B. At the outbreak of the Great War he was given command of the Plymouth Battalion of the Royal Naval Division which landed at Gallipoli in April, 1915. He was made a C.M.G. and was wounded in July of that year, but was in command of his battalion for the operations in August, 1915. In May, 1916, he was appointed to command the 198th Brigade which went to France in February, 1917. The diary[1] of the 198th Brigade for April, 1917, records: 'Cambrin. [36C N.W.1] 12th. Brigadier-General G. E. Matthews, C.B. C.M.G., (late R.M.L.I.), Cmd. 198th Inf. Bde. was wounded by the explosion of a shell and died on the 13 April, 1917 at the C.C.S. Béthune. Major C. W. Gordon-Steward, Bde.-Major 198th Brigade, was killed instantly by the same shell at 4.30 pm.' The funeral of Brigadier-General Matthews was attended by the band of the Chatham Division R.M.L.I. of which he had been Adjutant from 1891 to 1896. He is buried in Béthune Town Cemetery, France.

Officers Died In The Great War: Commands and Staff.
1 PRO WO 95/3138.

Maude, Sir Frederick S. K.C.B. C.M.G. D.S.O.   **Lieutenant-General**
G.O.C. 14th Brigade 5th Division   **Wounded: 12 April, 1915**
C. in C. Mesopotamian Expeditionary Force   **Died of Cholera: 18 November, 1917**

Frederick Stanley Maude was born at Gibraltar in 1864, the younger son of General Sir Frederick Francis Maude, V.C. G.C.B., who won his V.C. in the Crimea. He was educated at Eton and the R.M.C., Sandhurst, and was commissioned into the Coldstream Guards in June, 1884. After serving in the Sudan Campaign of 1885, he became Brigade-Major of the Guards Brigade and was responsible for much of the military organization for the Jubilee of 1887. He resigned his appointment and rejoined his battalion in 1899 at the Modder River in the South African War. He was seriously injured at Dreifontein when his horse fell and he injured his right shoulder; he never fully recovered the use of his right arm. He was awarded the D.S.O.[1] for his services in South Africa. As Military Secretary to Lord Munro, the Governor General of Canada, from 1901 to 1904, he made all the arrangements for the Royal Tour of Canada in 1901, and afterwards was made a C.M.G. From 1912 to 1914 he was a G.S.O. of the 5th Division at the Curragh. At the outbreak of the Great War he joined the Staff of III Corps and reached France during the retreat from Mons. In October, 1914, he was appointed to command the 14th Infantry Brigade of the 5th Division. His biography[2] contains an extract from his diary of events near St Eloi on 12 April. [The line ran from the east of the mound at St Eloi by the Bluff, Hill 60 and Zwartelen to the western edge of Armagh Wood.] 'Back for a hurried dinner and then down to the trenches again with Brigade-Major and Fleming. Started at 28 and then went along to 23, which is the right of my line. Wanted especially to see machine-gun positions. Twenty-eight is a curious trench, a series of bastions with nothing between. All trenches were badly deficient of parados and many of traverses. Bullets seemed to come from every direction and we have quite a few casualties. However, the men are working splendidly and we shall soon make the trenches better. On my way back got hit by a stray bullet, which went through my right arm and into my side, finally lodging close to my spine, pointing upwards. Walked as far as the East Surrey's dressing station, whence I was carried down on a stretcher to Lankhof Château. Here an ambulance met me and I was taken to 14th Field Ambulance at Ypres. Returned to England [with the bullet still in his back] to Lady Ridley's Hospital in Carlton House Terrace. 1st May received C.B. from The King. 3rd May returned to the front.' In July, 1915, he was appointed Major-General in command of the 31st Division, but at short notice he was sent to command the 13th Division in Gallipoli. When Gallipoli was evacuated he took his division to Egypt and to Mesopotamia in February, 1916. In July of that year he was appointed to command the Tigris Corps and in August he assumed command of the Army in Mesopotamia. For his services as a divisional commander he was created a K.C.B. He was promoted Lieutenant-General on 1 March, 1917, and on 11 March his Army occupied Baghdad. At an entertainment given in his honour by a Jewish School coffee was handed round. All partook, but General Maude alone took milk. Next morning he was down with cholera, and cholera in its severest type.[3] Lieutenant-General Sir Stanley Maude died on 18 November, 1917, and is buried in Baghdad (North Gate) War Cemetery, Iraq.

Officers Died In The Great War: Commands and Staff.
1 L.G. 27/9/01. 2 Callwell. *Life of Sir Stanley Maude.* 3 Macmunn. *Behind the Scenes in Many Wars.*

Maxwell, F. A. V.C. C.S.I. D.S.O.*   Brigadier-General
G.O.C. 27th Brigade 9th Division   Killed in action: 21 September, 1917

Francis Aylmer Maxwell was born in September, 1871, and gazetted to the Royal Sussex Regiment in November, 1891, but transferred to the Indian Staff Corps in December, 1893. He served in Waziristan and at Chitral in 1895 and on the north-west frontier of India, as A.D.C. to the G.O.C. the Tirah Expedition from 1897 to 1898. He was awarded the D.S.O.[1] in recognition of his services on the north-west frontier of India, and this was presented to him by Queen Victoria at Windsor on 25 June, 1898. In the South African War he served with Roberts Horse and as A.D.C. to Lord Kitchener. The *London Gazette* of 8 March, 1901, described the incident which earned him the Victoria Cross: 'Lieut. Maxwell was one of three officers, not belonging to 'Q' Battery, Royal Horse Artillery, specially mentioned by Lord Roberts as having shown the greatest gallantry and disregard of danger in carrying out the self-imposed duty of saving the guns of that battery during the affair at the Korn Spruit on 31st March 1900 [See Broadwood]. This officer went out on five different occasions and assisted to bring in two guns and three limbers, one of which he, Captain Humphreys and some gunners, dragged in by hand. He also went out with Captain Humphreys and Lieut. Stirling to get the last gun in, and remained there till the attempt was abandoned. During a previous campaign (the Chitral Expedition of 1885), Lieut. Maxwell displayed gallantry in the removal of the body of Lieutenant-Colonel F. D. Battye, Corps of Guides, under fire, for which, though recommended, he received no reward.' From 1909 to 1910 he was a Brigade-Major with the Indian Army, and in 1910 he was a Major with the Australian Commonwealth Military Forces. He was appointed Military Secretary to Lord Hardinge, Governor General of India, and in 1911 was created a C.S.I. He commanded the 12th Battalion Middlesex Regiment from June to October, 1916, and was appointed to command the 27th Infantry Brigade in October, 1916. He was awarded a Bar[2] to his D.S.O. for conspicuous bravery and leadership. On 20 September, 1917, the brigade made a successful attack on the Zonnebeke Redoubt, and a report of the attack in the brigade diary[3] reads: 'Unfortunately, however, Brigadier-General F. A. Maxwell, V.C. C.S.I. D.S.O., was killed by a rifle bullet when visiting the post at D.26.b.5.2. on September 21st, the morning after the attack.' The official history[4] has a footnote which describes how he died: 'On the 21st [September, 1917] Brigadier-General Maxwell, V.C. commanding the 27th Brigade (9th), whilst superintending consolidation, was killed by a sniper at 40 yards range. A born leader, he had always been regardless of personal safety and was at the time sitting on the front of the parapet watching wiring.' Brigadier-General Maxwell was buried at 9.30 am. on the 23rd at what was then known as Ypres Prison Cemetery; his grave is now in Ypres Reservoir Cemetery, Belgium.

Officers Died In The Great War: Indian Army.
1 L.G. 20/5/98.   2 L.G. 25/11/16.   3 PRO WO 95/1770.   4 Edmonds. *Military History France and Belgium, 1917*, Vol.2.

McMahon, N. R. D.S.O. — Brigadier-General
G.O.C. 4th Battalion Royal Fusiliers   3rd Division — Killed in action: 11 November, 1914

Norman Reginald McMahon was born in London in January, 1866, and was educated at Eton. He was commissioned into the Royal Fusiliers in May, 1885, and took part in the Burmese Expedition of 1886 to 1887. During the South African War, in which he served from 1899 to 1902, he was severely wounded in operations in Cape Colony, and for his services he was awarded the D.S.O.[1] He was Chief Instructor and Staff officer at the School of Musketry from 1905 to 1909. In November, 1914, the diary[2] of the 4th Battalion Royal Fusiliers records that the battalion was at Bailleul when it was inspected by Sir Horace Smith-Dorrien. He complimented the battalion on their work during the campaign, and he also said that Lieutenant-Colonel McMahon had been given a staff appointment some days before but that owing to the fact that there would be no one to command the battalion if he took up the appointment, he (Sir Horace) had very reluctantly to ask Sir John French to leave him in command for the present. A week later the diary entry reads: '11/11/14. Still in the same position. Terrible shelling started about 6.30 am. and continued for about 2½ hrs. (this is much the worst shelling I have seen during the war.) Infantry attack followed (it is said by the 15th Battalion of the German Imperial Guard) our line was driven in to a certain extent, but by the help of a very determined and successful counter attack by the Royal Scots Fusiliers and supported by the Royal Sussex Regiment the line was held. Colonel McMahon (now Brg-Genl.) was killed.' The history[3] of the Regiment records that it was east of Hooge, on the south side of the Ypres-Menin Road, on the edge of Herenthage Wood, and that 'Colonel McMahon went to them [battalion support troops who had only arrived on the day before the battle] and tried to rally them. Suddenly he was seen to sink to one knee and begin to remove his legging as though hit in the leg. At that moment a shell burst close to him and killed him.' Brigadier-General McMahon has no known grave; his name is commemorated on the Ploegsteert Memorial to the Missing, Belgium.

Officers Died In The Great War: The Royal Fusiliers.
1 L.G. 19/4/01.   2 PRO WO 95/1431.   3 O'Neill. *The Royal Fusiliers in the Great War*

Mercer, M. S. C.B.

G.O.C. 3rd Canadian Division

Major-General

Killed in action: 3 June, 1916

Malcolm Smith Mercer was a barrister-at-law who received his commission in the 2nd Regiment (Queen's Own Rifles of Canada) at Toronto in 1885, and after 26 years in that unit was gazetted to command. He passed the Militia Staff Course and had been Adjutant of the Canadian Bisley Team in 1909. At the outbreak of the Great War he was 55 years old and Lieutenant-Colonel Commandant of his Regiment [Militia]. From September, 1914, to November, 1915, he commanded the 1st Infantry Brigade of the 1st Canadian Division and in December, 1915, he was appointed G.O.C. 3rd Canadian Division. On the morning of 2 June, 1916, 'Major-General Mercer, accompanied by his aide-de-camp, Lt. Lyman Gooderham, had gone forward to inspect the positions of the 4th Canadian Mounted Rifles near Mount Sorrel, where the Germans had constructed some mysterious 'T' saps, evidently intending to use them as jumping-off places. On his way to the front General Mercer called for Brigadier-General Williams of the 8th Brigade. About 8.30 am, as the generals went forward, they were subjected to a bombardment by trench mortars, but the party passed through this without casualties and reached Lieutenant-Colonel J. H. F. Ussher's headquarters situated close to the front line. Led by Colonel Ussher, they at once proceeded on their tour of inspection.

Everything was found satisfactory. The trenches were in good shape and strongly held and the men eager for the fight. About nine o'clock, while the inspecting officers were standing in the communication trench known as "O'Grady Avenue", without a moment's warning a deluge of shells came over. They [the Germans] had a vast assemblage of guns from Pilckem Ridge to Wytschaete. They had planned to bombard the Canadian position later in the day, but due to information received they began their bombardment while the inspection was in progress. All their guns were now concentrated on the small sector held by the 4th Canadian Mounted Rifles. Immediately the bombardment opened Mercer sent Ussher to his headquarters to bring into action, in retaliation, the entire artillery of the 3rd Division, but the barrage put over by the Germans had destroyed all the wires. Ussher thereupon sent two pairs of runners with messages for the guns. While this work was in progress a shell struck the edge of the trench where the Canadian generals and Lt. Gooderham were standing. Williams was seriously wounded and both Mercer and Gooderham were thrown down and, for the moment, stunned. When they recovered from the shock they succeeded in having Williams carried into a sheltered trench known as the "Tube". General Mercer then made his way to Ussher's headquarters, but there was little security here. Hour after hour the bombardment continued; dugouts were crumpled in; trenches were obliterated; and the casualties were enormous. After a time the fire slackened and Mercer, who had miraculously escaped injury, determined to push his way back to his headquarters to organize resistance to the attack that the enemy would inevitably put over. He was still feeling the effects of the shock he had received, and as he went towards the rear, just before one o'clock, he had to be supported by Gooderham. The communications trenches had all been obliterated, and in this trip, made overland, there was but little shelter to be gained. Just as they reached Armagh Wood a chance shot hit Mercer in the leg, breaking a bone. His aide dragged him into a nearby ditch and did everything in his power to ease his suffering. Shortly after this event the bombardment lifted over Armagh Wood, and the Huns swarmed through the 4th Canadian Mounted Rifles. During the night eight attempts were made to recover the lost ground. While the fourth attack was on a British shell burst close to Mercer and a piece of shrapnel pierced his heart. Gooderham, who had gallantly stood by him until this moment, remained alone in no-man's-land until the morning of 4 June, when he was found by the Germans and taken prisoner.'[1] In a letter[2] written to the Historical Branch, Lieutenant-General Sir A. C. Macdonell (who had been Brigadier-General Commanding the 7th Canadian Infantry Brigade) states that splinters from the shell which killed General Mercer also broke Gooderham's arm but he stayed with the body of his General and at his request the Germans buried the body in a shallow grave, just removing all badges, buttons, etc. General Mercer's body was subsequently unearthed by a shell and found by the Canadians. The A. & Q.M.G. diary[3] of the 3rd Canadian Division records that it was not until 23 June that 'The body of Major-General M. S. Mercer was found in Armagh Wood.' On the following day he was buried in Lijssenthoek Military Cemetery, Poperinghe, Belgium.

1 Various Authorities. *Canada in the Great War.* 2 PRO CAB 45/147.
3 PRO WO 95/3842.

Napier, H. E. — Brigadier-General
G.O.C. 88th Brigade   29th Division — Killed in action: 25 April, 1915

Henry Edward Napier was born in September, 1861, and was educated at the United Services College, Westward Ho! and the R.M.C., Sandhurst. In May, 1882, he was gazetted to the Cheshire Regiment and served in the South African War in 1902. In 1907 he transferred to command the Royal Irish Rifles for four years, and in 1912 was appointed Brigadier-General Commanding the Cheshire Infantry Brigade. In 1914 he commanded No. 11 District, Irish Command, until he took command of the 88th Infantry Brigade and led them at the 'V' Beach landings at Gallipoli. The events are recorded in the diary[1] of 88th Brigade: 'River Clyde 24th. Orders to land at 'V' Beach west of Sedd el Bahr next morning after covering fire. 25th. 8.30 am. Brigade H.Q. and some 500 Worcesters transferred to mine sweeper and steamed to within 500 yards of the shore; we then got into cutters and were rowed to shore. 10.30 am. As we neared the shore we came under heavy rifle fire; both Brigadier-General Napier and his Bde-Major, Major Costeker, were killed before landing.' Brigadier-General Napier has no known grave; his name is commemorated on the Helles Memorial, Gallipoli.

Officers Died In The Great War: Commands and Staff.
1 PRO WO 95/4312.

Nickalls, N. T. — Brigadier-General
G.O.C. 63rd Brigade   21st Division — Killed in action: 26 September, 1915

Norman Tom Nickalls was born in April, 1864, and was educated at Eton. He was commissioned into the 17th Lancers from the Militia in November, 1886, and served in the South African War from 1901 to 1902. He was promoted to the rank of Brigadier-General on 5 August, 1914, and appointed to command the 63rd Infantry Brigade of the 21st Division. The 21st Division was one of the reserve divisions about which there was much controversy concerning their use at the Battle of Loos. The diary[1] of the 63rd Brigade has the following entry for 26 September, 1915: 'Action at the Chalk Pit. Brigadier-General N. T. Nickalls, commanding the Brigade, wounded and missing,' and in an appendix to the diary: 'It must have been about this time that Brigadier-General Nickalls was hit. One officer (Major Bullock, West Yorks. Regt.) states that he saw him hit near the Chalk Pit, but all efforts to find his body proved unavailing.' Brigadier-General Nickalls has no known grave; his name is commemorated on the Loos Memorial to the Missing, France.

Officers Died In The Great War: Commands and Staff.
1 PRO WO 95/2157.

Nugent, G. C. M.V.O. — Brigadier-General
G.O.C. 141st Brigade 47th Division — Killed in action: 31 May, 1915

George Colborne Nugent was born in February, 1864, the eldest son of Sir Edmund Nugent Bt., of West Harlington Hall, Norfolk. Educated at Eton and the R.M.C., Sandhurst, he was commissioned into the Grenadier Guards in 1882 and received his Majority in the Irish Guards on their formation in 1900. He served in the South African War from 1899 to 1900. In 1908 he was appointed to the command of a battalion. In 1909 he was made an M.V.O., and from 1909 to 1911 he was Colonel Commanding the Irish Guards and Regimental District. He became Commandant of the Duke of York's Royal Military School in July, 1913. In August, 1914, he was appointed to command the 141st Infantry Brigade. The A.Q.M.G. diary[1] of the 4th Division records: 'May 31st [1915]. Béthune. Major-Gen. [In the casualty list he is listed as Brg-Gen.] C. G. Nugent, M.V.O., Cmnd. 141st Inf. Bde. was killed in "Sidbury" Trench near Point Fixe. He was buried at 5.30 pm. in Béthune Cemetery. Major-Gen. Munro, Gen. Sergeant, Maj-Gen. Barter and representatives of units were present at the funeral. One Coy. of the 24th Btn. [London Regiment] in the Béthune area acted as escort. The Buglers of the 6th London Field Ambulance sounded the Last Post.' He is buried in Béthune Town Cemetery, France.

Officers Died In The Great War: Commands and Staff.
1 PRO WO 95/2706

Ormsby, V. A. C.B. — Brigadier-General
G.O.C. 127th Brigade 42nd Division — Killed in action: 2 May, 1917

Vincent Alexander Ormsby was born in July, 1865, and commissioned into the East Surrey Regiment in February 1885, and then transferred to the Indian Army (3rd Gurkha Rifles) in March, 1890. He saw service on the north-west frontier of India in 1897 and 1898 and was in the Tirah Campaign of 1898. In 1915 he was made a C.B., and in February, 1916, he was promoted to the rank of Brigadier-General and appointed to command the 127th Infantry Brigade. The diary[1] of the 127th Brigade describes the events that led to his death: 'St. Emilie. 1/5/17. During the night of 1/2 May a reconnaissance of the Green Line [in the vicinity of Little Priel Farm and Catelet Copse] was made by General Ormsby and several Staff and R.E. officers of both the 42nd Div. and the Corps in view of the line becoming on the 6th inst. the main line of resistance, whilst the Div. would by then have relieved the 48th Div. in the line. The night had passed quietly as regards shelling when shortly after midnight, possibly – it is said – owing to the sound of wheeled transport bringing up R.E. stores, the enemy opened fire on ground near the reconnaissance party who took cover in a sunken road. A shell, however, fell into the road, striking the slope of the bank. Pieces struck the general, one severing the jugular vein; he became unconscious at once and died shortly afterwards.' The history[2] of the 42nd Division states that, 'On May 3 [1917] the Division took over from the 48th Division a sector in the neighbourhood of Ronnsoy, southeast of Epehy. As Brigadier-General Ormsby was engaged in marking out the new front line of his brigade near Catelet Copse, the enemy suddenly opened a bombardment and he was struck in the head by a piece of shell and killed.' Various dates are recorded for the death of Brigadier-General Ormsby, the casualty list in the A. & Q.M.G. diary[3] of the 42nd Division says that it occurred on 2 May; the C.W.G.C. Register gives the date as 1 May; the Probate Register gives the date as 2 May and *The Times* for 18 May said that he fell on 7 May. He is buried in Villers-Faucon Communal Cemetery and Extension, France.

Officers Died In The Great War: Indian Army.
1 PRO WO 95/2659. 2 Gibbons. *The 42nd Division.* 3 PRO WO 95/2674.

Peake, M. C.M.G.   **Brigadier-General**
B.G.R.A. I Corps   **Killed in action: 27 August, 1917**

Malcolm Peake was born in March, 1865, and was educated at Charterhouse and the R.M.A., Woolwich, from which he passed into the Royal Artillery in December, 1884. For 10 years, from 1895 to 1905, he was attached to the Egyptian Army and served with the expedition to Dongola in 1896. In the Nile Expedition of the following year he was in command of a battery of Egyptian Artillery, and in the expedition of 1898 he commanded a battery of native artillery at the Battles of Atbara and Khartoum and again commanded artillery in 1899 in the first advance against the Khalifa. He was made a C.M.G. in 1900. From 1914 to 1916 he was A. A. G. at the War Office until, in April, 1916, he went to France to command the Artillery of the 29th Division, and in December of that year was appointed to command the Artillery of I Corps. The C.R.A's. diary[1] of I Corps records: 'La Buissiere. 27th August, 1917. While out on reconnaissance on Hill 70 [Loos], General Peake, G.O.C. R.A., and Major Trench were killed by an enemy shell.' Brigadier-General Peake and Major Trench are buried in adjacent graves in Noeux-les-Mines Communal Cemetery and Extension, France.

Officers Died In The Great War: Commands and Staff & Royal Regiment of Artillery (R.H.A. and R.F.A.).
1 PRO WO 95/619.

Phillpotts, L. M. C.M.G. D.S.O. — Brigadier-General
C.R.A. 24th Division — Killed in action: 8 September, 1916

Louis Murray Phillpotts was born in June, 1870, and passed out of the R.M.A., Woolwich, into the the Royal Artillery in February, 1890. He served in the South African War from 1899 to 1901 and was awarded the D.S.O.[1] in recognition of his services. He was appointed C.R.A. of the 24th Division in October, 1915, and was made a C.M.G. The C.R.A.'s diary[2] of the 24th Division contains an entry on 8 September: 'General Phillpotts and Captain Crippin go out to reconnoitre and are both killed in the Maltz Horn valley.' In September, 1916, Lieutenant-Colonel The Hon Ralph Hamilton, an artillery brigade commander of the 24th Division, entered in his diary[3]: 'We have just heard the sad news that General Phillpotts and Cripen (sic), the Brigade-Major, have both been killed this afternoon at Guillemont. 9th September. This morning practically all the officers of the Divisional Artillery rode over to the Citadel for the General's funeral. The two coffins were carried by Sergeants of the various Brigades, and covered with Union Jacks. They were buried side by side in an already enormous military cemetery there.' The cemetery where they are buried is Citadel New Military Cemetery, Fricourt, France.

Officers Died In The Great War: Royal Regiment of Artillery (R.H.A. and R.F.A.).
1 L.G. 27/9/01. 2 PRO WO 95/2195. 3 Hamilton. *The War Diary of The Master of Belhaven*

Prowse, C. B. D.S.O. — Brigadier-General
G.O.C. 11th Brigade 4th Division — Died of wounds: 1 July, 1916

Charles Bertie Prowse was born at West Monkton, Taunton, Somerset, in June, 1869. He was educated at Cornish's School, Clevedon, and at Marlborough, and entered the Army from the Militia in the Somerset Light Infantry. He served in the South African War from 1899 to 1902 where for part of the time he was Adjutant with the 2nd Battalion of his regiment. He was Adjutant of the 1st Volunteer Battalion Somerset Light Infantry at the time of change to the Territorial Army from 1904 to 1908. He took part in many of the actions which were fought in the early days of the Great War and trench maps bore his name when a farm just north of Ploegsteert Wood was named Prowse Point, it is now the name of a cemetery. In April, 1915, he was appointed Brigadier-General commanding the 11th Infantry Brigade. He was awarded the D.S.O.[1] for distinguished service in the field. On the first day of the Battle of the Somme, 1 July, 1916, the 11th Infantry Brigade attacked the German line just to the north of Beaumont Hamel, from 'Redan Redoubt' to 'The Quadrilateral'. In the regimental history[2] Captain G. A. Prideaux of the 1st Somerset Light Infantry states: 'At about 9.45 am. the General decided to move his H.Q. into the German front line, thinking that it was cleared of all the Germans. Just as he was getting out of our front line trench, near "Brett Street", he was shot in the back by a machine gun in the "Ridge Redoubt" and died in the afternoon.' In a letter[3] to the official historian, Lieutenant G. A. Robinson, M.C., who was with the 1st Rifle Brigade of the 11th Brigade on 1 July, 1916, wrote in April, 1930: 'Brigadier-General Prowse gave me orders to open the brigade ammunition dug-out that had been blown in. Immediately afterwards he was mortally wounded while assembling men of the Seaforth Highlanders in our front-line trench. Brigadier-General Prowse showed great gallantry in his efforts, ignoring the great breaches in our parapet, exposing himself to great danger.' Lieutenant-Colonel W. A. T. S. Somerville, D.S.O., who was Brigade-Major of the 11th Infantry Brigade on 1 July, 1916, in a letter[4] to the official historian, wrote: '2 enemy machine guns opened from Ridge Redoubt. These guns – to my mind – were the main cause of the failure of the 4th Division attack in the northern sector. The redoubt was never taken, and was strongly held throughout the morning.' This was the second loss that the Prowse family had to bear within a few weeks; his elder brother, Captain Cecil Irby Prowse, R.N., was the Captain of H.M.S. *Queen Mary* which exploded and sank at the Battle of Jutland on 31 May, 1916. Brigadier-General Prowse was buried at Vauchelles, but his grave is now in Louvencourt Military Cemetery, France. A plaque which was placed on his grave by his comrades of the 7/Somerset Light Infantry in 1919 now rests on his grave at Louvencourt.

Officers Died In The Great War: Somerset Light Infantry.
1 L.G. 3/6/16.   2 *History of the Somerset Light Infantry*.   3 PRO CAB 45/190.
4 PRO CAB 45/191.

Rawling, C. G. C.M.G. C.I.E. F.R.G.S.   Brigadier-General
G.O.C. 62nd Brigade   21st Division   Killed in action: 28 October, 1917

Cecil Godfrey Rawling was born in February, 1870, and was educated at Clifton College. He was commissioned from the Militia into the Somerset

Light Infantry in October, 1891, and served on the north-west frontier of India from 1897 to 1898. In 1903, with the Tibet Expedition, he surveyed 40,000 square miles of western Tibet, and in 1904 and 1905 commanded the Gartok Expedition across Tibet. He was awarded the Murchison Bequest by the Royal Geographical Society in 1909, and received the thanks of the Government of India, and the C.I.E. He was the Chief Survey Officer and afterwards leader of the British Expedition to Dutch New Guinea from 1909 to 1911. He wrote *The Great Plateau* in 1905 and *The Land of the New Guinea Pygmies* in 1913. He received the Patron's Gold Medal of the Royal Geographical Society. In the Spring of 1915 he took a new service battalion of his regiment to France. Just before the Battle of the Somme he was given command of a brigade and made a C.M.G. He was present at many of the actions on the Somme. In October, 1917, as the diary[1] of the 62nd Brigade records: 'The Brigadier was killed by a shell in Hooge Crater.' His divisional commander said that 'he had shown himself devoid of fear, and was always risking his life in exposed positions.' He was killed as he was talking with friends outside his brigade headquarters, and is buried at Huts Cemetery, Dickebusch (now Dikkebus), Belgium.

Officers Died In The Great War: The Somerset Light Infantry.
1 PRO WO 95/2152.

Riddell, J. F.   Brigadier-General
G.O.C. 149th Brigade   50th Division   Killed in action: 26 April, 1915

James Foster Riddell was born in October, 1861, and was educated at Wellington and the R.M.C., Sandhurst. He was commissioned into the Fifth Foot in August, 1880, and became a Lieutenant in the Northumberland Fusiliers in July, 1881. He served throughout the Hazara Campaign in 1888, with the 2nd Battalion Northumberland Fusiliers. He commanded successively the 3rd and 2nd Battalions Northumberland Fusiliers, the former he raised during the South African War in which he served from 1899 to 1900. In 1911 he was appointed to command the Northumberland Infantry Brigade, and in August, 1914, was one of the first Colonels to be gazetted Brigadier-General. Throughout the winter of 1914–1915 his brigade guarded the north-east coast and he prepared it for service abroad. On the night of 20–21 April, 1915, he crossed with his brigade to France, and less than a week later he was killed in action. It was intended to billet the brigade at a base in France, but on 22 April the Germans delivered their first gas attack and the brigade was rushed up to help fill the gap torn in the British line. On 26 April it was ordered to take the village of St Julien. The divisional history[1] describes the events which led to his death: 'Just when the 6th Battalion [Northumberland Fusiliers] had reached its furthest point in the direction of St. Julien, i.e. at 3.45 pm., their Brigadier met his death. General Riddell (accompanied by his Brigade-Major), for the purpose of getting into closer touch with his battalion commanders, left the support trench in which he had established his headquarters at about 3.30 pm. and proceeded towards "Vanheule Farm". At about one hundred and fifty yards south of the farm he received a bullet through the head and fell dead.' Brigadier-General Riddell is buried in Tyne Cot Cemetery, Belgium.

Officers Died In The Great War: Commands and Staff.
1 Wyrall. *History of the 50th Division*

Sanders, A. R. C. C.M.G. D.S.O.*   Brigadier-General
G.O.C. 50th Brigade   17th Division   Killed in action: 20 September, 1918

Arthur Richard Careless Sanders was born in January, 1877, and commissioned into the Corps of Royal Engineers in January, 1897. He served on the north-west frontier of India in 1908. In the Great War he served as a Staff officer in various capacities and was made a C.M.G and awarded the D.S.O.[1] for distinguished service in the field. On 9 September, 1918, he was appointed Brigadier-General Commanding the 50th Infantry Brigade and less than two weeks later his brigade's diary[2] contained the following entry: '20th September. Lowland Support [Lowland Support was a trench south-west of Gouzeaucourt and half-way to Heudecourt.] 8.30 am. Brigadier-General A. R. C. Sanders, C.M.G. D.S.O., killed by enemy machine-gun fire while on the way back to brigade headquarters after visiting our posts in "Quentin Redoubt" [which had been captured the night before].' Both the History of the 17th Division and the History of the 50th Infantry Brigade confirm that he was shot in the back and killed by a machine gun in Gouzeaucourt as he crossed the railway line. The A & Q.M.G. diary[3] of the 7th Division and *The Times* report that he died of wounds. After his death the *London Gazette* announced a Bar[4] to his D.S.O. which he was awarded as a Lieutenant-Colonel, R.E., attached to the 1st Essex Regiment, 'for conspicuous gallantry and devotion to duty. He led his battalion with great courage and determination in an attack, capturing and consolidating all his objectives in spite of heavy fire. It was due to his initiative that a battery of enemy guns in front of the objective was captured. His personal influences and good leadership were largely responsible for the success achieved by the battalion.' Brigadier-General Sanders is buried in Five Points Cemetery, Lechelle, France.

Officers Died In The Great War: Corps of Royal Engineers.
1 L.G. 3/6/16.   2 PRO WO 95/1999.   3 PRO WO 95/1986.   4 L.G. 2/12/18.

Scott-Moncrieff, W.   **Brigadier-General**
G.O.C. 156th Brigade 52nd Division   Killed in action: 28 June, 1915

William Scott-Moncrieff was born in June, 1858, and was educated at Wimbledon School and the R.M.C., Sandhurst. He was first commissioned in the 57th Foot in May, 1878. In 1879 he served in the Zulu Campaign with the Middlesex Regiment and from 1899 to 1900 he was in the South African War and was severely wounded at Spion Kop, a wound that left him permanently lame. After commanding his regiment in South Africa and Hong Kong, he was appointed to the command of the Lothian Brigade at Edinburgh. When the Great War broke out he had retired to live in the family home in the Ochill Hills of Fife, but he answered the call of duty and returned as a temporary Brigadier-General in August, 1914. His name, however, still appeared in the *Quarterly Army List* of April, 1915, as a non-effective officer. In January, 1915, he was given command of the 156th Brigade of the 52nd (Lowland) Division, and in the division's history[1] is an account of his death: 'Gallipoli. Attack on H 12 Trenches. Shortly after noon Brigadier-General Scott-Moncrieff decided to go forward to the firing line himself, telling Captain E. Girdwood, his Brigade-Major, that he was only going to the observation post to see how things were going, and would be back in half-an-hour. Brigadier-General Scott-Moncrieff saw that this last attack stood even a smaller chance of success than the others, and those that knew him best think that for this reason he intended to place himself in order to lead his men into that hurricane of fire, and it is certain that he, noble and sensitive man that he was, wished to take the same risk.' Lieutenant-Colonel W. C. Peebles, D.S.O., wrote[2] in May, 1929: 'General Scott-Moncrieff borrowed my pocket book to write his last message. After despatching same to his headquarters he personally led these last two companies [of the 1/7th Cameronians] by a forward sap, now marked sap 30, and was killed as the sap began to emerge on to the surface level.' His body lay in no-man's-land and was not recovered; he is commemorated on Special Memorial C. 132 in Twelve Tree Copse Cemetery, Helles, Gallipoli.

Officers Died In The Great War: Commands and Staff.
1 Thompson. *The Fifty-Second (Lowland) Division 1914–1918.*   2 PRO CAB 45/264.

Shephard, G. S. D.S.O. M.C.   **Brigadier-General**
G.O.C. 1st R.F.C. Brigade 1st Army   Killed: 19 January, 1918

Gordon Strachey Shephard was born in Madras in July, 1885, the second son of Sir Horatio and Lady Shephard. He was educated at Summerfields, Eton and the R.M.C., Sandhurst, and was commissioned into the Royal Fusiliers in January, 1905. Before the Great War he did a great deal of yachting and became a member of the Royal Cruising Club. In 1912 he joined the Royal Flying Corps and flew to France with the first five squadrons on 13 August, 1914. He received the Legion of Honour from General Joffre for good reconnaissance work during the retreat from Mons, and in January, 1915, he won the M.C. He was later awarded the D.S.O.[1] for distinguished service in the field. Sholto Douglas [Lord Douglas of Kirtleside] wrote[2] of him: 'There was one other man under whom we came to serve at that time who was also to provide me with a lesson in this matter of leadership. We were in the 1st Brigade of the Royal Flying Corps, which was commanded by Gordon Shephard, a Brigadier who, for all his exalted rank, was only about 35 years of age. One of the earliest of the pilots in the Flying Corps, he was somewhat vacuous in appearance with a receding chin and afflicted with a slight lisp – physically a colourless personality – but that was the only thing about him that was lacking in colour. Although he was not a good pilot, Gordon Shephard's mind was of a brilliance that would undoubtedly have led to his becoming one of the great leaders in the Air Force; but that poor flying of his brought about his death in an accident before the end of the war, and so his name came only to play a minor role in the history of flying. In fact, it has come to be much better known for the part it is said to have played in the creation of the novel *The Riddle of the Sands*, by Erskine Childers, who used him, young though he must have been, as a model for Carruthers, the hero of that well known story.' The diary[3] of the 1st Brigade R.F.C. records: 'Bruay, January 19th, 1918. Casualties. Personnel: Brigadier-General G. S. Shephard, D.S.O., M.C. Commanding 1st Brigade R.F.C., killed in flying accident. Machines: Nieuport Scout No. B3160, wrecked.' The Casualty Report[4] for January includes the following: 'No. 40 Squadron. No. 10 Wing. Left Aerodrome [Bruay] to visit Auchel at 11.5 am. on 19/1/18. Spun into ground at about 11.15 am. on edge of Auchel aerodrome. Pilot admitted to hospital and died from injuries.' The A & Q.M.G. diary[5] of the 1st Canadian Division recorded his death: 'Auchel. 21st January, 1918. Brigadier-General Sheppard (sic), D.S.O. M.C., Commanding the Royal Flying Corps of the 1st Army, was buried at Lozinghem, death resulted from a flying accident. The firing party with bugles and pipes was furnished by the 16th Battalion Canadian Scottish and turned out very smart. The whole funeral rites were very impressive. General Sheppard (sic) was very popular in the Canadian Corps and it was understood by those who read *The Riddle of the Sands* that he was the hero of this tale.' Brigadier-General Shephard is buried in Lapugnoy Military Cemetery, France.

Officers Died In The Great War: Royal Flying Corps and The Royal Fusiliers
1 L.G. 4/6/17.   2 Douglas. *Years of Combat.*   3 PRO AIR 1 1443/204/36/2.
4 PRO AIR 1 852/204/5/398.   5 PRO WO 95/3732.

Stewart, C. E. C.M.G.
G.O.C. 154th Brigade 51st Division

Brigadier-General
Killed in action: 14 September, 1916

Charles Edward Stewart was born in September, 1868, and commissioned into the Royal Highlanders [Black Watch] in April, 1889. In the South African War he was a Brigade Signals Officer in 1900 and a Brigade-Major from 1900 to 1902. At the outbreak of the Great War he was a Lieutenant-Colonel commanding a battalion of the Black Watch. He was appointed to command the 154th Infantry Brigade in January, 1916, and in September of that year he was killed, as the divisional history[1] records: 'On the 14 September the division sustained a considerable loss in the death of Brigadier-General Stewart, commanding 154th Brigade. General Stewart and his Intelligence Officer [Lieutenant Kitson] were walking through Houplines when a chance shell burst within a few feet of them, killing them both. It was a case of the cruellest bad luck, as this was the only shell which fell in that vicinity during the day.' Brigadier-General Stewart is buried in Cité Bonjean Military Cemetery, Armentières, France. Lieutenant Kitson is buried next to him.

Officers Died In The Great War: The Black Watch.
1 Brewsher. *The History of the 51st (Highland) Division*

Tanner, J. A. C.B. C.M.G. D.S.O.
C.E. VII Corps

Brigadier-General
Killed in action: 23 July, 1917

John Arthur Tanner was born at Tidcombe Manor, Wiltshire, in February, 1858, and was educated at Cheltenham College and the R.M.A, Woolwich. He was first commissioned as a Lieutenant in the Corps of Royal Engineers in June, 1877, and saw service with the Expedition to Waziristan in 1881 and the Sudan Expedition of 1885. He was with the Burmese Expedition from 1885 to 1888, as Adjutant to the Royal Engineers, and for his services he was awarded the D.S.O.[1] He was with the Relief Force in the operations in Chitral in 1895 and served on the north-west frontier of India from 1897 to 1898. In 1911 he was made a C.B. and he retired on an Indian Army pension in April, 1914. In October, 1914, he volunteered his services and was appointed C.R.E. of the 22nd Division, and went with the division to France in September, 1915. In October, 1915, he became Chief Engineer of VII Corps, and was made a C.M.G. in 1916. The C.E.'s diary[2] of VII Corps for 23 July, 1917, records: 'The Chief Engineer was killed [by] a shell behind Wancourt whilst on his way to inspect the defences at "Cavalry Farm" with the C.R.E. 50th Division [Lt.-Col. Rathbone].' Brigadier-General Tanner is buried in Bucquoy Road Cemetery, Ficheux, France.

Officers Died In The Great War: Commands and Staff.
1 L.G. 25/11/87.   2 PRO WO 95/815.

105

Taylor, S. C. D.S.O.   **Brigadier-General**
G.O.C. 93rd Brigade 31st Division   **Died of wounds: 11 October, 1918**

Stuart Campbell Taylor was born in June, 1872, and was commissioned into the King's Own Yorkshire Light Infantry in December, 1892. He served on the north-west frontier of India from 1897 to 1898 and was with the Tirah Expedition, as Signals Officer of the 4th Infantry Brigade. In 1898 he became private secretary to Sir Charles Bruce, Governor of Mauritius. He served in the South African War from 1899 to 1902, and was Staff Officer British Troops Crete during the international occupation of 1903–04. He was seconded from the Army in 1907 as Political Officer Northern Nigeria. He retired from the Army in July, 1911, but was re-employed on the outbreak of war in 1914. He commanded the 11th Battalion K.O.Y.L.I. from November, 1914 to 1915, and was then transferred to command the 15th Battalion West Yorks Regiment (1st Leeds) until he was wounded on 20 May, 1916. He was awarded the D.S.O.[1] for gallantry at Gavrelle in May, 1917, 'when in command of the right of an infantry attack. The attacking troops having been compelled to fall back, he collected the remnants of his battalion, about 100 men of other units, and, regardless of heavy fire, he organized these in defence of a position, and by his fine example of courage and skill he successfully resisted three counter-attacks and thus saved a critical situation.' In April, 1918, he was appointed Brigadier-General Commanding the 93rd Infantry Brigade. On 1 October his brigade head-quarters was 1½ miles east of Messines and the brigade diary[2] records: 'Whilst making a tour of the battalions during the morning Brigadier-General Stuart Taylor, D.S.O., was seriously wounded in the head and body and the Brigade-Major, Captain C. G. Watts, was killed by hostile shell fire.' Brigadier-General Taylor died of his wounds on 11 October, 1918, and he is buried in La Kreule Military Cemetery, Hazebrouck, France.

Officers Died In The Great War: The King's Own (Yorkshire Light Infantry).
1 L.G. 18/7/17.   2 PRO WO 95/2360.

Thesiger, G. H. C.B. C.M.G.   **Major-General**
G.O.C. 9th Division   **Killed in action: 27 September, 1915**

George Handcock Thesiger, a grandson of the first Lord Chelmsford, was born in October, 1868, and was educated at Eton and the R.M.C., Sandhurst. In March, 1890, he was gazetted to the Rifle Brigade, and joined the 2nd Battalion. He served in the Nile Expedition of 1898, being present at the Battle of Khartoum, and subsequently served in Crete. He went to the South African War with the 2nd Battalion in October, 1899, and was at the siege of Ladysmith, where he took part in the action on 'Wagon Hill' on 6 January, 1900, and was severely wounded. During the years 1901–1902 he was at the Staff College and from 1902 to 1906 was D.A.A.G. for Musketry at Salisbury Plain. He was Assistant Military Secretary to the G.O.C. in Ireland from 1908 to 1909, and from this post he went to Africa as Inspector-General of the King's African Rifles. In December, 1913, he was appointed to command the 4th Battalion The Rifle Brigade in India. He returned with the battalion to England in the autumn of 1914 and took it to France in December of that year. In 1913 he was made a C.M.G., and in 1914 a C.B. He was appointed to command the 2nd Infantry Brigade in May, 1915, and in August, 1915, he was promoted to Major-General and given command of the 33rd Division, from which he was transferred, in September, to the 9th (Scottish) Division. The official history[1] records that during the Battle of Loos: 'Major-General Thesiger, commanding the 9th Division, having heard that the 73rd Infantry Brigade was unsteady, had gone forward, personally, to investigate the situation about Fosse 8, but on reaching the eastern face of the Hohenzollern he, with two of his Staff officers, was killed.' The Divisional Staff diary[2] records that news of General Thesiger's death was sent by the 26th Infantry Brigade and that brigade's diary[3] records that, 'General Thesiger, Major Le Mottee, G.S.O.2, and Lt. Burney, A.D.C. were all killed in the Hohenzollern Redoubt on the 27th not far from the western face.' General Thesiger has no known grave; he is commemorated on Panel 129 of the Loos Memorial to the Missing, France.

Officers Died In The Great War: The Rifle Brigade.
1 Edmonds. *Military History France and Belgium, 1915*, Vol. 2.   2 PRO WO 95/1733.
3 PRO WO 95/1762.

Wing, F. D. V. C.B.
C.R.A. 3rd Division
G.O.C. 12th Division

Major-General
Wounded: 22 September, 1914
Killed in action: 2 October, 1915

Frederick Drummond Vincent Wing was born in November, 1860, and was educated at the R.M.A., Woolwich, from where he was gazetted as a Lieutenant in the Royal Artillery in May, 1880. He saw active service in the South African War from 1899 to 1902, and in 1902 was made a C.B. He held a variety of Staff appointments, including that of A.D.C. to Lord Roberts in 1903, and command of the Royal Artillery of the 3rd Division, Southern Command, from 1913 to 1914. He had a number of near escapes before he was eventually killed. The casualty return of the 3rd Division lists him as slightly wounded on 22 September, 1914, as General Smith-Dorrien's diary[1] records: '23rd September 1914. I was glad to see General Wing this morning at his work as usual, in spite of the fact that he got a shrapnel bullet through the lower part of his leg yesterday.' *The Burgoyne Diaries* record an incident in 1915: 'General Wing, commanding the

Divisional Artillery here, had a narrow escape this morning. As his motor car came over the rise of the hill near Mount Kemmel, German shrapnel burst just over him; breaking the glass in his car and sending a bullet through his chauffeur's arm.' The A. & Q.M.G. diary[2] of the 12th Division reports his death: 'October 2nd, 1915. The G.O.C. 12th Division Major-General F. D. V. Wing, C.B., and his A.D.C., Lt. C. C. Tower, Essex Yeomanry, were both killed by a shell near the advanced reporting station about 3.45 pm., while in active superintendence of operations, and just after they had visited the front-line trenches (near Mazingarbe).' The Divisional diary[3] reports the incident as follows: 'October 2nd. The advanced Report Centre, being surrounded by batteries, came in for some heavy shelling during the afternoon. At 3.45 pm. General Wing and his A.D.C., Lt. Tower, were killed whilst crossing the road outside the Report Centre.' Major-General Wing and his A.D.C. are buried in adjacent graves in Noeux-les-Mines Communal Cemetery and Extension, France.

Officers Died In The Great War: Commands and Staff
1 PRO CAB 45/206. 2 PRO WO 95/1828. 3 PRO WO 95/1822.

Wormald, F. C.B.   Brigadier-General
G.O.C. 5th Cavalry Brigade   2nd Cavalry Division   Killed in action: 3 October, 1915

Frank Wormald was born in February, 1868. He entered the Army in November, 1889, obtaining his commission in the 12th Lancers from the Militia. He saw considerable service in the South African War, and he commanded a mobile column from October, 1901, to May, 1902. In 1912 he succeeded to the command of his regiment. General Wormald was a successful big-game hunter in India and Africa, and was well known in the hunting field and as a polo player. He took his regiment to France with the first part of the Expeditionary Force, and when leading a charge of the 12th Lancers, during the Battle of Moy, near Cerissy, on 28 August, 1914, he was wounded. Three weeks later he rejoined his regiment, which he commanded continuously until July, 1915. In February, 1915, he was made a C.B. and in July of the same year he was appointed to command the 5th Cavalry Brigade. The diary[1] of the 5th Cavalry Brigade of 2 October records that: '100 men per regiment [were required] to clear up battlefields and reconstruct trenches.' And on 3 October: 'Brigadier-General Frank Wormald killed by shrapnel whilst going round trenches of late battlefield, Vermelles.' In the history[2] of the 12th Lancers an officer comments, bitterly: 'If they will send up Brigadiers to superintend 800 men burying dead, what do they expect?' Brigadier-General Wormald is buried in Nedonchel Churchyard, France, north of the west end of the church.

Officers Died In The Great War: 12th Lancers
1 PRO WO 95/1138. 2 Stewart. *History of the XII Royal Lancers 1715–1945.*

CHAPTER 4

Wounded, Gassed and Prisoners of War

The rank, appointment and decorations stated at the beginning of each entry are those held at the time of wounding or capture. Subsequent promotions, appointments and decorations awarded are mentioned in the text.

Ardee, Lord C.B.   **Brigadier-General**
G.O.C. 4th Guards Brigade 31st Division   **Gassed: 27 March, 1918**

Reginald Le Normand Brabazon, Lord Ardee, was born in November, 1869, the eldest son of the 12th Earl of Meath. He was educated at Wellington College, entered the Army, in the Grenadier Guards, in 1889, and served in the South African War from 1900 to 1902. In 1914 he commanded the 1st Battalion Irish Guards until he was wounded on 7 November of that year. On 8 February, 1918, he was appointed to command the 4th Guards Brigade and was gassed on 27 March, 1918. On that date the brigade diary[1] records: 'Monchy au Bois. Meanwhile the Brigadier's voice had completely given out, as the result of being gassed by a shell.' He received the C.B in 1915 and the C.B.E. in 1919. Lord Meath succeeded his father in 1929 and died in March, 1949.

PRO WO 95/1255.

Asquith, A. M. D.S.O.*   **Brigadier-General**
G.O.C. 189th Brigade 63rd (R.N.) Division   **Wounded: 20 December, 1917**

Arthur Melland Asquith was born in April, 1883, the third son of the 1st Earl of Oxford and Asquith (Prime Minister from 1908 to 1916). He was educated at Winchester and New College, Oxford, and in 1914 he joined the R.N.V.R. (his three brothers joined the Army; Raymond was killed on the Somme in 1916). He served with the Royal Naval Division at Antwerp and Gallipoli, where he was wounded. In April, 1917, he was recalled from

Staff duties to lead the Hood Battalion in their attack upon Gavrelle. He was awarded the D.S.O.[1] , for his actions near Beaucourt when 'he obtained leave to go up to the front when he heard a fight was imminent. Later, although wounded, he returned to the Brigade Headquarters and gave a clear account of the situation and of the fighting, which had been going on during the night.' Two Bars[2] were added to the D.S.O.; the first was awarded 'for conspicuous gallantry and determination in the attack and clearance of a village, when he personally captured ten of the enemy, and later organized its defence, and, by his contempt of danger under heavy fire, contributed greatly to the success of the operations and the steadiness of all ranks with him.' The second was for conspicuous gallantry and devotion to duty during two days' operations. 'He went through a heavy barrage and made a successful reconnaissance of an advanced position. Later, in bright moonlight, he reconnoitred some buildings which were reported to be occupied by the enemy. His advance was observed, and the enemy opened fire, but he entered one of the buildings and found it occupied by an exhausted British garrison. He returned, under heavy fire, and brought up three platoons to relieve them. He showed great determination and resource.' On 16 December, 1917, he was promoted Brigadier-General in command of the 189th Infantry Brigade of the 63rd (R.N.) Division, but four days later he was wounded. The brigade diary[3] records the event: 'Bde. H.Q. Q.18.b.9.9 [just east of Beaucamp]. At 1.20 pm. 20th. The command of the brigade passed to Lt.-Col. Kirkpatrick vice Brigadier-General Asquith, D.S.O., evacuated wounded.' During the war he was wounded four times, the last wound resulted in the loss of a leg. He retired from the Army with the honorary rank of Brigadier-General and he died in August, 1939.

---

1 L.G. 17/4/17.   2 L.G. 8/7/17 & 18/1/18.   3 PRO WO 95/3112.

Bailey, V. T. D.S.O.   Brigadier-General
G.O.C. 142th Brigade   47th Division   Wounded & P.O.W.: 24 March, 1918

Vivian Telford Bailey was born in December, 1868, and was educated at St. Columba's College, Rathfarnham, Co. Dublin, and at King's College, London. He joined the 8th Battalion The King's Regiment from the 5th Battalion Connaught Rangers in 1891, and served in the South African War in 1901. From 1914 to 1917 he commanded the King's Liverpool Regiment (Pioneers) and was awarded the D.S.O.[1] for distinguished service in the field. In 1917 he was appointed to command the 142nd Infantry Brigade, and in the March Retreat of 1918 the brigade diary[2] records that at '2.40 Orders received from 47 Div. to withdraw to position E. of High Wood. Brigade H.Q. moved via Factory Corner – Flers – Longueval. 5.30 pm. Brigadier and Staff ran into enemy N. of Delville

Wood and were captured together with all records.' Brigadier-General Bailey was wounded and captured and Captain H. Peel, his Brigade-Major, was killed. Brigadier-General Bailey was made a C.M.G. in 1918, retired from the Army in 1919 and died in November, 1938.

1 L.G. 14/1/16.   2 PRO WO 95/2742.

Baldock, T. S. C.B.
G.O.C. 49th Division

Major-General
Wounded: 16 July, 1915

Thomas Stanford Baldock was born in January, 1854, and was educated at Cheltenham and the R.M.A., Woolwich, from which he entered the Royal Artillery in April, 1873. He served in the South African War from 1901 to 1902, and from April to May of 1902 he was in command of a column of mounted rifles, and was made a C.B. in the same year. In September, 1911, he was appointed to command the 49th Division. The A. & Q.M.G. diary[1] of the division records that on 16 July, 1915, when at the advanced headquarters of the 49th Division at Trois Tours, he was severely wounded in the head by shell fire. His brigade diary[2] describes the incident: 'Château des Trois Tours [N.W. of Ypres, near Brielen]. Friday 16th. The Germans shelled Inf. Bde. and Art. Bde H.Q.'s in the morning. At 4.15 pm. they suddenly fired 5 or 6 salvos of shrapnel and H.E. into Trois Tours Château grounds. General Baldock was outside at the time and in endeavouring to get back into the house, whilst the shelling was in progress, was wounded severely in the head by a fragment of shell. He was carried into a dugout and his wound was dressed by a medical officer. He was afterwards removed in a motor car to No.10 Clearing Hospital at Poperinghe.' Major-General Baldock retired from the Army in 1916 and died in August, 1937.

1 PRO WO 95/ 2769.   2 PRO WO 95/2765.

Ballard, C. R.
G.O.C. 95th Brigade   5th Division

Brigadier-General
Wounded: 20 July, 1916

Colin Robert Ballard was born in July, 1868, and was educated at the United Services College, Westward Ho! He was commissioned into the Norfolk Regiment in February, 1888, and served in Burma from 1891 to 1892 with the Bungshe Column. On the north-west frontier of India he served with the Relief Force in Chitral in 1895, and with the Tirah Expedition of 1898. He served in the South African War from 1899 to 1902, as Adjutant of Roberts' Light Horse and on the Staff, and then served in East Africa from 1903 to 1904 on operations in Somaliland. He commanded the 7th Infantry Brigade from November, 1914, to July, 1915, and then took command of the 95th Infantry Brigade in August, 1915. During the

Battle of the Somme his brigade headquarters was at Bécordel-Bécourt on 20 July, 1916, when, as the brigade diary[1] records: 'At 10 am. a shell landed in brigade headquarters and wounded General Ballard.' He was made a C.B. and when he recovered from his wounds he returned to command the 57th Infantry Brigade, 19th Division from December, 1916, to April, 1917, when he left the brigade to become Military Attaché in Roumania. He was made a C.M.G. in 1918. From 1920 to 1923 he was President of the Allied Police Commission in Constantinople. In 1923 he retired from the Army and wrote a number of books including one, in 1931, on General Smith-Dorrien. Brigadier-General Ballard died in June, 1941.

1 PRO WO 95/1575.

Beckwith, A. T. D.S.O.

Brigadier-General

G.O.C. 153rd Brigade   51st Division

Gassed (March): 11 April, 1918

Arthur Thackeray Beckwith was born in October, 1875, and was educated at Radley College. He was commissioned into the Hampshire Regiment in September, 1895, served in the South African War from 1899 to 1900 with the South Lancashire Regiment, and served in Aden and the Hinterland from 1903 to 1904. He was at Gallipoli in 1915, in command of the 2nd Battalion Hampshire Regiment, and was awarded the D.S.O.[1] for gallantry and devotion to duty. On 2 August, 1917, he was appointed to command the 153rd Infantry Brigade, and in March, 1918, he was gassed but remained at duty. In a letter[2] written in July, 1931, Lieutenant-Colonel L. M. Dyson wrote of the events of 11 April: 'About 9 am. Brigadier-General Beckwith gave orders for the H. Q. of 153rd Brigade to move back from Pacaut to Riez du Vinage, but just before leaving, collapsed and was obviously too ill to carry on. The Division was told, sent an ambulance for him and ordered me to take command.' He had already been wounded three times in the war. He returned to command the 35th Infantry Brigade from August to September, 1918, and the 13th Infantry Brigade from September, 1918, to May, 1919. He then commanded the 85th Infantry Brigade of the British Army of the Black Sea until February, 1920. He was made a C.M.G. in 1918 and a C.B. in 1919. Brigadier-General Beckwith retired from the Army in 1924 and died in October, 1942.

1 L.G. 3/6/16.   2 PRO CAB 45/122.

Bellingham, E. H. C. P. D.S.O.

Brigadier-General

G.O.C. 118th Brigade   39th Division

P.O.W.: 28 March, 1918

Edward Henry Charles Patrick Bellingham was born in January, 1879. He was educated at The Oratory School and the R.M.C., Sandhurst, and was commissioned into the Royal Scots in August, 1899. He served in the South African War from 1899 to 1902, but resigned from the Army in March, 1904, and became Vice Consul in Guatemala. At the outbreak of the Great War he returned to the Army and commanded the 8th(S) Battalion the Royal Dublin Fusiliers from February, 1916, to February, 1917. Whilst in command of this battalion he was awarded the D.S.O.[1] for conspicuous gallantry in action. 'He took command of two leading battalions when the situation was critical and displayed the greatest determination under shell and machine-gun fire. The success of the operation was largely due to his quick appreciation of the situation, and his rapid consolidation of the position.' On 3 February, 1917, he was appointed to command the 118th Infantry Brigade. The war diary of the 39th Division[2] records the events which led to his capture: '27 March [1918]. At 4 am. telephonic orders were received from XIX Corps that a withdrawal would be carried out immediately, before daylight if possible, to the line Vrely-Guillaucourt-Marcelcave. The withdrawal commenced in full daylight at 7 am., the 117th Infantry Brigade moving first, their withdrawal being covered by the 118th Infantry Brigade. The enemy was not slow to notice movement and put down a heavy and well directed barrage with artillery and machine guns, but fortunately did not inflict heavy casualties. He also advanced rapidly into Harbonnières and forced a large number of men to keep in a too westerly direction. Brigadier-General Bellingham remained to supervise the right flank and rear-guard of his brigade and, with his Brigade-Major (Major F. Gunner), was taken prisoner.' The brigade diary[3] records that, 'when the brigade was assembled on the Wiencourt – Marcelcave [S.E. of Villers-Bretonneux] line in the afternoon it was found that the B.-G.C. and the B-M were missing. They had left Bde. H.Q. about 6.30 am. They were last seen in a trench in R.25.c before withdrawal from that line, where they had taken cover from the shelling.' Brigadier-General Bellingham was repatriated in December, 1918, and was made a C.M.G. In 1921 he succeeded his father as the 5th Baronet. In the Second World War he was commissioned in the Royal Air Force, his name appears in the Air Force List for March, 1944, as F/Lt. Bellingham, Sir Edward H.C.P., Bt. C.M.G. D.S.O. He served on the Control Commission in Germany. Brigadier-General Sir Edward Bellingham died in May, 1956.

---

1 L.G. 20/10/16.   2 PRO WO 95/2567.   3 PRO WO 95/2589.

Borradaile, H. B.   D.S.O.   **Brigadier-General**
G.O.C. 36th Brigade   12th Division   **Wounded: 1 October, 1915**

Harry Benn Borradaile was born in October, 1860. He was educated at Charterhouse and was gazetted to the 25th Foot in January, 1880. In April,

1881, he was a Lieutenant in the King' Own Scottish Borderers. He served in Burma from 1885 to 1889 and was with the Sikkim Expeditionary Force in 1889. In 1895 he was with the Chitral Relief Force and was awarded the D.S.O.[1] in recognition of his services. From 1902 to 1909 he commanded the 34th Sikh Pioneers of the Indian Army. In 1913 he retired, but he returned in 1914 and commanded the 36th Infantry Brigade until he was wounded in 1915. His name appears in the casualty list of the A. & Q.M.G. diary[2] of the 12th Division on 1 October as wounded but remaining at duty, however, on 9 November, 1915, he was ordered home. Brigadier-General Borradaile died in August, 1948.

1 L.G. 16/7/95.   2 PRO WO 95/1828.

Borrett, O. C. C.M.G. D.S.O.*
G.O.C. 197th Brigade 66th Division
G.O.C. 54th Brigade 18th Division

Brigadier-General
Wounded: 30 March, 1918
Gassed : 24 October, 1918

Oswald Cuthbert Borrett was born in March, 1878, and was educated at Wellington College. He entered the Army, in the King's Own Royal Lancashire Regiment, in May, 1898, and served in the South African War from 1899 to 1902. In 1914 he was a Major with the Royal Lancashire Regiment and in August, 1915, was Lieutenant-Colonel commanding the 5th K.S.L.I. until he returned to the 1st Battalion of his own Regiment in July, 1916. He was awarded the D.S.O.[1] in 1915 for distinguished service in the field, and a Bar[2] to the order in 1917 for conspicuous gallantry and devotion to duty. On 13 July, 1917, he was appointed to command the 197th Infantry Brigade. The Summary of Operations of 21 to 30 March, contained in the brigade diary[3], includes the following: '29th. At 7 pm. Brigade Headquarters withdrew to Domart. 30th. At 8.10 am. the enemy were reported to have broken through the Army Line, and Generals Borrett and Williams went out to form the troops up on Hangard Line. Bde. H.Q. moved to Gentiles. At about 10 am. Brigadier-General Borrett was wounded.' On 12 October he returned to command the 54th Infantry Brigade, but just under two weeks later, according to the A. & Q.M.G. diary[4], he was gassed and evacuated, although his brigade's diary[5] records that he was sick. He returned to his brigade once again on 15 November, 1918. He was made a C.M.G. in 1918, a C.B.E. in 1922 and was created a K.C.B. in 1937. From 1936 to 1939 he was Lieutenant of the Tower of London. Lieutenant-General Sir Oswald Cuthbert Borrett retired from the Army in 1938 and died in July, 1950.

1 L.G. 23/6/15.   2 L.G. 18/7/17.   3 PRO WO 95/3123   4 PRO WO 95/2018.
5 PRO WO 95/2024.

Brand, C. H. C.M.G. D.S.O.
G.O.C. 4th Australian Brigade 4th Australian Division

Brigadier-General
Wounded: 6 July, 1917

Charles Henry Brand was born in September, 1873. He served for 18 years in the Australian Education Department, Queensland, and for 10 years on the Administrative and Instructional Staff of the Australian Forces. He served in the South African War from 1900 to 1901. In the Great War he was with the Australian Forces in Gallipoli, where, as a Captain with the 3rd Australian Infantry Battalion, he was awarded the D.S.O.[1] for gallantry and devotion to duty in connection with the operations at the Dardanelles. He was appointed Brigadier-General Commanding the 4th Australian Infantry Brigade in August, 1916, and was made a C.M.G. In the Australian history[2] of the war and the diary[3] of the General Staff of the 4th Australian Division the events of 6 July, 1917, are described: 'Steenwerck. 7 pm. While 4th Aust. Inf. Bde. H.Q. were dining [H.Q. Mess was at English Farm, Ploegsteert], a shell aimed at 6 howitzers which were in the vicinity of Bde. H.Q., in spite of numerous requests for their removal, landed in the mess. The Intelligence Officer was killed and Brigadier-General Brand, his Brigade-Major, Major C. M. Johnson (Glenhuntly, Victoria.), the acting Staff-Captain, Captain H. Thompson (Adelaide) and the Signals Officer, Lieut. W. Beazley (Perth, W. Australia.) were wounded.' Brigadier-General Brand returned from the hospital rest station on 17 July. He was made a C.B. in 1918. After the war he became Second Chief of the General Staff of the Australian Military Forces from 1926 to 1930, and from 1930 to 1932 he was Quartermaster General. In 1927 he was made a C.V.O. He retired from the Army in 1933, and from 1934 to 1947 he was Senator for Victoria. Major-General Brand died in July, 1961.

1 L.G. 3/6/15. 2 *Official History of Australia in the War of 1914–1918*, Vol. 4.
3 PRO WO 95/3444.

Bray, R. N. D.S.O.
G.O.C. 189th Brigade 63th Division

Brigadier-General
Gassed: 12th March, 1918

Robert Napier Bray was born in December, 1872, and was educated at the United Services College, Westward Ho! He entered the Army in December, 1894, when he was gazetted from the Militia to the 1st Battalion The Duke of Wellington's Regiment. He served in China in 1900, at the relief of Tientsin and Peking. At the outbreak of the Great War he commanded a battalion of the West Riding Regiment until, in December, 1916, he was appointed to command the 87th Infantry Brigade, and in April, 1917, he transferred to command of the 171st Infantry Brigade. He held this command until September, then in January, 1918, he took command of the 189th Infantry Brigade. On 12 March the brigade was on Flesquiéres

Ridge when the whole of the salient was drenched with gas shells, mustard gas, and Brigadier-General Bray, his Brigade-Major, Captain Barnett, and the entire clerical staff and signal section, were gassed.[1] The brigade diary[2] describes the event. 'Trescault. Again a quiet day, but from 11 pm. 12th March till 2.30 pm. 13th March. Trescault and Ribcourt were again heavily bombarded with gas shells and further heavy casualties were incurred including the total personnel of brigade headquarters who were all evacuated on the 13th inst.' However, Bray returned once again in June, 1918, to command the 48th Infantry Brigade until May, 1919. He received the D.S.O.[3] for distinguished service in the field, and the C.M.G. in 1919. Brigadier-General Bray died in October, 1921.

1 Jerrold. *The Royal Naval Division.*   2 PRO WO 95/3113.   3 L.G. 1/1/17.

Bremner, A. G. C.M.G.

C.E. XIX Corps

Brigadier-General

Wounded: 22 March, 1918

Arthur Grant Bremner was born in June, 1867. He was educated at the R.M.C., Canada, and commissioned into the Royal Engineers in July, 1888. He served with the Dongola Expedition of 1896 as the Assistant Field Engineer. From 1914 to 1916 he was a Lieutenant-Colonel of Royal Engineers and was made a C.M.G. in 1916. In February, 1917, he was appointed Chief Engineer of XIX Corps. On 22 March, 1918, his head-quarters was at Villers Carbonnel and his Corps engineers were busy destroying bridges to delay the enemy's advance. The C.E.'s diary[1] records: 'Chief Engineer, Brigadier-General A. Bremner, severely wounded by aeroplane bomb about 10 pm.' A letter[2] written to the official historian in May, 1929, refers to the incident: 'Brigadier-General Haig, D.S.O., and I proceeded to XIX Corps H.Q. Just as we arrived a German aeroplane flew over the camp and dropped a bomb which fell on the "G" office, killing and wounding most of the General Staff.' The official history[3] mentions the event and states that the G.S.O.2 was killed and 'the Chief G.S.O., Brigadier-General C. N. Macmullen, though not wounded, received a shock, the effects of which were not without influence on the fortunes of the Corps during the next few days.' Brigadier-General Bremner retired from the Army in 1920 and died in March, 1950.

1 PRO WO 95/969.   2 PRO CAB 45/193.   3 Edmonds. *Military Operations France & Belgium 1918.*

Bridges, G. T. M. C.M.G. D.S.O.

G.O.C. 19th Division

Major-General

Wounded: 20 September, 1917

George Tom Molesworth Bridges was born in August, 1871, was educated at Newton Abbot College and the R.M.A., Woolwich, and was com-

1. Brigadier-General Findlay's grave at Vailly. The first British general killed in action in the Great War.

2. (*Below Left*) Brigadier-General McMahon. Killed at Ypres.

3. (*Below*) Brigadier-General Wormald. G.O.C. 5th Cavalry Brigade. Killed at Vermelles.

4. (*Above Left*)Major-General Thesiger. G.O.C. 9th Division. Killed at Loos.

5. (*Above*) Major-General Wing. G.O.C. 12th Division. Killed at Loos.

6. (*Left*) Major-General Sir William Throsby Bridges. G.O.C. 1st Australian Division. Mortally wounded at Gallipoli.

7. (*Above*) Brigadier-General Prowse. G.O.C. 11th Infantry Brigade. Died of wounds on the first day of the Battle of the Somme.

8. (*Above Right*) Brigadier-General Cole. G.O.C. 25th Infantry Brigade. Killed in action near Fromelles.

9. (*Right*) Brigadier-General Dawson. G.O.C. South African Brigade. Surrendered only when the ammunition was expended.

10. (*Right*) Major-General Mercer. G.O.C. 3rd Canadian Division. Killed in Armagh Wood, aged 57.

11. (*Below*) Brigadier-General Johnston. G.O.C. 3rd New Zealand Division. Killed by a sniper east of Ploegsteert Wood.

12. (*Below Right*) Brigadier-General C. W. E. Gordon. G.O.C. 123rd Brigade, killed by shellfire.

13. Memorial to Brigadier-General Scott-Moncrieff in Twelve Trees Copse Cemetery, Gallipoli.

14. The grave of Brigadier-General Kenna in Lala Baba Cemetery, Gallipoli.

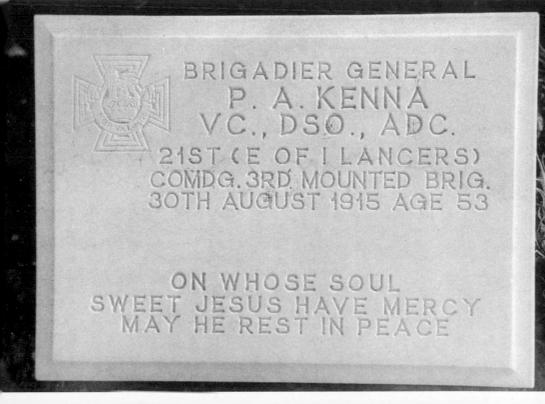

15. Brigadier-General Lumsden, V.C. C.B. D.S.O. & three Bars. G.O.C. 14th Infantry Brigade. Killed near Ransart.

17. 'Bury me between a soldier and a subaltern'. The grave of Lieutenant-General R.G. Broadwood. Anzac Cemetery, Sailly-sur-la-Lys.

16. Lieutenant-General Sir Frederick Stanley Maude. C.-in-C. Mesopotamian Expeditionary Force. Died of cholera.

18. The grave of Brigadier-General Brown at Bailleul Communal Cemetery Extension.

19. Brigadier-General A. E. Stewart. G.O.C. 3rd New Zealand (Rifle) Brigade. Wounded by a sniper on the Somme in 1918.

20. Brigadier-General Maclachlan. G.O.C. 112th Infantry Brigade. Killed by a sniper while going round the line.

21. Major-General Paris. G.O.C. 63rd (R.N.) Division. Wounded on the Somme in 1916.

22. Brigadier-General Clifford. G.O.C. 149th Infantry Brigade. Killed by a sniper firing from High Wood.

23. Major-General Bridges. G.O.C. 19th Division. Wounded at Hill 60.

24. The funeral of Major-General Lipsett. G.O.C. 4th Division. The last General to be killed in the Great War.

missioned into the Royal Artillery in 1892. He served in the South African War from 1899 to 1901 with the Imperial Light Horse and then in command of Australian Mounted Infantry. During the campaign he was severely wounded by a rifle bullet in the shoulder. He received the D.S.O.[1] for his services. From 1902 to 1904 he served in East Africa where he was engaged in operations in Somaliland, being severely wounded at Jidballi by a bullet which went through his shoulder and passed close to his spine. In 1914 he was a Major in the 4th Dragoon Guards and was at Casteau when the first British shot of the of the Great War was fired. He became famous for his rallying of exhausted British troops at St Quentin with a tin whistle and a drum taken from a local toy shop, an episode remembered in Sir Henry Newbolt's poem 'The Toy Band – A Song For the Great Retreat: You that mean to fight it out, wake and take your load again, Fall in! Fall in! Follow the fife and drum!' However, a statement[2] by Lt. Colonel F. W. Sopper, who was a Captain and 2nd i/c 'B' Squadron XVIII Hussars in 1914, to the official historian, describes another incident at St Quentin in which Major Bridges used firmer measures to get rebellious troops under control. On 27 August, 1914, Captain Sopper was in St Quentin when Major Bridges collected the stragglers. 'Major Bridges and a small party of cavalry reached St. Quentin when about 500 men of two Battalions (1st Royal Warwicks and 2nd Dublin Fusiliers) were looting the place. Major Bridges placed the two C.O.'s (Elkington and Mainwaring) in arrest and he took command of the town; ordering all cavalry officers to take small parties and round up the infantry and get them into the Town Hall and lock them in there. When all were collected Major Bridges went and spoke to them. He said he had enough men and ammunition to shoot them down and he gave them an hour to decide whether they would take their rifles and march or be shot down where they were. The men at once decided to march. Outside the town some carts had been collected and the men were told they could get into them. They refused, saying they were men again and would march.' Apparently, Major Bridges made them a speech which Captain Sopper considered one of the finest things he had ever heard. Captain Sopper considered the whole episode a triumph for Major Bridges' personality, determination and grasp of a nasty situation. He was promoted Lieutenant-Colonel in the 4th Hussars in 1914. In 1917 he was Military Representative on the Mission to the U.S.A., and on his return he was appointed to command the 19th Division. During the Third Battle of Ypres, on 20 September, 1917, he went from his headquarters at the Sherpenburg to visit one of his brigade commanders, Brigadier-General Cubbitt of the 57th Infantry Brigade, who had his headquarters in a dugout in Hill 60. When he left the dugout during a German barrage a shell exploded nearby and shattered his right leg. That night, at Wulveringham, his leg was amputated. Not wanting to go to England, he spent six weeks at a base hospital in Montreuil, near Bologne. 'Nearly everyone I knew in the Army came to see me here, except Douglas Haig.'[3] He recovered and within three months he took over the Trench Warfare Department of the Ministry of Munitions. He returned to the U.S.A with another War Mission in 1918, and then became Chief of the British Military Mission (Salonika), and from 1922 to 1927 he was Governor of New South Wales. He retired from the Army in 1922. Lieutenant-General Sir George Tom Molesworth Bridges, K.C.B. K.C.M.G. D.S.O. F.R.G.S. D.Sc., died in November, 1939. His ashes were placed in the the church-yard at St. Nicholas-at-Wade, Isle of Thanet, Kent, and a memorial was placed upon the wall of the Lady Chapel, popularly known as the Bridges Chapel since it contains memorials to several members of his family.

1 L.G. 8/2/01.   2 PRO CAB 45/189   3 Bridges. *Alarms and Excursions*

Brooke, Lord C.M.G. M.V.O. — Brigadier-General
G.O.C. 12th Canadian Brigade   4th Canadian Division — Wounded: 11 September, 1916

Leopold Guy Francis Maynard, Lord Brooke, was born in September, 1882, the eldest son of the 5th Earl of Warwick, and was commissioned from the Militia into the 1st Life Guards in November, 1900. He served in the South African War as an A.D.C. from 1901 to 1902 and as A.D.C. to the Inspector General to the Forces from 1907 to 1912. He was present, as a newspaper correspondent, in the Russo-Japanese war from 1904 to 1905 when he was made a M.V.O. In 1913, when he had become a Lieutenant-Colonel in the Territorial Army (Essex Regiment), he went to Canada, at the request of the Minister of Militia, to command the 2nd Canadian Cavalry Brigade in its annual training, and in the summer of 1914 was in charge of Petawawa Camp. When the Great War started he went to France as A.D.C. to the C. in C. of the B.E.F. In June, 1915, he was a Brigadier-General and had been made a C.M.G. when he took command of the 4th Canadian Infantry Brigade of the 2nd Canadian Division. The division was needed at the front with the least possible delay and was sent by short cut across the Channel from Folkstone to Boulogne. The brigade diary[1] records the event: 'Brigade Headquarters and the four battalions left Folkestone for Boulogne [on the] night of 14/15th. Destroyer rammed military leave boat which had on board brigade headquarters and right half of 18th Battalion and Battalion H.Q.'s.' The collision carried away part of the paddle box and veered the crowded mail boat over to a very dangerous angle. The ship stayed afloat and was eventually towed into Boulogne harbour. Lord Brooke returned to England in November, 1915, to become G.O.C. of the training camp of the Canadian Division at Bramshott. In May, 1916, he returned to France to command the 12th Canadian Brigade of the 4th Canadian Division. The division's General Staff diary[2] for 11 September, 1916, records: 'Westoutre. Enemy rather more active than usual with trench mortars and artillery. Particular attention was paid to Kemmel and near the Château. Several 5.9 in. shells were dropped, one wounded Brigadier-General The Lord Brooke and Colonel Clerk of the 72nd Battalion (slightly). Major-General Watson [G.O.C. 4th Canadian Division], who was with them, had a lucky escape.' Lord Brooke succeeded his father as 6th Earl of Warwick in January, 1924, and died in January, 1928.

1 PRO WO 95/3905.   2 PRO WO 95/3880.

Bruce, C. D.   Brigadier-General
G.O.C. 27th Brigade   9th Division   P.O.W.: 25 September, 1915

Clarence Dalrymple Bruce was born at North Berwick, Scotland, in 1862. He was educated at Haileybury College and the R.M.C., Sandhurst, and was commissioned into the Duke of Wellington's Regiment in 1882. He served in India from 1883 to 1889 as A.D.C. Sirhind Division to General MacFain, and was on the Staff of Sir Francis Grenfell, in Cairo, during the Atbara Campaign. He raised the Chinese Regiment at Wei Hai Wei in 1898 and afterwards commanded the regiment for six years. In 1900 he was dangerously wounded in the fighting around Tientsin for the relief of Peking. He was Commissioner of the International Police at Shanghai from 1907 to 1914. In January, 1915, he was appointed to command the 27th Infantry Brigade of the 9th Division. At the Battle of Loos, as is recorded in the divisional history[1]: [The Germans] 'penetrated during the night between the 9th and 7th Divisions and attacked and captured the Quarries from the rear. To the Seventh Division this came as a complete surprise, and amongst the prisoners was Brigadier-General Bruce, while Captain Buchan, his Brigade-Major, was killed.' The diary[2] of the 27th Brigade recorded the events: 'Later German bombers succeeded in working round the flank of the troops in "Pekin Trench" and this position was abandoned; the brigade being withdrawn to "Fosse Alley". Brigade headquarters was established in the Quarries. During the night the Quarries were attacked and occupied by the Germans and, the line of "Fosse Alley" becoming untenable, the Brigade fell back to our own first line trench. Brigadier-General C.D. Bruce and Captain Buchan, Brigade-Major, were reported missing.' In a letter[3] written in March, 1927, Brigadier-General Bruce describes the events that led to his capture. He had been ordered by his Divisional Commander, Major-General Thesiger (q.v.), to attack Haisnes. He wrote: 'I went into the Quarries because poor Buchan, my Brigade-Major, said he had been told (he had gone over to the Quarries) that a telephone was still working down underground in the Quarries. Buchan and I descended into the bottom of the Quarries. ------ I could not get on to 9th Division in their phone dug-out, still deeper down

119

in the bowels of the earth, but waited while Buchan kept trying. I cannot say how long we were down in the phone dug-out, a sort of low cave room, possibly 30 or 40 minutes. We could hear the heavy firing overhead by artillery. Suddenly, we heard infantry shooting and shouting. Then we tried to crawl out up the underground way and found men were shooting down it. At that we went back to the cave place when a gas bomb or bombs were thrown in, through the roof I presume. It was pitch dark. Buchan and most of the phone operators were blown to pieces; some, from their cries, dreadfully wounded. Those of us left, 3 or 4, were knocked silly. I remember trying to get out through the passage; the firing down it had stopped. The next thing I recall clearly was voices shouting *Heraus*! *Heraus*! or words to this effect, then I realised what had happened.' Bruce was a prisoner of war. Eventually, he was interned in Holland from April, 1918, and was repatriated in April, 1919. He was made a C.B.E. in 1919 and was a F.R.G.S. Brigadier-General Bruce died in December, 1934.

1 *History of the 9th (Scottish) Division.* 2 PRO WO 95/1769. 3 PRO CAB 45/120.

Bulfin, E. S. C.V.O.   **Brigadier-General**
G.O.C. 2nd Brigade 1st Division   **Wounded: 1 November, 1914**

Edward Stanislaus Bulfin was born in November, 1862, and was educated at Stonyhurst and Trinity College, Dublin. He entered the Army as a Lieutenant in the Yorkshire Regiment from the Militia in November, 1884, and served in the Burma Expedition of 1893, where he was in command of a column, and in the South African War where he was a D.A.A.G on the Staff. He was A.A. & Q.M.G. in Cape Colony from 1906 to 1910, and was made a C.V.O. He commanded the Essex Infantry Brigade from 1911 to 1913, and the 2nd Infantry Brigade from 1913 until he was wounded near Ypres in 1914. His brigade diary[1] records that on 1 November the brigade's headquarters was in 'woods E. of Zillebeke [when at] 12 noon Major-General (sic) Bulfin was wounded.' In his diary[2] for November, 1914, General Bulfin recorded: 'I was walking with Frith and an orderly when a shell came and killed the orderly, smashed up Frith and I got hit in the head and side and so went down. I told Pakenham to put the brigade under Lord Cavan and got away into Ypres after I had been patched up. Left Ypres that night, hospital being shelled, also the station. Our train badly shelled and several of the wounded killed. [On 2 November] Got to Boulogne at 7 pm. and went to Hotel 4 miles out, [it had been] turned into a hospital. Took a lot of metal from my head. [3 November] Embarked on board the St. Andrew at 6 pm. and left for England.' He returned to command the 28th Division in 1915 and the 60th Division from 1915 to 1917, served in Egypt and Mesopotamia and from

120

1917 to 1919 was in command of the 21st Corps in Palestine and Syria He was created a K.C.B. in 1918 and was promoted to General in 1925, the year that he took retired pay. General Sir Edward Bulfin died in August, 1939.

1 PRO WO 95/1267. 2 PRO CAB 45/140

Burt, A. D.S.O.   **Brigadier-General**

G.O.C. 7th Cavalry Brigade   3rd Cavalry Division   Carbon Monoxide Poisoning: 1 July, 1918

Alfred Burt was born in April, 1875, and was educated at Oundle and Heidelberg. He joined the Artist Volunteers in 1894, and was with the 3rd Battalion Royal Warwickshire Regiment from 1895 to 1896. In June, 1896, he was commissioned into the 3rd Dragoon Guards. He attended the Turco – Greek War of 1897, and served in the South African War from 1899 to 1902. He was a war correspondent in the Spanish Morocco War of 1910, and was Brigade-Major of the Welsh Border Mounted Infantry Brigade from 1912 to 1914. During the Great War he commanded the 3rd Dragoon Guards until 1918 when he was appointed to command the 7th Cavalry Brigade. He had the unusual distinction of being the recipient of the Albert Medal, which was awarded by the King for his gallantry on 30 June, 1918. The events which led to the award were described in the *London Gazette* of 8 November, 1918: 'Whitehall. 6 November 1918. The King has been pleased to award the Albert Medal to Lt.-Col. (temp. Brig.-Gen.) Alfred Burt, D.S.O., and Sergeant Victor Brooks, Canadian Cavalry Field Ambulance; and (posthumous awards) to Private Arthur Johnson and Driver Alfred Horn, late of the Army Service Corps in recognition of their gallantry in saving life in France in June last. The circumstances are as follows:

On 30 June, 1918, a Corporal of the Royal Air Force, who had been lowered by a rope into a crater caused by a bomb which had been dropped by a hostile aeroplane, was overcome by carbon monoxide gas, which had accumulated in large quantities in the crater. Endeavours were made to haul him out, but his head became caught, and Private Johnson volunteered to descend and re-adjust the rope, which he did successfully, and the Corporal was rescued, but Johnson was himself overcome. Driver Horn at once put on his respirator and lowered himself to the rescue, but was likewise overcome. Sergeant Brooks then volunteered to attempt to rescue both men, but was overcome by gas; fortunately he was hauled out. At this stage Brigadier-General Burt refused to permit anyone else to descend, but he did so himself, and succeeded in dragging one of the unconscious men someway towards the rope; he, however, became unconscious and had to be pulled out. There can be no doubt that all knew the

121

risk that they were running, and willingly incurred it in the hope of saving life.'

The brigade diary[1] for 1 July, 1918, says that four bombs were dropped in a field N. W. of St Oaken, which was where the 7th Cavalry Brigade had its headquarters. The R.A.F. Corporal was sent from 102 Squadron to examine two bombs which were supposed to be duds. While digging up the first, it was found that it had exploded about 11 feet below the surface, making a large cavity. The rest of the story is as is recorded in the *Gazette*. General Burt did not go to hospital until 16 July and after 14 days he went on leave. He was awarded the D.S.O.[2] for conspicuous gallantry and devotion to duty. 'His regiment was ordered forward when the situation was most obscure, and by his skilful leading he was able to seize an important position and thus prevent the enemy from counter-attacking. His personal bravery was a fine example to all.' He received a Bar[3] to the order 'for conspicuous gallantry and devotion to duty during a hostile attack when although his left flank was exposed and the enemy well in his rear, by his personal courage and example he so cheered and inspired his men that he was able to keep his portion of the defence intact and inflict severe casualties on the enemy.' After the war he was Chief of the Military Mission to Latvia and Lithuania until February, 1920. He died in February, 1949.

---

1 PRO WO 95/1154.   2 L.G. 18/6/17.   3 L.G. 26/7/18.

Butler, The Hon. L. J. P. C.M.G. D.S.O.   Brigadier-General
G.O.C. 4th Guards Brigade 31st Division   Gassed: 24 April, 1918

Lesley James Probyn Butler was born in April, 1876, a son of the 26th Baron Dunboyne, and was educated at Winchester and New College, Oxford. He entered the Army from the Militia in March, 1900, as a Second-Lieutenant in the Durham Light Infantry, and in February of the following year he transferred to the Irish Guards. He served in the South African War from 1899 to 1900. In August, 1914, he was Brigade-Major of the 8th Infantry Brigade and in that capacity he went to France with the brigade. From March, 1915, until July, 1915, he was G.S.O.2 of the 4th Division, and in May, 1916, he was appointed to command the 60th Infantry Brigade and was awarded the D.S.O.[1] He was made a C.M.G. in 1917. In April, 1918, he was a brigade commander with the Home Forces, and on 4 April, 1918, he took command of the 4th Guards Brigade, but three weeks later, on 24 April, the brigade diary[2] records: 'Brigadier-General Butler, C.M.G. D.S.O. went to Div. H.Q. suffering from gas poisoning.' He returned to France to command the 94th Infantry Brigade from November, 1918, until March, 1919. After the war he served as G.S.O.1 with the British Military Mission to Schleswig, and in 1920 was appointed to command the Devon and Cornwall Infantry Brigade, Southern Command. He retired from the Army in 1922 and died in December, 1955.

1 L.G. 14/1/16.   2 PRO WO 95/1225.

Cameron, N. J. G. C.M.G. Brigadier-General
G.O.C. 103rd Brigade 34th Division Wounded: 1 July, 1916

Neville John Gordon Cameron was born in October, 1873. He was educated at Wellington College and was commissioned into the Cameron Highlanders in December, 1892. He served in the Nile Expedition of 1898, being present at the Battles of Atbara and Khartoum, then served in the South African War from 1900 to 1902. In the years between August, 1909, and September, 1913, he was a Brigade-Major with the 2nd Infantry Brigade, Aldershot Command, and a Staff officer at the War Office. In August, 1914, he went to France as the A.A. & Q.M.G. of the 1st Division of the B.E.F. He subsequently served as G.S.O.1 with Scottish Command and with the 34th Division before he was appointed to command the 103rd Infantry Brigade in December, 1915. On the first day of the Battle of the Somme he was wounded 20 minutes after his brigade had 'gone over the top.' His brigade diary[1] records: '1 mile east of Albert. July 1, 1916. 7.50 am. Brigadier-General N. J. G. Cameron, C.M.G. was wounded. Lt.-Col. Steward, 27th Nth. Fus. assumed command.' A letter[2] written by William Parr at the War Office in May, 1930, describes what happened: 'Brigadier-General Cameron was commander of the 103rd Brigade at the opening of the battle on 1 July. He had established his battle headquarters close to that of the 102nd Brigade, about half-way between the Tara – Usna line and the original British front line, and on the forward slope facing La Boisselle. At Zero plus 20 minutes he was wounded by a machine-gun bullet whilst watching the brigade advancing down the forward slope from its assembly position about the Tara Usna line, the whole of the ground being well covered by machine-gun fire from the positions in rear of the German front line. Lieut. Colonel G. V. R Steward assumed command of the brigade, but it took some hours and more than one orderly to be able to extract him [General Cameron] from the front line.' He returned to France in September, 1916, to command the 151st Infantry Brigade until, in October, 1917, he became Divisional Commander of the 49th Division. He was made a C.M.G. in 1916 and a C.B. in 1918. In 1925 he was promoted to Major-General, and took retired pay in 1931. His only son was killed in action in 1940, and Major-General Cameron died in December, 1955.

1 PRO WO 95/2464.   2 PRO CAB 45/136.

Campbell, H. M. C.B. C.M.G.   **Brigadier-General**

C.R.A. 46th Division   **Wounded: 13 March, 1918**

Herbert Montgomery Campbell was born in August, 1861, and was commissioned into the Royal Artillery in June, 1881. From 1899 to 1902 he served in the South African War. On 5 August, 1914, he was appointed C.R.A. of the 46th Division. An entry in the division's C.R.A.'s diary[1] on 13 March, 1918, reads: 'Fouquiéres. Hostile artillery very active – a 77 mm. battery E. of Auchy fired short bursts on our trenches in the Cambrin Sector throughout the day. Brigadier-General Herbert M. Campbell, C.B. C.M.G. R.A., was wounded in the left eye by a 77 mm. shell when returning from the Hohenzollern Sector. [The A. & Q.M.G. diary[2] of 1 Corps records that he was visiting the O.P.'s and T.M. positions.] He was taken to No. 1 C.C.S.' The A. & Q.M.G. diary[3] states that 'he was operated on on the same evening – result the loss of the left eye.' Brigadier-General Campbell retired from the Army in January, 1919, and died in April, 1937.

1 PRO WO 95/2669.   2 PRO WO 95/613   3 PRO WO 95/2666.

Campbell, L. W. Y. C.M.G.   **Brigadier-General**

9th (Sirhind) Brigade   3rd (Lahore) Division   **Wounded: 18 December, 1916**

Leslie Warner Yule Campbell was born in August, 1867, was educated at Boulogne-sur-Mer and Cheltenham College. He entered the Army, in the King's Own Scottish Borderers, in 1886, transferred to the Indian Staff Corps in February, 1888, and served in the Tirah Campaign of 1897 and 1898, in which he was wounded. He commanded the 89th Punjabis at the taking of Shaik Syed in 1914 and then served in Gallipoli. From 1916 to 1918 he fought in Mesopotamia in the battles for the relief of Kut, and on 18 December, 1918, when his brigade's headquarters was in the Dujaila depression [east of Kut], he was wounded by a sniper whilst going round the line.[1] After the war he was given Brigade command in India and took part in the 3rd Afghan War. He retired from the Army in 1921 and died in July, 1946.

1 PRO WO 95/5110.

Carton de Wiart, A. V.C. D.S.O.   **Brigadier-General**

G.O.C. 12th Brigade   4th Division   **Wounded: 23 November, 1917**

G.O.C. 105th Brigade   35th Division   **Wounded: 20 April, 1918**

Adrian Carton de Wiart was born in Brussels in May, 1880, and was educated at the Oratory School, Edgbaston, and at Balliol College, Oxford, where he studied law. When the South African War broke out in 1899 he gave up his studies and enlisted as a Trooper in the Middlesex Yeomanry (Duke of Cambridge's Hussars). He was twice wounded. He afterwards obtained a commission in the 4th Dragoon Guards in September, 1901. From July, 1914, to March, 1915, he was with the Somaliland Camel Force and during operations he lost an eye and was awarded the D.S.O.[1] 'for distinguished service in the field in connection with the operations against Dervish Forces at Shimber Berris, Somaliland, during the months of November, 1914 and February, 1915.' He then went to France where he lost an arm at the Second Battle of Ypres. As a Lieutenant-Colonel commanding the 8th Battalion Gloucestershire Regiment he won the Victoria Cross at La Boisselle on the Somme. The *London Gazette* of 9 September, 1916, announced the award: 'Captain (Temporary Lt. Colonel.) Adrian Carton de Wiart, D.S.O. For the most conspicuous bravery, coolness and determination during severe operations of a pro-longed nature. It was owing in great measure to his dauntless courage and inspiring example that a serious reverse was averted. He displayed the utmost energy and courage in forcing our attack home. After three other battalion commanders had become casualties, he controlled their commands, and ensured that the ground won was maintained at all costs. He frequently exposed himself in the organisation of positions and of supplies, passing unflinchingly through fire barrage of the most intense nature. His gallantry was inspiring to all.'

His name kept appearing in casualty lists. In the A. & Q.M.G. diary[2] of the 4th Division: '8/9 November. Brigadier-General Carton de Wiart gassed. Arras. 23 November, 1917. Brigadier-General Carton de Wiart, V.C. D.S.O., Cmnd. 12th Inf. Bde., wounded', and in the diary[3] of 105th Infantry Brigade: '20 April, 1918. Brigadier-General Carton de Wiart wounded in the left leg while reconnoitring near Martinsart.' He was wounded eight times in the Great War. He was made a C.M.G. in 1918 and a C.B. in 1919. From 1918 to 1924 he commanded the British Military Mission to Poland, and then retired from the Army. In the War of 1939–1945 he returned to command the Central Norwegian Expeditionary Force. He was in a Wellington aircraft which came down in the Mediter-ranean when on its way to the Middle East and he became a Prisoner of War of the Italians from 1941 to 1943. He was a military representative with General Chiang Kai-Shek from 1943 to 1946, and was created a K.B.E in 1945. He took retired pay in 1947. Lieutenant-General Sir Adrian Carton de Wiart, V.C. K.B.E. C.B. C.M.G. D.S.O., died in June, 1963.

---

1 L.G. 5/5/15.   2 PRO WO 95/1451.   3 PRO WO 95/2486.

Casson, H. G. C.M.G.   **Brigadier-General**
G.O.C. 157th Brigade   52th Division   **Wounded: 3 September, 1915**

Hugh Gilbert Casson was born in January, 1866, and was commissioned into the South Wales Borderers in August, 1886. He served in the South African War from 1899 to 1901. In July, 1915, he was appointed to command the 157th Infantry Brigade, and at Gallipoli on 3 September, 1915, he 'was wounded in the thumb while looking through a periscope'.[1] On the next day he went to the Hospital Ship *Dunluce* for a few days. His divisional commander, Major-General Egerton, recorded in his diary[2] that Casson was wounded as a result of his periscope being hit and the splinters cutting both his thumbs. 'He has two nasty big holes in the top of his thumbs, and they might go septic.' He was made a C.M.G. in 1915 and a C.B. in 1916. He retired from the Army in October, 1919, and died in February, 1951.

1 PRO WO 95/4321.   2 PRO CAB 45/244.

Cayley, D. E. C.M.G.   **Brigadier-General**
G.O.C. 88th Brigade   29th Division   **Gassed: 24 April, 1917**

Douglas Edward Cayley was born in July, 1870. He was educated at Clifton College and was commissioned into the Worcestershire Regiment in March, 1890. He served in the South African War from 1900 to 1902. In 1914 he was Lieut.-Colonel commanding the 4th Battalion Worcestershire Regiment, and then went all through the Gallipoli Campaign. He became commander of the 88th Brigade and was gassed on 22 April, 1917, as the brigade's diary[1] records: 'April 21st. The enemy put over a good deal of gas shells between 1 am. and 3 am. April 22. Brigade headquarters moved forward to the caves and deep dugouts east of Monchy, the Brigadier went away sick having been slightly gassed the night before.' Cayley was made a C.M.G. in 1915, promoted to Major-General in March, 1918, and made a C.B. in 1919. Major-General Cayley retired from the Army in November, 1919, and died in December, 1951.

1 PRO WO 95/2306.

Clemson, W. F. D.S.O.   **Brigadier-General**
G.O.C. 124th Brigade   41st Division   **Wounded: 9 June, 1916**

William Fletcher Clemson was born in March, 1866, and was gazetted to the York and Lancaster Regiment in November, 1887. He commanded the 2nd Battalion of his Regiment in 1915 and was awarded the D.S.O.[1] In September, 1915, he was promoted to command of the 124th Infantry

Brigade. At 2 am. on 9 June, 1916, he was wounded by machine-gun fire near Ploegsteert Wood while on a night tour of the trenches[2], but he returned to command the brigade on the 24th of that month. He served in Italy from November, 1917, to March, 1918,, was made a C.M.G. in 1917 and received a Bar[3] to his D.S.O. The *London Gazette* of 22 March, 1918, gave the following citation: 'When his Brigade appeared to be held up in attack owing to hostile machine-gun fire he proceeded to the front of the attack and, rallying the leading troops, he led them successfully to their objectives.' Brigadier-General Clemson retired from the Army in 1920 and died in December, 1946.

1 L.G. 23/6/15.   2 PRO WO 95/2640.   3 L.G. 19/11/17 (citation to follow).

Colvile, G. N.   D.S.O.
G.O.C. 68th Brigade   23rd Division

Brigadier-General
Wounded: 30 May, 1917

George Northcote Colvile was born in July, 1867, and was gazetted to the Oxfordshire Light Infantry in February, 1887. In the South African War, from 1899 to 1902, he served with mounted infantry, was severely wounded and was awarded the D.S.O.[1] in recognition of his services during operations in South Africa. He was promoted to Major in 1906 and retired from the Army in July, 1907. Recalled in 1914 he served first with the 7th Sherwood Foresters and later with the 52nd Oxfordshire and Buckinghamshire Light Infantry. He was Colonel of the 7th Duke of Cornwall's Light Infantry in July, 1915, and became a Brigadier-General Commanding the 68th Infantry Brigade in August, 1916. In the Casualty List in the A & Q diary[2] of X Corps he is listed as wounded on 2 June, but the divisional history[3] records that in the Ypres Salient on 30 May: 'the headquarters of the 68th Infantry Brigade at Railway Dugouts were practically demolished by bombardment. A direct hit on the signal dugout killed the operator. Fortunately, none of the brigade staff was seriously injured, but Brigadier-General Colvile was severely bruised by a shell splinter.' He remained at duty and continued to command his brigade until September, 1917. Brigadier-General Colvile died in May, 1940.

1 L.G. 27/9/01.   2 PRO WO 95/858.   3 Sandilands. *The 23rd Division 1914 – 1919.*

Congreve, W. N.   V.C.   C.B.   M.V.O.
G.O.C. XIII Corps

Lieutenant-General
Wounded: 12 June, 1917

Walter Norris Congreve was born at Chatham in November, 1862, and was educated at Harrow and the R.M.C., Sandhurst. He entered the Rifle Brigade in February, 1885, and served in the South African War. As a Brigade-Major of an infantry brigade he was wounded at Colenso, where he won his Victoria Cross. The *London Gazette* of 7 February, 1900, gave the following citation: 'Walter Norris Congreve, Capt., The Rifle Brigade. Date of Act of Bravery: 15 Dec. 1899. At Colenso, on the 15th Dec.1899, the detachment serving the guns of the 14th & 66th Batteries, Royal Field Artillery, had all been either killed or wounded, or driven from their guns by infantry fire at close range, and the guns were deserted. About 500 yds. behind the guns was a donga, in which some of the few horses and drivers left alive were sheltered. The intervening space was swept with shell fire and rifle fire. Capt. Congreve, Rifle Brigade, who was in the donga, assisted to hook up a gun. Being wounded he took shelter, but seeing Lieut. Roberts fall badly wounded, he went out and brought him in. Capt. Congreve was shot through the leg, the toe of his boot, grazed on the elbow and shoulder, and his horse shot in three places.'

He became Assistant Military Secretary to the G.O.C.-in-C. the Forces in South Africa. In 1903 he was made a M.V.O., and in 1911 he was made a C.B. In 1914 he was in command of the 18th Infantry Brigade which he took to France and served with until he was appointed to command the 6th Division in May, 1915. He was appointed Lieutenant-General Commanding XIII Corps in November, 1915, and held the command until he was wounded on 12 June, 1917. One of his divisional commanders, writing[1] after the war, said: 'His personal courage was extraordinary. He was always amongst the front line troops, and was a magnificent example to the men of a complete disregard of shelling or any other form of Boche hatred. Of course you cannot go on – for four years – at this game and not get hit, and Squibs (Regtl. nickname) and his A.D.C. were hit practically full pitch by a 5.9 H.E. shell, just in front of the railway line at the foot of Vimy Ridge, between the Ridge and Arleux. This was a notoriously bad place. The Vimy Ridge had a long, gentle, forward slope all in plain view of the Boche, and they used to snipe with their artillery at anyone who exposed himself there. Nevertheless, Squibs would walk across these two miles of open most unconcernedly and, of course, they got him at last. His left hand was almost completely blown off, and he was a good deal cut and knocked about.' He had an iron hook fitted to the stump of his left arm. In 1917 he was created a K.C.B., and in January, 1918, he returned to France to command VII Corps. After the war he commanded North Force of the Egyptian Expeditionary Force in Palestine and later he was G.O.C. of the Egyptian Expeditionary Force until 1923. In June, 1925, he became Governor of Malta. General Sir Walter Congreve died in February, 1927, at the Military Hospital, Imtarfa, and was buried at sea, from *H.M.S. Chrysanthemum*, off the coast of Malta.

---

1 Thornton and Fraser. *The Congreves, Father and Son*

Cooper, R. J. C.V.O.　　　　　　　　　　　　　　　　**Brigadier-General**

G.O.C. 29th Brigade 10th Division　　　　　　　　**Wounded: 10 August, 1915**

Richard Joshua Cooper was born in July, 1860, and was commissioned into the Grenadier Guards in 1880. He served in the Egyptian Expedition of 1882 and saw action at the Battle of Tel-el-Kebir. He served in the South African War from 1899 to 1900 and transferred to the Irish Guards, later commanding the 1st Battalion of the Regiment. He was made a C.V.O. and retired from the Army in 1910, but returned at the outbreak of the Great War. He commanded the 29th Infantry Brigade in Gallipoli, and the divisional history[1] records that on 10 August, 1915, 'the dawn was misty and just as it began to grow light General Baldwin (q.v.) was killed. Almost at the same instant General Cooper fell, severely wounded in the lungs.' The brigade diary[2] records: 'Anzac. 10/8/15. A general Turkish counter-attack was delivered at about 04.30 against our lines, which were below the crest of the Chunuk Bair ridge. The H.Q. of the Brigade had come up on the 9th and taken up a position in the firing line near the R.I. Rgt. They were just below the bank on which the firing line was posted. They were all therefore much exposed on the morning of 10th and all the officers and 16 of the staff were casualties. Brig-Gen. R. G. (sic) Cooper, C.V.O., wounded. Capt. McCleverty, Bde-Major, wounded. Capt. G. W. Nugent, Staff-Capt., killed. Capt. C. C. Waddington, M.G.O., wounded & Lt. M. W. Prettyman, Signal Off., wounded.' The Australian official history[3] records that 'Brigadier-General Cooper was wounded through the lungs. Lieutenant-Colonel Bradford of the Royal Irish Rifles, upon whom the command fell, had no sooner been informed of the fact than he too was seriously wounded as was his second-in-command.' Brigadier-General Cooper was made a C.B. in 1917. He returned to retirement from the Army in January, 1920, and died in May, 1938.

---

1 Cooper. *The Tenth (Irish) Division in Gallipoli.*　2 PRO WO 95/4296.
3 *Official History of Australia in the War of 1914 – 1918.* Vol. 2.

Cowans, E. A.　　　　　　　　　　　　　　　　　　**Brigadier-General**

G.O.C. 159th Brigade 53rd Division　　　　　　　**Wounded: 14 August, 1915**

Ernest Arnold Cowans was born in December, 1865, and was commissioned from the Militia into the Seaforth Highlanders in November, 1886. He served in the Hazara Expeditions of 1888 and 1891. In the South African War he was severely wounded at Paardeburg in February, 1900. In June, 1914, he was Brigade Commander of the Cheshire Infantry Brigade, Western Command, and then became Brigadier-General Commanding the 159th Infantry Brigade. A year later he was wounded, as the General Staff diary[1] of the 53rd Division records: 'Suvla Bay to Sulajic. 14

August, 1915. Sniping continued day and night causing a steady drain in casualties, amongst the numbers was Brigadier-General Cowans, Commanding 159th Infantry Brigade.' He received retired pay from May, 1916, and died in October, 1942.

1 PRO WO 95/4322.

Cox, H. V.   C.B.   C.S.I.   Major-General
G.O.C. 29th Indian Brigade   G.H.Q. Troops   Wounded: 7 & 8 August, 1915

Herbert Vaughan Cox was born at Watford, Herts., in July, 1860. He was educated at Charterhouse and the R.M.C., Sandhurst, and was commissioned into the 25th Foot in January, 1880. In July, 1881, he became a Lieutenant in the K.O.S.B. and transferred to the Indian Army in 1883. He served in the Afghan War of 1879 and 1880; with the Burmese Expedition from 1885 to 1889; and with the Mohmand Force and the Tirah Expedition in 1897 and 1898, and then served with the China Expedition in 1900 and 1901. He held various Staff appointment in India including that of a Military Member of the Central Committee for the Delhi Durbar in 1911 and 1912. He was made a C.S.I. in 1911 and a C.B. in 1912. At the outbreak of war in 1914 he held brigade command in the Indian Army and in October he was appointed Brigadier-General Commanding the 29th Indian Infantry Brigade of the Mediterranean Expeditionary Force. In Gallipoli his brigade was part of G.H.Q. Troops, but for the attack on Sari Bair the brigade came under the command of General Sir Arthur Godley, G.O.C. New Zealand and Australian Division. The General Staff diary[1] of the 13th Division records: 'Anzac. 7 August, 1915. 7 am. Orders received by 39th Brigade to reinforce General Cox with two battalions. General Cayley conferred with General Cox and found he had been hit with a spent bullet and was unable to walk.' The brigade diary[2] for 7 August states that he had been hit in the ankle and it much interfered with his free movement. On the following day the diary states that he had been hit in the knee by a spent bullet. It is not clear whether the second entry corrects the first or whether he was hit twice by spent bullets. He was created a K.C.M.G. in 1915 and went on to command the 4th Australian Division in Egypt and France until January, 1917, when he became Military Secretary at the India Office. He was created a K.C.B. in 1918 and a G.C.B. in 1921, when he retired from the Army. General Sir Herbert Vaughan Cox died in October, 1923.

1 PRO WO 95/4300.   2 PRO WO 95/4272.

130

Davies, H. R. C.B.   **Major-General**

G.O.C. 11th Division   **Wounded: 13 September, 1918**

Henry Rodolph Davies was born in September, 1865. He was educated at Eton and was commissioned into the Oxfordshire Light Infantry in August, 1884. He served in the Burmese Expedition of 1887 and 1888, and saw service on the north-west frontier of India with the Mohmand Field Force and, the Tirah Expedition of 1897 and 1898. He was a Special Service Officer in China in 1900 and in the South African War from 1901 to 1902. He was in China again from 1906 to 1909 as D.A.A.G. North China. He commanded the 2nd Ox. and Bucks. Light Infantry from 1911 until he was appointed to command the 3rd Infantry Brigade from 1915 to 1916, and the 33rd Infantry Brigade in 1917. Promotion to Major-General and appointment to command the 11th Division came in 1917. It was whilst he was with this division that he was wounded on 13 September, 1918, as the divisional diary[1] records: 'Arras. Major-General H. R. Davies, C.B., Cmd. the Division, was wounded while going round one of the forward companies, and was evacuated to C.C.S.', but he returned to his division a month later. After the war he commanded the 49th Division until 1923 when he retired. Major-General Davies died in January, 1950.

---

1 PRO WO 95/1782.

Dawson, F. S. C.M.G.   **Brigadier-General**

G.O.C. South African Brigade   9th Division   **P.O.W.: 24 March, 1918**

Frederick Stewart Dawson was born at Hove, Sussex, in November, 1873. At the outbreak of the Great War he commanded the 1st Regiment of the South African Defence Corps, and in 1916 he was made a C.M.G. and appointed to command the South African Infantry Brigade, which was part of the 9th Division. The Australian history[1] describes the stand made by the South African Infantry Brigade on 24 March, 1918: '27 March, 1918. General Dawson of the South African Infantry Brigade had, three mornings before, held, as ordered, "at all costs", a position near Marrieres Wood, and towards evening had been captured with a small remnant of his surrounding troops.' The brigade diary[2] describes the action, which was confirmed by General Dawson in a report in 1919: 'Combles. 24th March, 1918. At 8 o'clock on the morning of the 24th the Enemy was seen advancing over the ground which had been evacuated the night before. About 9 am. the battle commenced. Time after time he hurled his troops against our position but each time he was repulsed with enormous losses. At 11.30 am. he appeared to give up the attempt to dislodge them, but concentrated his energies on the troops on the Left and Right, with the result that he forced his way through and so was able to bring enfilade fire to bear from both flanks. General Dawson sent a message through to say that he could not withdraw in daylight. The enemy had worked around both flanks, the British Front Line had withdrawn to the ridge east of Combles, nearly 1000 yds. behind, but Lewis Gun and rifle fire could still be heard coming from behind Marrières Wood. The story of the magnificent stand made by the Brigade after it was surrounded can only be told by those who were with it to the last. But this much can be certain, that it was shortage of ammunition alone which made the survivors surrender.' Brigadier-General Dawson was awarded the D.S.O.[3] whilst he was in captivity, and after he was repatriated, in December, 1918, he received a Bar[4] to his D.S.O. The citation in the *London Gazette* said: 'He displayed gallantry of the highest degree during the fighting about Chapel Hill, Revlon Farm and Sorrel on 21 –22 March, 1918. On the afternoon of the 22nd he skilfully withdrew his brigade north to the Green Line. He and members of his staff after personally preventing the enemy from entering Sorrel for some time, retired through Sorrel, fighting under heavy rifle fire at close range. On the 24th when his brigade only mustered 470 bayonets, they held 1,200 yards of front against overwhelming numbers until 4.30 in the afternoon, when ammunition was expended. He and his brigade did splendidly, and rendered most valuable service.' On 29 October, 1920, *The Times* reported from Dar-es-Salaam that Brigadier-General Dawson had died at Irangi from enteric fever while on a shooting trip.

---

1 *Official History of Australia in the War of 1914–1918*, Vol. 5.   2 PRO WO 95/1779.
3 L.G. 3/6/18. 4 L.G. 8/8/19.

Delamain, W. S. C.B. D.S.O.   **Major-General**
G.O.C. 16th Brigade   6th Indian Division   **P.O.W.: 29 April, 1916**

Walter Sinclair Delamain was born in February, 1862. He was commissioned into the Royal Berkshire Regiment in October, 1881, and served in the Egyptian Expedition of 1882. He then transferred to the Indian Staff Corps in February, 1885, and was with the Burmese Expedition from 1885 to 1888. He saw service on the Somali Coast with the Zaila Field Force in 1890, served in China in 1900, and in Waziristan from 1901 to 1902. In 1904 he was with the Aden Boundary Commission and was awarded the D.S.O.[1] for his services. He held a brigade command in India in 1914 and was made a C.B. He commanded the 16th Infantry Brigade of the 6th Indian Division in Mesopotamia and was captured at the fall of Kut-el-Amara in 1916. Repatriated in November, 1918, he was created a K.C.M.G., and held a divisional command in India in 1919, was Adjutant General from 1920 to 1923, and was created a K.C.B. in 1922. Lieutenant-

General Sir Walter Sinclair Delamain retired in 1923 and died in March, 1932.

1 L.G. 17/2/05.

Dick-Cunyngham, J. K. C.M.G. D.S.O.   Brigadier-General
G.O.C. 152th Brigade   51st Division   P.O.W.: 12 April, 1918

James Keith Dick-Cunyngham was born at Cheltenham in March, 1877, the third son of Sir R. K. A. Dick-Cunyngham, 9th Bt. and Lady Dick-Cunyngham. He was educated at Cheltenham College, and was gazetted to the Gordon Highlanders in May, 1898. In the South African War, in which he served from 1899 to 1902, he was awarded the D.S.O.[1] When war broke out in 1914 he was Assistant Provost Marshal of 2nd Army Corps, but went to France as Brigade-Major of the 14th Infantry Brigade. In September, 1915, he became G.S.O.2 with 1st Army Corps, and G.S.O.1 with the 51st Division in November, 1916. In 1918 he was made a C.M.G. He was appointed Brigadier-General of the 152nd Infantry Brigade in April, 1918, and shortly afterwards was a prisoner. The divisional history[2] records that he 'was wounded and taken prisoner at Le Cornet Malo on the 12th April after only six days with his new command.' The Australian history[3] describes the incident at 'the village of Riez du Vinage, in the cottages of which were the headquarters of the two Scottish Brigades. --- Dyson [G.O.C. 153 Bde.], who was lame, limped across the road, tapped on a cottage window and called through it to his colleague, Brigadier-General Dick-Cunyngham of the 152 Brigade: "Come on Dick – it's time to be going." Cunyngham waved and said he was coming, but did not come; before he opened the door, the Germans were in the house.' In the brigade diary[4] it is recorded that 'At 5 am. enemy lights were seen in the vicinity of brigade headquarters and there was no further communication with brigade.' The A. & Q.M.G. diary[5] of the 51st Division records in the Casualty List: H.Q. 152nd Inf. Bde. Brg-Gen. J. F. Dick-Cunyngham, C.M.G. D.S.O., Missing. Captain Berney-Ficklin, Bde-Major, Missing. Captain W. Drummond, M.C., Staff-Captain, Missing. Dick-Cunyngham was repatriated in December, 1918, and was made a C.M.G. In 1932 he was made a C.B. and promoted to Major-General. He commanded the 53rd (Welsh) Division, Territorial Army, until he died in November, 1935.

1 L.G. 27/9/01. 2 Farrell. *51st (Highland) Division War Sketches.* 3 *Official History of Australia in the War of 1914–1918*, Vol. 5. 4 PRO WO 95/2863 5 PRO WO 95/2849.

Dugan, W. J. D.S.O.   **Brigadier-General**

G.O.C. 184th Brigade 61st Division   **Wounded accidentally: 8 September, 1916**

Winston Joseph Dugan was born in May, 1877, and was educated at Lurgan College, and Wimbledon, Surrey. He served in the ranks for nearly 4 years before being commissioned as a Second-Lieutenant in the 2nd Battalion Lincolnshire Regiment in January, 1900. He served in the South African War from 1899 to 1902. At the outbreak of the Great War he was on the Staff of the East Anglian Division. He commanded the 2nd Battalion Royal Irish Regiment in 1915 and in that year he was wounded and awarded the D.S.O.[1] for distinguished service in the field. In 1916 he was appointed to command the 184th Infantry Brigade until he was wounded accidentally as the brigade diary[2] records, 'La Gorgue 6.50 am. 8 September, 1916. Brg-Gen. J. H. (sic) Dugan, D.S.O., wounded whilst watching demonstration by Stokes Mortar. Taken to hospital at Merville.' He returned to France in December, 1916, to command the 73rd Infantry Brigade until July, 1918, when he became Inspector of Training. In a letter[3] written in July, 1937, he described how he nearly became a prisoner of war: 'I remember going up with John Capper, our divisional commander, and my Brigade-Major – none of us armed or accompanied by an orderly – to visit one of our posts in the Bois de Riaumont, overlooking Lens and just beyond the Cité de Bureaux. It was snowing all the time and fairly thickly and before we knew where we were, we found ourselves face to face with a German sentry group who, fortunately, were as surprised as ourselves and so gave us just time to clear back down the slope for all our worth to the tune of whistling bullets cracking on the bare tree trunks. That was a shake up and no mistake and I shall never forget the choking off I got from John Capper when we foregathered at my brigade headquarters in Angres an hour or so afterwards. Another step forward and we might have found ourselves prisoners in Berlin.' He was made a C.M.G. in 1918. After the war he commanded the 10th Infantry Brigade, and in 1931 commanded the 56th (1st London) Division of the Territorial Army until his retirement in 1934. He was made a C.B in 1929 and was created a K.C.M.G. in 1934. From 1934 to 1939 he was Governor of South Australia, and from 1939 to 1949 was Governor of Victoria, Australia. In 1944 he was created G.C.M.G., and in 1949 he was created the first Baron Dugan of Victoria and of Lurgan in the County of Armagh. He died in August, 1951.

---

1 L.G. 23/6/15.   2 PRO WO 95/3063.   3 PRO CAB 45/133.

Eden, A. J. F. C.M.G. D.S.O.　　　　　　　　　　　**Brigadier-General**
G.O.C. 24th Brigade 8th Division　　　　　　　Wounded: 23/29 October, 1916
G.O.C. 57th Brigade 19th Division　　　　　　　　Wounded: 10 August, 1918

Archibald James Fergusson Eden was born in January, 1872. He was educated at Haileybury College and the R.M.C., Sandhurst, and was gazetted Second-Lieutenant in the Oxfordshire Light Infantry in June, 1892. He served in the West African Field Force from 1898 to 1901, including service in the Niger Hinterland and the Ashanti Expedition of 1900. He served in the South African War from 1901 to 1902. He was a brigade commander from 1916 to 1924 during which time he commanded the 24th Infantry Brigade and was wounded in the Battle of the Somme in October, 1916. The brigade diary[1] has no reference to him being wounded, although his name does appear in the Casualty Return as being wounded but at duty. In August, 1918, he commanded the 57th Infantry Brigade and the brigade diary[2], which was written in the vicinity of Béthune, describes the circumstances of his second wound: 'Considerable enemy bombing activity throughout the night [of] 10/11th. 57 Infantry Brigade H.Q. attacked and owing to one bomb falling within 15 feet of the building, portions of it were blown in. Brigadier-General Eden, C.M.G. D.S.O., the Brigade Cmdr. was wounded in the head and evacuated to Field Ambulance.' He was awarded the D.S.O.[3] in 1916 and he was made a C.M.G. in 1918. Brigadier-General Eden retired from the Army in 1924 and died in May, 1956.

---

1 PRO WO 95/1717.　2 PRO WO 95/2084.　3 L.G. 3/6/16.

Evans, H. J.　　　　　　　　　　　　　　　　**Brigadier-General**
G.O.C. 115th Brigade 38th Division　　　　　　　　　　Wounded: July, 1916

Horatio James Evans was born in June, 1859. He was commissioned into the 8th Foot in January, 1878, and became a Lieutenant in the Liverpool Regiment in February, 1880. He served in the Afghan War from 1878 to 1879, and in the South African War from 1899 to 1900. At the outbreak of the Great War he was O.C. No. 4 District, Western Command, but in 1915 he was appointed Brigadier-General Commanding the 115th Infantry Brigade of the 38th (Welsh) Division. Brigadier-General Evans did not do his reputation any good when he saved his brigade from annihilation at Mametz Wood by insisting on withdrawing his troops from an untenable position. The General Staff diary[1] for 7 July, 1916, records: '2 am. The 16th Welsh Regiment and the 11th South Wales Borderers were held up by machine-gun fire and had to fall back on their original positions. At 11 am. after another artillery bombardment another attempt was made to enter the wood, but again machine-gun fire from the flank and front made

135

progress impossible. The enemy were reported to be holding a trench from S.20.a.1½ .8 to S.20.a.0.0., strongly. A third attack was then ordered and an artillery bombardment was arranged for at 4.30 pm. Meanwhile, during the day it had poured with rain, the ground was sodden and the trenches [were] many inches deep in mud – telephone wires had been cut and progress was extremely difficult. The artillery bombardment was also inaccurate and ineffective, and the battalions of the 115th Brigade were disorganised. The G.O.C. 115th Infantry Brigade accordingly decided not to attack.' Two days later the diary recorded: 'Major-General Ivor Phillips, D.S.O., vacated command of division and proceeded to England.' In the brigade diary[2] the Casualty List of 5 to 12 July, 1916, contains the names of: Brigadier-General H. J. Evans, wounded – at duty; Capt. C. L. Veal (Bde.Major), wounded; Capt. H. V. Huiton (Staff-Captain), wounded. It also contains the following comment: 'Owing to the nature of the under-growth it would have been impracticable to have carried out the pro-gramme for the attack as laid down by the times given even had no opposition been encountered.' Brigadier-General J. R. Caussen, who was a Lt. Colonel commanding the 11th South Wales Borderers of the 115th Brigade in 1916, wrote, in a letter[3] to the official historian: '11 July [1916]. Knowing it was impossible to get orders from Brigadier-General Evans, (he was weak from loss of blood from a headwound and had no staff officers left), I took it upon myself to take over any detachments of 10th/ S.W.B. and amalgamate them with the 11th/S.W.B. as a support.' The A. & Q.M.G. diary[4] of the 38th Division records: 'Casualty List 5th July to 12th July 1916. Brigadier-General Evans wounded. 27 August, 1916. Brigadier-General Evans granted leave of absence to England.' The Army List shows that he went on retired pay on 28 August, 1916. He was made a C.M.G. in 1919 and died in February, 1932.

1 PRO WO 95/2539.   2 PRO WO 95/2560.   3 PRO CAB 45/189.   4 PRO WO 95/2541.

Evans, U. W. C.B.   **Brigadier-General**
G.O.C. 17th Brigade 6th Indian Division   **P.O.W.: 29 April, 1916**

Usher Williamson Evans was born in June, 1864, and was commissioned into the Royal Engineers in December, 1884. He served in Chin-Lushai Expedition of 1889 and 1890 and the Tirah Campaign of 1897 and 1898. He served on the Staff and held brigade command in India at the beginning of the Great War and then served in Mesopotamia as G.S.O.1 of the 6th Indian Division and then as commander of the 17th Brigade of the same division. He was captured at the fall of Kut-el-Amara and was held prisoner in Turkey for 2 years 8 months. He was made a C.B. in 1915 and a C.M.G. in 1919. He retired from the Army in 1920 and died in June, 1946.

Fagan, E. A. D.S.O.   **Brigadier-General**

G.O.C. 46th Brigade   15th Division   **Gassed: 18 July, 1917**

Edward Arthur Fagan was born in November, 1871, and was commissioned into the South Staffordshire Regiment in May, 1891. In 1893 he transferred to the Royal West Kent Regiment and in the following year transferred again to the Indian Army Corps. He served in the Tirah Expedition in 1897 and 1898 and the Tibet Expedition in 1903 and 1904. He was appointed to command the following infantry brigades in France: the 93rd Brigade from August, 1916, to March, 1917, the 46th Infantry Brigade from March, 1917, to July, 1917, and the 12th Infantry Brigade from November, 1917, to October, 1918. It was whilst he commanded the 46th Infantry Brigade that he was gassed on 18 July, 1917, the circumstances are described in the brigade diary[1]: 'July 18, 1917. Brandhoek. The Brigadier proceeded by motor car at 4 am. to H.Q. 45th Brigade at Ypres to discuss impending relief. The enemy was shelling "Dead End" and "Diximude Street" with mustard oil gas shells. The effects of these shells [resulted in] the evacuation of Brigadier-General Fagan to hospital.' He was awarded the D.S.O.[2] in 1917 and a Bar[3] to the order in 1918, 'for conspicuous gallantry and devotion to duty. When his front battalion was being overwhelmed he personally directed the action to be taken by other battalions with the utmost disregard for his own safety. He inspired all ranks with enthusiasm, and the success of the defence was largely due to his fine example.' He was made a C.M.G. in 1918. After the war he held brigade command in the Indian Army and took part in the Afghan War of 1920, and for his services he was made a C.S.I. He was made a C.B. in 1923 and created a K.C.B. in 1932. Major-General Sir Edward Fagan retired from the Army in 1931 and died in June, 1955.

1 PRO WO 95/1950.   2 L.G. 1/1/17.   3 L.G. 26/7/18.

Feilding, G. P. T. D.S.O.   **Brigadier-General**

G.O.C. 1st Guards Brigade   Guards Division   **Wounded accidentally: 8 December, 1915**

Geoffrey Percy Thynne Feilding was born in September, 1866. He was educated at Wellington College and was commissioned into the Coldstream Guards in April, 1888. He served in the South African War from 1899 to 1902 and was awarded the D.S.O.[1] for his services. He was A.D.C. to the Viceroy of India from November, 1905 to July, 1907. In 1914 he commanded the 3rd Battalion Coldstream Guards, and in April, 1915, he was appointed to command the 149th Infantry Brigade. In August of the same year he was transferred to command the 1st Guards Brigade. On 8 December the brigade diary[2] records that the headquarters was at La Gorgue and that Brigadier-General Feilding was accidentally wounded, but does not explain the circumstances of the accident. However, he returned to the brigade on the 13th, but two days later 'he went to England owing to the wound in his leg.' He was made a C.B. in 1916, promoted to Major-General and appointed to command the Guards Division, a position that he held until October, 1918. He was made a C.M.G. in 1917 and created a K.C.B. and K.C.V.O. in 1919. He was G.O.C. London District from 1918 to 1920 and retired from the Army in 1927. Major-General Sir Geoffrey Feilding died in October, 1932.

1 L.G. 27/9/01.   2 PRO WO 95/1212.

Fell, R. B.
G.O.C. 51st Brigade   17th Division

Brigadier-General
Wounded: 20 December, 1915

Robert Black Fell was born in November, 1859, and was educated at Windermere College. He was commissioned into the 90th Perthshire Light Infantry in 1878, served in the Zulu War of 1879, and served as second in command of the 2nd Battalion Scottish Rifles in the South African War from 1901 to 1902. He commanded the Scottish Rifles from 1903 to 1907, and the Scottish Rifle Brigade Territorial Force from 1908 to 1912. In 1913 he commanded the Ceylon Volunteers, but in 1914 he returned to England to command the 102nd Infantry Brigade. In 1915 he was appointed to command the 51st Infantry Brigade and it was while he was with this brigade that he was wounded on 20 December, 1915. The A. & Q.M.G. diary[1] of the 17th Division records that the wound was slight and that he remained at duty. In 1917 he commanded the 16th Training Reserve Brigade, and then returned to the Ceylon Defence Forces. He was made a C.B. in 1916 and a C.B.E. in 1919. He retired from the Army in 1918 and died in March, 1934.

1 PRO WO 95/1986.

Fisher, B. D.   D.S.O.*
G.O.C. 8th Brigade   3rd Division

Brigadier-General
Gassed: 21 August, 1918

Bertie Drew Fisher was born in July, 1878. He was educated at Marlborough and New College, Oxford, and was commissioned into the 17th Lancers in May, 1900. He served in the South African War from 1900 to 1902. From 1913 to 1914 he was a G.S.O.3 in the Military Aeronautics Department, and from September, 1914, until May, 1915, he was Brigade-Major with the 6th Cavalry Brigade and was awarded the D.S.O.[1] He then served as a G.S.O.2 until June, when he became a Lieut.-Colonel Commanding the Leicestershire Yeomanry. He was awarded a Bar[2] to his D.S.O. 'for conspicuous gallantry and devotion to duty, while commanding his battalion. The battalion on his right had been penetrated, and he was outflanked by the enemy. He withdrew his men with great skill under very heavy shell fire to a fresh position, which he held throughout the day and handed over practically intact to another division next morning. The importance of this position was great, and by holding it as he did he rendered fine service.' In April, 1918, he was appointed Brigadier-General of the 8th Infantry Brigade and he was gassed on 21 August, 1918. The brigade diary[3] describes events that occurred when the brigade made an attack, the object of which was the capture of the Arras – Bapaume railway line: '21 August, 1918. Heavy gas shelling between Ayette and Brigade H.Q. It is estimated that over 1000 gas shells (Yellow Cross) fell in this vicinity. 22nd August. 9 am. Brigadier-General Fisher and Capt. B. W. W. Gostling, Bde-Major, had to go back owing to effects of gas on morning of 21. Aug. 28th: Brigadier-General Fisher and Capt. Gostling returned from hospital.' This was the second time that he was wounded in the Great War. He was made a C.M.G. in 1919. In 1938 he was created a K.C.B. and in the same year he retired from the Army, but returned in 1939 to become G.O.C. Southern Command from 1939 to 1940. Lieutenant-General Sir Bertie Drew Fisher died in July, 1972.

---

1 L.G. 18/2/15.   2 L.G. 26/7/18.   3 PRO WO 95/1419.

Fowler, F. J.   C.B.   D.S.O.   **Brigadier-General**
G.O.C 37th Brigade   14th Indian Division   **Wounded: 8 March, 1916**

Francis John Fowler was born at Mian Mir, India, in July, 1864, and was educated at the King William College, Isle of Man; Bedford Modern School and the R.M.C., Sandhurst. He was commissioned into the North Lancashire Regiment in August, 1883, but transferred to the Indian Staff Corps in November, 1885. He served in the Zhob Valley Expedition of 1884, and was with the Burmese Expedition from 1887 to 1889. He was awarded the D.S.O.[1] for his services in Burma. From 1897 to 1899 he was in Uganda where he commanded a column in pursuit of mutineers and rebels. He served in China in 1900 and in East Africa (Somaliland) from 1908 to 1910. He was A.Q.M.G. Indian Army from 1913 to November, 1914. In 1916 he commanded the 37th Infantry Brigade of the Indian Expeditionary Force 'D' in Mesopotamia, and on 8 March, 1916, he was wounded in the attack on the Dijailah Redoubt. The diary[2] of the 37th Brigade contains a 'Report on Operations of 8/9 March, 1916,' which describes the event: 'By 5.45 pm. the assault had failed and the Somersets and Gurkhas fell back to their trenches. It was during this withdrawal that Brigadier-General Fowler C.B. D.S.O. was wounded.' On 1 July, 1916, he rejoined from hospital at Amara and resumed command of the brigade, but was invalided in September, 1916, and returned to India, where he was appointed to Divisional Area Command. He was made a C.B. in 1916. Major-General Fowler retired from the Army in 1921. He became a J. P. in the Isle of Man and died in June, 1939.

---

1 L.G. 29/11/89.   2 PRO WO 95/5179.

Freyberg, B. C. V.C. D.S.O.
G.O.C. 173rd Brigade 58th Division

Brigadier-General

Wounded: 19 September, 1917

Bernard Cyril Freyberg was born in London in March, 1889, and was educated at Wellington College, New Zealand, and New Zealand University. He joined the Army in November, 1909, as a Second-Lieutenant in the 6th Hauraki Regiment, New Zealand Military Forces, and later transferred to the British Army. He was a company commander in the Hood Battalion of the Royal Naval Division in 1914 and 1915 and commanded the battalion from 1915 to 1917. He was in the retreat from Antwerp and was in Gallipoli from the landing to the evacuation. It was at the landing in Gallipoli that he earned his D.S.O.[1]: 'For most conspicuous gallantry and devotion to duty during the landing on the Peninsula on the night of 24–25 April, 1915, when he swam ashore at night, alone, and lit flares on the beach to distract attention from the landing operations which were happening elsewhere. He was several hours in the water before being picked up.' [He was a good swimmer; he won the New Zealand Swimming Championships from 100 yards to a mile in 1905–06.] He was twice wounded at Gallipoli; in the leg on 8 May and in the stomach on 25 July, 1915. It was in France, where he commanded the Hood Battalion in the advance on Beaucourt, in November, 1916, that he won his Victoria Cross[2]: 'For conspicuous bravery and brilliant leading as a battalion commander. By his splendid personal bravery he carried the initial attack straight through the enemy's front system of trenches. Owing to mist and heavy fire of all descriptions, Lieut.-Colonel Freyberg's command was much disorganised after the capture of the first objective. He personally rallied and reformed his men, including men from other units who had become intermixed. He inspired all with his own contempt of danger. At the appointed time he led his men forward to the successful assault of the second objective, many prisoners being captured. During this advance he was twice wounded, he again rallied and reformed all who were with him, and although unsupported in a very advanced position, he held his ground throughout the day and the following night under heavy artillery and machine-gun fire. When reinforced on the following morning he organised the attack on a strongly-fortified village, and showed a fine example of dash in personally leading the assault, capturing the village and 500 prisoners. In this operation he was again wounded severely, but refused to leave the line till he had issued his final instructions. The personality, valour and utter contempt of danger on the part of this single officer enabled the furthermost objectives of the Corps to be permanently held, and on this point d'appui the line was eventually formed.'

On 21 April, 1917, he returned to France on his appointment to Brigadier-General Commanding the 173rd Infantry Brigade, and on 20 September of that year he was wounded yet again when the brigade attacked the enemy lines east of St Julien. An Operations Report for 19–21 September in the brigade diary[3] describes his wounds: 'At 8 pm. Brigadier-General B. C. Freyberg, V.C. D.S.O., was brought to Brigade Headquarters by stretcher bearers, having been severely wounded at 6 pm. near 2/4th Bn. London Rgt. headquarters at St Julien. His wounds had been dressed at the R.A.P. and he continued to command his Brigade though wounded in 10 places by an H.E. shell, which burst almost at his foot. At 11 am. the A.D.M.S. 58th Division visited General Freyberg whose wounds had again been dressed during the night by a M.O. of the 2/3rd H.C. Field Ambulance, and ordered his evacuation. As our objective had been gained and consolidated, General Freyberg, who had maintained communications by telephone with O.C. 2/4th Bn. London Rgt. throughout the battle and inspired everyone with his own cheerful courage and example, was persuaded to hand over the command to Lieut.-Colonel Dann, D.S.O., commanding 2/4th Bn. London Rgt.' He transferred to the Grenadier Guards in September, 1917, and was appointed to command the 88th Infantry Brigade in January, 1918. He was awarded a Bar[4] to his D.S.O. 'for most conspicuous bravery and devotion to duty in the attacks which led up to the capture of Gheluvelt on 28 September, 1918.' Brigadier-General Freyberg won a second Bar[5] to his D.S.O. in the last five minutes of the Great War. 'In an action at Lessines he led the cavalry in a dash to save the bridge over the river Dendre, and with nine men only he rushed a village on horseback, and captured a village and 104 prisoners two minutes before the beginning of the armistice.' He was wounded nine times in the Great War. After the war he went to the Rhine with the Army of Occupation and then served in various capacities with the British Army until the war of 1939–45 when he became G.O.C. New Zealand Forces, and in 1941 was C.-in-C. Allied Forces in Crete, and later in North Africa and Italy. He was awarded a third Bar to his D.S.O. in 1945, and from 1946 to 1952 he was Governor-General of New Zealand. Over the years he was the recipient of many honours and awards, Lieutenant-General Lord Freyberg of Wellington, New Zealand, and of Munstead in the County of Surrey, V.C., G.C.M.G., K.C.B., K.B.E., D.S.O., LL.D.(St. Andrews), D.C.L. (Oxford), LL.D. (New Zealand) died in July, 1963.

---

1 L.G. 3/6/15. 2 L.G. 16/12/17. 3 PRO WO 95/2999. 4 L.G. 1/2/19. 5 L.G. 8/3/19.

Gellibrand, J. D.S.O.   **Brigadier-General**
G.O.C. 6th Australian Brigade 2nd Australian Division   **Wounded 21 May, 1916**

John Gellibrand was born in December, 1872, and was educated at King's School, Canterbury, and the R.M.C., Sandhurst. In October, 1893, he was commissioned into the South Lancashire Regiment. He served in the South African War from 1899 to 1900, and then became a Captain and the Adjutant of the Manchester Regiment. He was Garrison Adjutant in St Helena from September, 1902, to 1904 and D.A.A. & Q.M.G. in Ceylon in 1908. In May, 1912, he retired from the Army. He served in the Great War on the Staff of the 1st Australian Division, and the official history[1] records that at Gallipoli on 8 May, 1915, 'Major Gellibrand was hit through the chest by shrapnel.' He was awarded the D.S.O.[2] in 1916 for distinguished service in the field and in that same year became the commander of the 6th Australian Infantry Brigade. The official history[3] again records that he was wounded on 21 May, 1916, when 'the enemy shelled Fleurbaix Church and Erquinghem village, General Gellibrand was wounded'. On 22 May he was evacuated. He was awarded a Bar[4] to his D.S.O. 'for conspicuous gallantry and devotion to duty. His brigade reached its third objective, but was ordered back owing to the division on the right being held up at the first objective. His brigade repelled several counter-attacks and held on when the brigade on the right was in difficulties. It was largely owing to his influence and presence in this advanced position that the operations were successful.' He was made a C.B. in 1917. From December, 1917, he commanded the 12th Brigade of the 4th Australian Division until, in May, 1918, he was made a Major-General in the A.I.F. and commanded the 3rd Australian Division. He was created a K.C.B. in 1919. From 1920 to 1922 he was commissioner of Police in Victoria, and from 1925 to 1928 was Member for Denison in the Australian Federal Parliament. Major-General Sir John Gellibrand died in June, 1945.

---

1 & 3 *Official History of Australia in the War of 1914–1918*, Vols. 1 & 2.   2 L.G.2/5/16.
4 L.G. 18/6/17

Glasgow, A. E. D.S.O.   **Brigadier-General**
G.O.C. 58th Brigade 19th Division   **Wounded: 30 May, 1918**

Alfred Edgar Glasgow was born in 1870, and was educated at Nelson and Wellington Colleges, New Zealand. He was commissioned into the Royal Sussex Regiment in 1891 and was Adjutant from 1895 to 1899. He served with the Chitral Relief Force in 1895 and was with the Tirah Expedition of 1897–1898. He commanded the 8th (S) Battalion Royal Sussex Regiment in the early part of the Great War and was awarded the D.S.O.[1] in 1916. He later served on the Staff from January, 1917, until the end of the war.

The A. & Q.M.G. diary[2] of the 19th Division records that at Chaumuzy on 30 May, 1918, Brigadier-General Glasgow was 'slightly wounded, upper lip', but remained at duty. This was the second time he had been wounded in the war. On the next day he was ordered to go to hospital at Chalons, but on 3 June he returned to his brigade. He was made a C.M.G. in 1918 and a C.B. in 1923. Brigadier-General Glasgow took retired pay in 1927 and died in February, 1950.

1 L.G. 3/6/16.   2 PRO WO 95/2058.

Gordon-Lennox, Lord Esme   M.V.O.   D.S.O.

G.O.C. 95th Brigade   5th Division

Brigadier-General

Wounded: 14 April, 1918

Lord Esme Charles Gordon-Lennox was born in January, 1875, the second son of the 7th Duke of Richmond. He entered the Army, as a Second-Lieutenant in the Scots Guards, in December, 1896, saw service in the South African War from 1900 to 1902, and in West Africa (Southern Nigeria) in 1903. He was made a M.V.O. in 1907. He was wounded at Ypres in 1914, and in 1916 was appointed to command the 95th Infantry Brigade. He was awarded the D.S.O.[1] in January, 1918. On 14 April, 1918, when the 95th Brigade's headquarters was in a house N.E. of Bois Moyen, the brigade diary[2] records: '1 pm. A direct hit was obtained on Bde. H.Q. Brig-Genl. Gordon-Lennox was severely wounded +6 of the Signal Section. Capt. Gotto (Bde. Major) was also slightly wounded. All were taken down to 14 F. Amb.' He was made a C.M.G. in 1919. After the war, from 1926 to 1946, he was Yeoman Usher of the Black Rod and Secretary to the Lord Great Chamberlain. Lord Esme Gordon-Lennox died in May, 1949.

1 L.G. 1/1/18.   2 PRO WO 95/1576.

Gorringe, Sir George F.   K.C.B.   C.M.G.   D.S.O.

G.O.C. 12th Indian Division

Major-General

Wounded: 23 February, 1916

George Frederick Gorringe was born at Southwick, Sussex, in February 1868. He was educated at Lee's School, Brighton, and at Wellington College. He was commissioned into the Royal Engineers at Chatham in February, 1888, and was employed with the Egyptian Army from January, 1893, to December, 1899. During these years he was D.A.A.G. on the Headquarters Staff in the Dongola Expedition of 1896 when he was awarded the D.S.O.[1] for his services, and he was with the Nile Expeditions of 1897, 1898 and 1899. In the South African War, in which he served from 1899 to 1901, he was A.D.C. to Lord Kitchener and in command of a flying column of the Loyal Farmers' Light Horse. He was made a C.M.G. in 1900. From 1909 to 1911 he held Brigade Command of the 18th Infantry

Brigade, Northern Command. He became a Major-General in September, 1911, and commanded the Bombay Brigade in India. In 1915 he was created a K.C.B., and from April of that year to March, 1916, he commanded the 12th Indian Division in Mesopotamia. It was during this time that he was wounded, as recorded in the D.A.A.G.'s diary[2] of the 12th Indian Division: '23 February, 1916. This morning about 6.15 am., General Gorringe was wounded in the buttock, just after he mounted his horse, by a sniper's bullet from the other side of the river – handed over command to Major-General Keary, 3rd (Lahore) Div. 6 pm. Left for treatment at Amara.' When he had recovered he became Chief-of-Staff of the Tigris Force and in March, 1916, he commanded the 3rd Army Corps of the Kut Relief Force. In September, 1916, he went to France where he commanded the 47th Division until 1919. He was created a K.C.M.G. in 1918. After the war he commanded the 10th Division in Egypt from 1919 to 1921 and was promoted to Lieutenant-General. He retired from the Army in 1924 and died in October, 1945.

1 L.G. 17/11/96.   2 PRO WO 95/5142.

Green, H. C. R.   D.S.O.   **Brigadier-General**
G.O.C. 20th Brigade   7th Division   **Wounded: 5 October, 1917**

Henry Clifford Rodes Green was born in May, 1872, and was commissioned into the K.R.R.C. in November, 1891. He served in the South African War from 1899 to 1902. From 1914 to 1916 he commanded the 8th Battalion K.R.R.C. and was awarded the D.S.O.[1] for distinguished service in the field. In August, 1916, he was appointed to command the 20th Infantry Brigade and was wounded while commanding the brigade at the 3rd Battle of Ypres. His wound was slight and he remained at duty and continued to command his brigade until the end of the war. He was made a C.M.G. in 1918, a C.B. in 1919, and he retired from the Army in 1928. Brigadier-General Green died in April, 1935.

1 L.G. 3/6/16.

Grier, H. D.   **Brigadier-General**
C.R.A. 6th Indian Division   **Wounded: 24 December, 1915**
                                                                    P.O.W.: 29 April, 1916

Harry Dixon Grier was born in May, 1863, and was commissioned into the Royal Artillery in July, 1892. He saw much overseas service: in Burma from 1889 to 1891; with the Isazai Expedition of 1892; operations in Chitral in 1895, and as a Staff-Captain R.A. with the Malakand Force, and with the Tirah Expedition from 1897 to 1898. In the Great War he served in

Mesopotamia where he was wounded twice. One of his wounds was incurred when the Turks attacked the fort at Kut on 24 December, 1915, just as he had taken over as the C.R.A. of the division. [Lieutenant-Colonel Courtney who took over as acting C.R.A., was mortally wounded on the same day.] He was made a C.B. in 1916, whilst he was in captivity, and was awarded the D.S.O.[1] in 1918 for distinguished service in connection with military operations in Mesopotamia. Brigadier-General Grier retired from the Army in 1919 and died in October, 1942.

---

1 L.G. 23/8/18.

Griffin, C. J. C.M.G. D.S.O.* Brigadier-General
G.O.C. 7th Brigade 25th Division Wounded: 29 May, 1918

Christopher Joseph Griffin was born in December, 1874, and was commissioned into the Lancashire Fusiliers in September, 1895. He served in the South African War from 1899 to 1902, being severely wounded at Spion Kop in January, 1900. In the Great War he commanded the 2nd Battalion Lancashire Fusiliers until, in April, 1917, he was appointed to command the 103rd Infantry Brigade. He was awarded the D.S.O.[1] in 1915 and a Bar[2] to the order in July, 1917, 'for conspicuous gallantry and devotion to duty. He commanded his battalion with great ability and determination. When the left brigade was out of touch he was mainly responsible for communication being re-established at a critical moment when conditions were most trying. The successful issue was largely due to his splendid example.' In August, 1917, he took command of the 7th Infantry Brigade and on 29 May, 1918, he was wounded. The 7th Infantry Brigade diary[3] records the event: 'Rosnay [west of Rheims] 29th. 12 noon. Brigade H.Q. moved to sunken road about 1000 yards S. of Rosnay. 1.30 Capt. S. Hawkins (Staff-Captain) killed. Brigadier-General C. J. Griffin wounded' [by the same shell]. This was the fourth time that he had been wounded in the war. He held a command in Ireland from June, 1918, and he was made a C.M.G. Brigadier-General Griffin retired from the Army in 1923 and died in July, 1957.

---

1 L.G. 18/2/15. 2 L.G. 18/7/17. 3 PRO WO 95/2242.

Haggard, H. Brigadier-General
G.O.C. 32nd Brigade 11th Division Wounded: 7 August, 1915

Henry Haggard was born in July, 1864. He was commissioned into the East Yorkshire Regiment in March, 1883. In 1888 he was Garrison Adjutant in Trinidad, and from 1895 he spent four years as Adjutant of the 1st Battalion in India. He was Adjutant of Volunteers until 1902 when he went to serve in the South African War with the 3rd Battalion East Yorkshire Regiment. In the spring of 1914 he had returned home from India, where he had commanded the 2nd Battalion for four years, and with the outbreak of war in August, 1914, he was appointed Brigadier-General Commanding the 32nd Infantry Brigade. At Suvla, at 12 noon on 7 August, 1915, the brigade diary[1] records that he was 'wounded in the leg by a shell.' He recovered from his wounds and was given command of a training brigade in England. He retired from the Army in August, 1918, and died in September, 1933.

---

1 PRO WO 95/4299.

Haking, R. C. B. C.B.   Brigadier-General
G.O.C. 5th Brigade 2nd Division   Wounded: 16 September, 1914

Richard Cyril Byrne Haking was born in January, 1862. He entered the Army, as a Second-Lieutenant in the 62nd Foot, in January, 1881, and became a Lieutenant in the Royal Hampshire Regiment in July of that year. He served with the Burmese Expedition from 1885 to 1887, and was D.A.A.G., Cork District, from 1898 to 1899. He served in the South African War from 1899 to 1901, and then became a Professor at the Staff College until 1906. He was a G.S.O. with the 3rd and 4th Divisions, Southern Command, until 1908, when he became a Brigadier-General General Staff, Southern Command. He held command of the 5th Infantry Brigade, Aldershot Command, in September, 1911, and took the brigade to France in 1914 as part of the 2nd Division. The diary[1] of the 5th Brigade describes their situation on 16 September, 1914: 'Verneuil. Enemy located in strength on line just south of Tilleut de Courteçon [on the Chemin des Dames]. Heavy shelling commenced at daybreak and continued almost unceasingly until 11.15 am. Mostly howitzer. (General Haking slightly wounded and obliged to go to hospital.)' Three months later he returned to command the 1st Division and, in September, 1915, until the end of the war, to command XI Army Corps. After the war he was Chief of the British Armistice Commission until August, 1919, and in 1920 was G.O.C. Plebiscite Area, East Prussia. He retired from the Army in 1927 and died in June, 1945.

---

1 PRO WO 95/1343.

Hamilton, W. G. C.B. D.S.O.   Brigadier-General
G.O.C. 18th Brigade 6th Indian Division   Wounded: 19 February, 1916
P.O.W.: 29 April, 1916

William George Hamilton was born in January, 1860. He was commissioned into the 30th Foot in May, 1878, and was a Lieutenant in the

East Lancashire Regiment in June, 1880. In 1889 and 1890 he was a Staff Officer in Bengal, and in 1892 was a Brigade-Major with the Isazai Expedition. For his services with the Chitral Relief Force in 1895 he was awarded the D.S.O.[1] He held various Staff appointments in India until 1913, when he held Brigade Command in India until 1915, the year that he was made a C.B. He went to Mesopotamia as Brigadier-General Commanding the 18th Infantry Brigade of the 6th (Indian) Division. On 19 February, 1916, he 'was wounded when on the roof of his office in Kut by a stray bullet from a sniper during a raid by a Turkish aeroplane, but luckily the bullet only passed through the muscles of his back and he was able to return to duty in a few weeks'.[2] He became a prisoner of war in April, 1916, when the Kut garrison surrendered. Repatriated in November, 1918, and made a C.S.I., he retired from the Army in January, 1919, and died in August, 1940.

1 L.G. 21/1/96.   2 Sandes. *In Kut and Captivity*

Hare, S. W.

G.O.C. 86th Brigade   29th Division

Brigadier-General

Wounded: 25 April, 1915

Steuart Welwood Hare was born September, 1867. He was educated at Eton and the R.M.C., Sandhurst, and commissioned into the K.R.R.C. in 1886. He served in the Hazara Expedition and the Miranzai Expedition in 1891, the Isazai Expedition in 1892, and on operations in Chitral in 1895. In 1912 he was Brigade Commander of the Scottish Rifle Brigade. He commanded the 86th Infantry Brigade at the landing of the 29th Division on the Gallipoli Peninsula at 'W' beach. Brigadier-General Hare and his Brigade-Major [Major Frankland] were so anxious to be ashore at the first possible moment that they obtained the somewhat unwilling permission of the divisional commander to land with the first tows at 'W' Beach. They accordingly transferred to the *Implacable* during the afternoon of the 24th. 'To the north of the bay, as soon as the Turks on the cliff had been put to flight, Brigadier-General Hare and his Brigade-Major, with a small party of signallers, pushed on towards 'X' Beach, to establish touch with the Royal Fusiliers. But this was no task for the commander of the covering force. Before his little party had gone 200 yards it was fired on from Hill 114, and Brigadier-General Hare was severely wounded'.[1] Captain H. H. King [Signals Officer 86th Brigade] wrote in his diary[2]: 'Once ashore we got together under the cliff and I went off with the Staff-Captain and found Frankland, the Brigade-Major, who told us General Hare was wounded in the leg. We found him in a gully looking very bad, but had to leave him. He and the Brigade-Major had come ashore in the first tow from the *Implacable* and when the Lancashire Fusiliers had hesitated at

147

the barbed wire, General Hare had encouraged them under terrific fire.'
The Brigade-Major, Major T. H. Frankland of the Royal Dublin Fusiliers,
was killed. From 1916 to 1919 Major-General Hare commanded the 54th
Division in Egypt and Palestine. He was made a C.B. in 1917 and created
a K.C.M.G. in 1918. After the war he commanded the East Anglian
Division, Territorial Force from 1919 until he retired from the Army in
1923. Major-General Sir Steuart Hare died in October, 1952.

1 Aspinall-Oglander. *Military Operations Gallipoli.* 2 *Great War Magazine*

Hart, H. E. D.S.O.   Brigadier-General
G.O.C. 2nd N.Z. Brigade N. Z. Division   Gassed: 19 February, 1918

Herbert Ernest Hart was born at Wairarapa, New Zealand, in October,
1882. He was educated at Wellington, New Zealand, for the Law, entering
the profession in civil life as Barrister and Solicitor. He served in the South
African War with the New Zealand Forces from 1901 to 1902, and in
October, 1907, he joined the 17th (Ruahine) Regiment, New Zealand
Forces. He served at Gallipoli and was awarded the D.S.O.[1] in 1915, for
gallantry and devotion to duty in connection with the operations at the
Dardanelles. In March, 1917, he took command of the 4th New Zealand
Brigade until it was broken up in February, 1918, when he was appointed
to command the 2nd New Zealand Brigade. Two weeks after his appointment the brigade diary[2] records: 'The Butte. 18th February. On the night
of the 18/19 the whole of the 2nd N. Z. Inf. Brigade H.Q. stationed at the
Butte de Polygon were gassed together with the majority of the Battalion
stationed in the Butte (2nd Canterbury) with the result that the whole of
Brigade Headquarters were evacuated wounded.' He returned to command the 3rd New Zealand Division in July, 1918. Brigadier-General Hart
was made a C.M.G. in 1918, a C.B. in 1919, and retired from the Army in
1930. From 1931 to 1935 he was Administrator of Western Samoa, and
from 1936 to 1943 he was Chief Administrative Officer, Imperial War
Graves Commission, Eastern District. He was created a K.B.E. in 1935.
During the Second World War he served as Assistant Director at G.H.Q.
Middle East from 1940 to 1942. Brigadier-General Sir Herbert Hart died
in March, 1968.

1 L.G. 3/6/15. 2 PRO WO 95/3696.

Hart-Synnot, A. H. S. D.S.O.   Brigadier-General
G.O.C. 6th Brigade 2nd Division   Wounded: 11 May, 1918

Arthur Henry Seton Hart-Synnot was born in July 1870, and was educated
at Clifton College, King William's College and the R.M.C., Sandhurst. He
was commissioned into the East Surrey Regiment in October, 1890. He

was at the Relief of Chitral in 1895, when he was in command of the Maxim Gun Section, and from 1897 to 1898 he was with the Tirah Expedition as A.D.C. to the G.O.C. 1st Brigade. He served in the South African War from 1899 to 1902, first with the mounted infantry and afterwards as Brigade-Major with the Irish Brigade – he was wounded twice. For his services he was awarded the D.S.O.[1] He was British Military Attaché with the Japanese Army in Manchuria from 1904 to 1905, and a G.S.O.2 in South China from 1907 to 1911. At the outbreak of the Great War he was on the General Staff in India, but went to France in 1916 and served on the Staff of the 17th and 40th Divisions, and then commanded the 1/4th East Lancashire Regiment at the 3rd Battle of Ypres. He commanded the 6th and 25th Brigades before he was appointed to command the 86th Infantry Brigade on 28 April, 1918, and just two weeks later the brigade diary[2] records that when the brigade was in the trenches west of Boyelles, 'Brig-Genl. A. H. S. Hart-Synnot, D.S.O., wounded and Captain E. L. Wright, M.C., Bde. Major, killed.' Brigadier-General Hart-Synnot had both legs blown off. He was awarded a Bar[3] to his D.S.O. for his distinguished service, and in 1919 he was made a C.M.G. He died in November, 1942.

1 L.G. 19/4/1900.   2 PRO WO 95/1357.   3 L.G. 3/6/18.

Heneker, W. C. G. D.S.O.   **Brigadier-General**
G.O.C. 54th Brigade   18th Division   **Wounded: 10 December, 1915**

William Charles Giffard Heneker was born in August, 1867, and was educated at Bishop's College School, Lennoxville, Canada, and at the R.M.C., Kingston, Canada. He was commissioned into the Connaught Rangers in September, 1888, served in the Niger Coast Protectorate from 1897 to 1899, and with the West African Frontier Force until 1903. In 1902 he was 2nd i/c the Southern Nigeria Regiment, West African Frontier Force, when he commanded the Ulia and Ishan Expeditions, and he also commanded columns in the Ibeku – Olokro country in 1902 in operations against Chief Adukukaiku of Iggara. For his services he was awarded the D.S.O.[1] In 1912 he commanded the 2nd Battalion North Staffordshire Regiment at Peshawar in India, and the Rawalpindi Infantry Brigade in 1913 and 1914. At the outbreak of the Great War he commanded the 1st Infantry Brigade at Quetta. He was appointed to command the 54th Infantry Brigade in March, 1915, and in December of the same year he was wounded whilst his brigade was stationed on the Somme. The brigade diary[2] records the incident: 'Méaulte. 10th December. 3 pm. Brigadier wounded in left leg by long-range indirect machine-gun fire whilst walking down the hill south of Canterbury Avenue. Wound severe but apparently not serious, bullet entered leg but did not come out. He was taken to dressing station at Citadel thence to Corbie.' He recovered from his wound and returned to France to command the 190th Infantry Brigade of the Royal Naval Division in October, 1916. After the war he was created a K.C.B. in 1919 (C.B. 1918) and a K.C.M.G. in 1922. He commanded a division of the Rhine Army until 1922. His last command was that of G.O.C. Southern Command, India, until he retired from the Army in 1932. General Sir William Heneker died in May, 1939.

1 L.G. 12/9/02. 2 PRO WO 95/2041.

Heywood, C. P. C.M.G. D.S.O. Brigadier-General
G.O.C. 3rd Guards Brigade Guards Division Wounded: 5 November, 1918

Cecil Percival Heywood was born in May, 1880, and was educated at Eton and the R.M.C., Sandhurst. He was commissioned into the Coldstream Guards in August, 1899, and in the South African War, in which he served from 1900 to 1902, he was wounded. He was then employed with the Egyptian Army in the Sudan from 1907 to 1908, and as A.D.C. to the G.O.C. 3rd Division, Southern Command from 1910 to 1912. In the Great War he was a Brigade-Major and General Staff Officer until 1918 when he was appointed to command the 3rd Guards Brigade. He was awarded the D.S.O.[1] in 1916. He was wounded in the the last few days of the war as the brigade diary[2] records: 'Lebracmar. 23.50 Brigadier wounded by a shell which came through the house which Brigade H.Q. were sharing with gunners, killing 2 and wounding 6. Captains Penn [Brigade-Major] and Keith [Staff-Captain] were in the same room as the Brigadier but neither were wounded.' He was awarded the C.M.G. in 1918, and served as a G.S.O.1 at G.H.Q. North Russian Force in 1919. He commanded the Coldstream Guards from 1927 to 1930, and then became Director of Military Training, India, from 1930 to 1932. In 1932 he became Director of Staff Duties at the War Office until he died in October, 1936.

1 L.G. 3/6/16. 2 PRO WO 95/1222.

Hibbert, G. L. D.S.O. Brigadier-General
G.O.C. 154th Brigade 51st Division Wounded: 1 October, 1915

Godfrey Leicester Hibbert was born in January, 1864, and was educated at Cheltenham College. He was commissioned into the Northamptonshire Regiment in February, 1884, but shortly afterwards he transferred to the Royal Lancaster Regiment. He served in the South African War from 1900 to 1901 as Adjutant to the 4th Battalion of his Regiment and was awarded the D.S.O.[1] in recognition of his services during operations in South Africa. In the Great War he commanded the 154th Infantry Brigade in France, and the 77th Infantry Brigade in Salonika. It was whilst he was Brigadier-General of the 154th Infantry Brigade that he was wounded near Aveluy, on the Somme, on 1 October, 1915. In 1917 and 1918 he commanded a brigade at home until demobilization. He was made a C.B. in 1917, a C.M.G. in 1919, and died in March, 1924.

1 L.G. 27/9/01.

Hoare, R. D.S.O.
Brigadier-General
G.O.C. 229th Brigade 74th Division
Wounded: 9 September, 1918

Reginald Hoare was born in September, 1865. He was educated at Eton and was commissioned into the 4th Hussars in January, 1886, and served in the South African War from 1901 to 1902, commanding a mobile column in the latter year. He held various Staff appointments in India before his appointment to Brigade Command was made in 1912, when he commanded the 2nd South-Western Mounted Brigade. His appointment to Brigadier-General came at the outbreak of war when his brigade became the 229th Infantry Brigade. He was awarded the D.S.O.[1] in January, 1918. 'The Narrative of Operations', included in the brigade diary[2], reports: 'Brigadier-General R. Hoare, D.S.O., was wounded near his Headquarters in Longavesnes on the 9 September.' He retired from the Army and was made a C.M.G. in 1919, and died in October, 1947.

1 L.G. 1/1/18   2 PRO WO 95/3152.

Holmes, H. G. C.M.G.
Brigadier-General
G.O.C. 8th Brigade 3rd Division
Wounded: 30 April, 1917

Hardress Gilbert Holmes was born in July, 1862, and was commissioned into the Yorkshire Regiment in May, 1885. He served on the north-west frontier of India from 1897 to 1898 and was with the Tirah Expeditionary Force. In the South African War, in which he served from 1899 to 1902, he was in command of a mounted infantry battalion. He retired from the Yorkshire Regiment in February, 1908, but at the outbreak of war in 1914 he rejoined the Army and commanded the 9th Battalion Yorkshire Regiment until December, 1916, when he was appointed to command the 8th Infantry Brigade and was made a C.M.G. in the same year. The diary[1] of 8th Brigade records that, near Monchy, on 30 April, 1917, at 10.30 am. 'Brig-General H. G. Holmes, C.M.G., slightly wounded in the eye by a direct hit on H.Q. dug-out. Lt. Col. A. F. Lumsden assumed command.' [As Brigadier-General Lumsden (q.v.) he was killed in 1918.] Brigadier-General Holmes returned to command the 8th Infantry Brigade on 15

May, 1917. He was made a C.B.E. in 1919 when he retired from the Army and he died in September, 1922.

1 PRO WO 95/1417.

Hornby, M. L. C.M.G. D.S.O.
G.O.C. 116th Brigade 39th Division

Brigadier-General
Wounded: 23 March, 1918

Montague Leyland Hornby was born in July, 1870, and was educated at Shrewsbury and the R.M.C., Sandhurst. He was commissioned into the East Lancashire Regiment in January, 1889, and transferred to the Indian Staff Corps in March, 1892. He served in the Waziristan Expedition from 1894 to 1895, was severely wounded at the action at Wano, and was awarded the D.S.O.[1] for his services. From 1897 to 1898 he was with the Tirah Expedition and was then employed with the King's African Rifles in East Africa until 1904, serving with the Nandi Expedition of 1900. He took retired pay in April, 1909, but returned to the Army at the outbreak of hostilities. From 1914 to 1915 he was Brigade-Major of the 70th Infantry Brigade, and then commanded the 8th Battalion Yorks and Lancs. Regiment until April, 1916, when he was appointed to command the 116th Brigade. He was made a C.M.G. in 1917. When Brigadier-General Cape (q.v.) [Acting divisional commander] was killed on 18 March, 1918, Brigadier-General Hornby assumed command of the 39th Division. The diary[2] of the 39th Division describes the events of 23 March, 1918: 'At 8 am. Major-General Feetham (q.v.) returned from leave and took over command of the division from Brigadier-General Hornby who resumed command of the 116th Infantry Brigade. At 1 pm. orders were issued to Inf. Bdes. to prepare to withdraw to the La Maisonnette – Beaches line. The 118th Infantry Brigade moved back ---- the 116th Infantry Brigade followed shortly afterwards. The river was crossed at Halle and Clery and the retirement successfully effected, though the crossing of the river was constantly harassed by machine-gun fire from hostile aeroplanes and constant shell fire. During these operations Brigadier-General M. L. Hornby, C.M.G. D.S.O., Cmd. 116th Brigade, was severely wounded.' He returned to command his brigade in October, 1918, until November, 1918, when he took command of the 137th Infantry Brigade. Brigadier-General Hornby was made a C.B. in 1922 and retired from the Army, for the second time, in 1927. He died in November, 1948.

1 L.G. 27/8/95. 2 PRO WO 95/2567.

Hubback, A. B. C.M.G.   **Brigadier-General**
G.O.C. 2nd Brigade 1st Division   **Wounded: 1 July, 1917**

Arthur Benison Hubback was born in Liverpool in April, 1871. He was educated at Fettes College, Edinburgh, and articled to T. Shelmerdine, City Architect of Liverpool. He worked in the Public Works Department of the Federated Malay States, and in 1902 he joined the Malay States Volunteer Rifles. He was in command of the contingent representing the Federated Malay States at the Coronation of King George V. In 1914 he was a Major in the 19th Battalion London Regiment (T.F.) and in 1915 he commanded the 20th London Regiment (T.F.). He was made a C.M.G. and appointed Brigadier-General Commanding the 2nd Brigade in March, 1916. On 1 July, 1917, he was wounded, as the brigade diary[1] records: 'Coxy de Bains. 1 July. Brigadier-General A. B. Hubback and Brigade-Major, Captain E. E. Calthrop, M.C., Royal Engineers, both wounded slightly visiting the line.' Brigadier-General Hubback returned to command the 118th Infantry Brigade and then 63rd Infantry Brigade in 1918. After the war he was awarded the D.S.O. for distinguished service in connection with military operations in France and Flanders. He commanded the 5th London Infantry Brigade from 1920 to 1924, and died in May, 1948.

_____

1 PRO WO 95/1268.

Hulke, W. B. D.S.O.   **Brigadier-General**
G.O.C. 115th Brigade 38th Division   **Wounded: 30 August, 1918**

Walter Backhouse Hulke was born in September, 1872. He was first commissioned in November, 1892, and he retired from the Lincolnshire Regiment in February, 1911. He was recalled in 1914 to command a battalion of the Yorkshire Regiment, and in 1917 he was awarded the D.S.O.[1] for distinguished services in the field. In 1918 he was appointed to command the 115th Infantry Brigade, and on 30 August the A. & Q.M.G. diary[2] of the 38th Division records that he 'was wounded whilst reconnoitring for an attack on Morval.' The brigade diary[3] gives the map location of his H.Q. (Sheet 57c SW. S.12.b.55.60.) [N.E. of Delville Wood] and records that he 'was wounded and evacuated.' He died in January, 1923.

_____

1 L.G. 1/1/17.   2 PRO WO 95/2541.   3 PRO WO 95/2560.

Jacob, C. W. C.B.   **Major-General**
G.O.C. 21st Division   **Wounded: 4 March, 1916**

Claud William Jacob was born in November, 1863, and was educated at Sherborne School and the R.M.C., Sandhurst. He was commissioned into the Worcestershire Regiment in 1882 and transferred to the Indian Staff Corps in December, 1884. He served in the Zhob Valley Expedition in 1890, and in Waziristan from 1901 to 1902. He was a General Staff Officer in India in 1912. In 1915 he commanded the Dehra Dun Brigade and later, in the same year, commanded the Meerut Division, and the 21st Division and was made a C.B. The A. & Q.M.G. diary[1] of the 21st Division records the events of 4 March, 1916: 'Armentières. The enemy bombardment of the town commencing at 5 pm. with shells of all calibres up to 5.9'. The billet of the L-G.O.C. was hit and the G.S.O.1, Lieut.-Colonel Daniell, killed and his G.O.C. wounded.' Major-General Jacob returned to his division in April, 1916, and in the same year took command of the 2nd Army Corps, a command which he held until 1919. He was created a K.C.B. in 1917 and a K.C.M.G. in 1919. He was created a K.C.S.I. in 1924, a G.C.B. in 1926 and a G.C.S.I. in 1930. He was appointed Chief of the General Staff, India, in 1925, and in 1926 was promoted to Field Marshal. He was Constable of the Tower of London from 1933 to 1943 and died in June, 1948.

---

1 PRO WO 95/2135.

Jeffreys, G. D.   Brigadier-General
G.O.C. 58th Brigade   19th Division   Wounded: 14 April, 1916

George Darell Jeffreys was born in March, 1878, and was educated at Eton and the R.M.C., Sandhurst. He was commissioned into the Grenadier Guards in March, 1897, and saw service with the Nile Expedition, being present at the Battle of Khartoum in 1898. He served with the Grenadier Guards in the South African War from 1900 to 1902. From 1911 to 1914 he was Commandant of the Guards Depot. In 1914 he went to France and in June, 1915, was Lieut.-Colonel commanding a battalion of his Regiment. As a Brigadier-General he took command of the 58th Infantry Brigade in January, 1916, and in April of that year the brigade diary[1] records: 'Cense du Raux. 14/4/16. Brigadier-General G. D. Jeffreys was wounded by shrapnel on Rue du Bois while returning from the trenches with G.O.C. 19th Division [Major-General Bridges (q.v.)]. General Jeffries (sic) was removed to the No. 2 Casualty Clearing Station at Merville.' He was back with his brigade eight days later and assumed command once more. He took command of the 57th Infantry Brigade in July, 1916, before commanding the 1st Guards Brigade from December, 1916. In 1916 he was made a C.M.G. He commanded the 19th Division from 20 September, 1917, after Major-General Bridges was wounded, until February, 1919. In 1918 he was made a C.B. After the war he commanded the Light Division in the British Army on the Rhine and then became G.O.C. London District in February, 1920. He was created a K.C.V.O. in 1924 and a

K.C.B. in 1932. From 1941 to 1951 he was M. P. for the Petersfield Division of Hampshire. His only son was killed in action in 1940. In 1952 he was created the first Baron of Burkham and he died in December, 1960.

1 PRO WO 95/2087.

Johnston, A. C. D.S.O. M.C.
Brigadier-General
G.O.C. 126th Brigade 42nd Division
Wounded: 16 September, 1917

Alexander Colin Johnston was born in January, 1884, and was educated at Winchester College and the R.M.C., Sandhurst. He was commissioned into the Worcestershire Regiment in November, 1903. From April, 1907, until October, 1910, he was employed with the West African Frontier Force. He played cricket for Hampshire during the years from 1902 to 1914. In the Great War he was a G.S.O.3 with the 25th Division, then a Brigade-Major with the 7th Infantry Brigade in 1916, before commanding the 10th Battalion Cheshire Regiment from August, 1916, to September, 1917. He was awarded the M.C. and the D.S.O.[1] On 14 September, 1917, he was appointed to command the 126th Infantry Brigade and two days later he was shot by a sniper. The brigade diary[2] records the event: 'Railway Wood. 16/9/17. Brigadier-General A. C. Johnston, D.S.O. M.C., was wounded at 5 am. at Sans Souci Farm by a German sniper and was evacuated. Capt. B. Sanderson, Brigade-Major, was slightly wounded and remained at duty.' He was awarded a Bar[3] to his D.S.O. for distinguished service in the field. Johnston was wounded four times during the war. After the war he became Commandant of the Duke of York's Royal Military School, Dover, and Chief Education Officer of the R.M.C.

1 L.G. 4/6/17. 2 PRO WO 95/2656. 3 L.G. 1/1/18.

Kelly, G. C.
Brigadier-General
G.O.C. 2nd Brigade 1st Division
Wounded: 26 September, 1918

George Charles Kelly was born in October, 1880, and was educated at Wellington College and the R.M.C., Sandhurst. He was commissioned into the K.R.R.C. in November, 1899, served in the South African War from 1899 to 1902, and was severely wounded in operations on Tugela Heights. In 1903 and 1904 he served in East Africa, in Somaliland, and saw action at Jidballi. From 1914 he was Staff-Captain and then Brigade-Major with the 6th Infantry Brigade until August, 1915, and in 1918 he was Lieutenant-Colonel Commanding the 2nd Battalion K.R.R.C. In March, 1918, he was appointed to command the 2nd Infantry Brigade. In September he was wounded in operations, the object of which was 'to deny enemy observation from the high ground south-east of Pontruet [Sht.62bS.W.1. M.9]

155

from which he could have seen and interfered with preparations for the big attack in contemplation against the Hindenburg Line from Bellenglise northwards.'[1] At 3.30 pm. on the 26th Brigadier-General Kelly was evacuated wounded. He was awarded the D.S.O.[2] for conspicuous gallantry and devotion to duty. 'When his brigade met with unexpected resistance he promptly made a personal reconnaissance, and, by handling his brigade in a masterly way under very heavy fire gained his objective and repulsed several counter attacks. His powers of command and brilliant example were admirable.' This was the second occasion on which he was wounded in the war, but he returned to his brigade ten days after the armistice. In 1934 he became Major-General Commanding the 15th Infantry Brigade and in 1936 he was made a C.B. He died in April, 1938.

1 PRO WO 95/1268.   2 L.G. 11/1/19.

Kemball, G. V. C.B. D.S.O.
Major-General
G.O.C. 28th Indian Brigade 7th Indian Division
Wounded: 6 April, 1916

George Vero Kemball was born in October, 1859, and was educated at Harrow. He was commissioned into the Royal Artillery in December, 1878, and served in many campaigns including: the Afghan War in 1878 and 1879; operations in Chitral in 1895; the north-west frontier of India in 1897 and 1898, including the Tochi Expedition; and West Africa, Northern Nigeria, from 1900 to 1903, including the Kaduna Expedition and the Kano Sokoto Expedition. In the latter expedition he was in command and for his services he was awarded the D.S.O.[1] and was made a C.B. in 1903. From 1909 to 1913 he was a Director at the War Office. In 1914 he held Brigade Command in India and in 1915 became Major-General Commanding the 28th Indian Brigade which served in Mesopotamia as part of the 7th Indian Division. The brigade diary[2] includes an account of operations of the 28th Brigade from 4–11 April, 1916, in the attack on Sannaiyat, on the river Tigris: 'April 15th. No move was made by the brigade till 2.30 pm. when it advanced in rear of 13th Division which had assaulted and captured the Hannah position at dawn. April 16th. [During the advance] at 5.45 am. a withering burst of rifle and machine-gun fire was opened on the advancing lines – it soon became evident from the number of casualties, that it was quite impossible to cross the open plain. --- General Kemball accordingly ordered the rearmost lines, which had already come under rifle and shell fire, to halt and dig themselves in. At this point General Kemball and three officers with him were wounded. --- Late in the afternoon General Kemball, who till then had remained in command of the Brigade, was transferred to the Field Ambulance.' He was created K.C.M.G. in 1916 and returned to India where he commanded a division from 1917 to 1919. Major-General Sir George Kemball died in January, 1941.

1 L.G. 25/4/02.   2 PRO WO 95/5140.

Kemp, G. C. C.B. **Brigadier-General**
G.O.C. 2nd Brigade 1st Division **Wounded: 2 March, 1918**

Geoffrey Chicheley Kemp was born in March, 1868, and was commissioned into the Royal Engineers in July, 1886. He served with the Chitral Relief Force in 1895 and was present at the storming of the Malakand Pass. At the outbreak of the Great War he was a Lieutenant-Colonel until, in August, 1915, he was appointed Brigadier-General Commanding the 138th Brigade, a post which he held until he became sick in June, 1917. In 1916 he was made a C.B. He returned to command the 2nd Brigade in July, 1917, and remained in this command until 2 March, 1918, when his brigade's diary[1] recorded: 'During a reconnaissance of the Army Battle Zone, Brigadier-General G. C. Kemp, C.B., Captain Gordon-Cumming M.C., [Brigade-Major], and of the King's Royal Rifles, Major Sir J. V. E. Lees, Bart., Captain C. H. Hordan and Lieutenant G. E. McCabe were all wounded by the same shell on the St. Julien – Wietje road.' Command of the brigade passed to Brigadier-General Sir William Kay (q.v.), who was wounded 12 days later, and then to the acting command of Lieutenant-Colonel Bellamy who only lasted 3 days before he was wounded. Brigadier-General Kemp was made a C.M.G. in 1918, the year that he retired from the Army. He died in August, 1943.

1 PRO WO 95/1268.

Kennedy, Alfred Alexander. C.M.G. **Brigadier-General**
G.O.C. 230th Brigade 74th Division **Wounded: 23 September, 1918**

Alfred Alexander Kennedy was born in December, 1870, and was educated at Harrow and the R.M.C., Sandhurst. He was commissioned into the 3rd Hussars in October, 1891. He was Brigade-Major to the 2nd Cavalry Brigade, Eastern Command, in 1911, and G.S.O.1 the 2nd Cavalry Division in 1915, the year in which he was made a C.M.G. Command of the 7th Cavalry Brigade followed in May, 1915, and in November, 1916, he commanded the 1st Indian Cavalry Division. He was then appointed to command infantry brigades, the 75th, in May, 1918, and the 230th in July, 1918. It was whilst he commanded the 230th Brigade that he was wounded. The brigade diary[1] records: 'Templieux Quarries. 23 Sept.[1918]. While at mess shell struck mess hut wounded BG-C, Staff-Capt., Bde. Intl. Off., Bde. Signal Off. B.M. wounded very slightly, remaining at duty, all remainder evacuated.' After the war he commanded a brigade in the Army on the Rhine, and was Military Governor of Cologne until January, 1920. He was made a C.B. in 1921. Major-General Kennedy died in March, 1926.

1 PRO WO 95/3153.

Kenyon, E. R. C.B.   **Major-General**
C.E. 3rd Army   **Wounded: 2 May, 1917**

Edward Ranulph Kenyon was born in November, 1854, and was educated at Winchester and the R.M.A., Woolwich. He entered the Army, as a Lieutenant in the Royal Engineers, in February, 1874. He was employed in Cyprus from 1880 to 1886, and employed under the Admiralty from 1896 to 1901. In 1906 he was Chief Engineer at Gibraltar until he retired with the rank of Colonel in 1911. He was re-employed in 1914 as Deputy Chief Engineer, Southern Command, and then as C.R.E. of the 20th Division. In February, 1916, he was appointed Chief Engineer of IV Corps, and in July of the same year became Chief Engineer of the 3rd Army, and was made a C.B. On 2 May, 1917, he was wounded at Arras by a shell splinter in the arm and was sent to Hospital No. 24 at Etaples before being sent to England, but he returned in June and resumed his post, which he held until December. From January to July, 1918, he was Deputy Controller Chemical Warfare. He was made a C.M.G. in 1918 and retired from the Army. Major-General Kenyon died in May, 1937.

Knatchbull, G. W. C.   **Brigadier-General**
G.O.C. 38th Brigade 13th Division   **Wounded: 17 November, 1915**

George Wyndham Chichester Knatchbull was born at Morah, Gwalior, India, in March, 1862. He was educated at the R.M.C. Sandhurst, and was commissioned into the Welsh Regiment in March, 1883, and transferred to the Indian Staff Corps in July, 1885. He served in the Burmese Expedition from 1885 to 1887, and in China from 1900 to 1902. At the outbreak of the Great War he commanded the 6th Battalion Royal Lancashire Regiment, which he commanded at Gallipoli until August, 1915. When Brigadier-General Baldwin (q.v.) was missing on 11 August, Lieut. Colonel Knatchbull was appointed to temporary command of the 38th Infantry Brigade, and this command was confirmed a few days later with his promotion to Brigadier-General. He held the command for just three months before he was wounded. The brigade diary[1] records: 'Chocolate Hill. 17/11/15. 9.45 am. Brigadier-General G. W. Knatchbull was wounded by shrapnel bursting over Chocolate Hill.' He was hit by two

shrapnel bullets – one through the chest and the other through the foot.[2]
Brigadier-General Knatchbull retired from the Army in October, 1918,
and died in June, 1943.

1 PRO WO 95/4302.   2 PRO CAB 45/247.

Leckie, R. G. E.

Brigadier-General

G.O.C. 3rd Canadian Brigade   1st Canadian Division

Wounded: 18 February, 1916

R. G. E. Leckie was a Canadian officer who was born in 1869 and
graduated from the R.M.C., Kingston, Ontario and passed the Militia Staff
course. From 1890 to 1900 he served in both the infantry and cavalry
branches of the active Militia, and afterwards transferred to the Reserve
of Officers. In 1902 he saw active service as a Captain with a Canadian
unit in the South African War. He rejoined the active Militia in 1910 to
organize the 72nd Regiment (Seaforth Highlanders of Canada) which he
was still commanding at the outbreak of the Great War. He commanded
the 16th Canadian (Scottish) Battalion in 1915 and fought in many of the
early battles of the war. In August, 1915, he was appointed Brigadier-
General Commanding the 3rd Canadian Infantry Brigade and commanded
it until he was wounded in February, 1916. At this time the H.Q. of the
3rd Canadian Infantry Brigade was at La Petite Monque (Sheet 27.
X.17.c.3.4) and the brigade diary[1] records: 'Brg-Gen. Leckie who was
down in the 8th Bde. area inspecting sites for defended localities at
Stinking and Gabion Farms, was reported to be wounded through both
legs with a G.S. wound. The bullet penetrated the upper part of his right
thigh, cutting a secondary artery. A flesh wound was also made in his left
thigh. The only danger was due to loss of blood incurred through the
General having no field dressing with which to bind the wound.'

1 PRO WO 95/3772.

Leveson Gower, P.   D.S.O.

Brigadier-General

G.O.C. 49th Brigade   16th Division

Gassed: 15 August, 1917

Phillip Leveson Gower was born in February, 1871, and commissioned
into the Derbyshire Regiment in September, 1891. He served on operations on the north-west frontier of India in 1897 and 1898, and was with
the Tirah Expeditionary Force. He served in the South African War from
1899 to 1901, and in the Great War he commanded the 2nd Notts. and
Derby Regiment until he was appointed to command the 49th Infantry
Brigade in February, 1916. On the day before his brigade was to attack the
Frezenberg Ridge he was gassed. The brigade diary[1] records the event:
'Millcott. [½ mile N.E. of Potijze]. 15/8/17. Bde. Hdqrs. Staff and Signal

Section relieved the 47th Bde. Hdqrs. in the line. The dugout at Millcott was apparently full of gas as the Brigadier and Staff-Capt. had to be evacuated to hospital suffering from gas poisoning. 23/8/17. The brigadier returned from hospital and assumed command.' This was the second time that he had been wounded in the war. He was awarded the D.S.O.[2] in 1917 and was made a C.M.G. in 1918. He took retired pay in November, 1919, and died in June, 1939.

---

1 PRO WO 95/1976.   2 L.G. 1/1/17.

Lewis, F. G.   C.B.   C.M.G.   T.D.   Brigadier-General
G.O.C. 166th Brigade   55th Division   Wounded: 1 December, 1917

Frederick Gustav Lewis was born in 1873. He was educated at Haileybury College and Trinity Hall, Cambridge, where he obtained his B.A. In civilian life he was a partner in a firm of solicitors, and he was also a Territorial Army officer. He commanded the 13th (Princess Louise's) Kensington Battalion London Regiment until August, 1915, when he took command of the 142nd Infantry Brigade until December, 1916. He was made a C.M.G. in 1916 and a C.B. in 1917. In April, 1917, he was appointed to command the 166th Infantry Brigade and held the command until he was wounded on 1 December, 1917. The brigade diary[1] records: 'Epehy. Dec.1, 1917. Hostile artillery very active throughout the day. Brigade H.Q. heavily shelled. General Lewis wounded at 3.30 pm.' He became Deputy Director Demobilisation at the War Office and afterwards commanded the 46th London Infantry Brigade, Territorial Force. Brigadier-General Lewis died in July, 1967.

---

1 PRO WO 95/2928

Lloyd, F. C.   Brigadier-General
G.O.C. 158th Brigade   53rd Division   Wounded: 17 August, 1915

Frederick Charles Lloyd was born in October, 1860, and was educated at Haileybury. He was commissioned into the 10th Foot in January, 1880, and became a Lieutenant in the Lincolnshire Regiment in July, 1881. He served in the South African War from 1900 to 1902, during which time he commanded the 7th Mounted Infantry. From 1908 to 1912 he commanded the 2nd Battalion Lincolnshire Regiment, and held brigade command from July, 1912. At the outbreak of war in 1914 he was appointed Brigadier-General Commanding the 158th Infantry Brigade. In Gallipoli, where he served from July, 915, he was wounded on 17 August, 1915, and his Brigade-Major was slightly wounded at the same time.[1] Brigadier-General

Lloyd was made a C.B. and retired from the Army in April, 1918, and died in June, 1957.

---

1 PRO WO 95/4323.

Longbourne, F. C. D.S.O.

G.O.C. 171st Brigade 57th Division

Brigadier-General

Wounded: 5 October, 1918

Francis Cecil Longbourne was born in June, 1883, and was commissioned from the Militia into the Royal West Surrey Regiment in April, 1902. He served in the South African War, and with the Mounted Infantry of the West African Frontier Force from 1911 to July, 1914. As a Captain in the Queen's Regiment he was severely wounded in October, 1914, and was awarded the D.S.O.[1] in 1915 for his services in the field. He was Brigade Machine-Gun Officer, 22nd Infantry Brigade, from October, 1915, to February, 1916, and then commanded the 2nd Battalion Royal West Surrey Regiment until September, 1917. His appointment to command the 171st Brigade came in September, 1917, he held this command until he was wounded in October, 1918. The A. & Q.M.G. diary[2] of the 57th Division records his wounding: 'Near Cambrai [171 Brigade H.Q. was at Proville]. 5 October, 1918. Brigadier-General Longbourne, D.S.O., and Lt.-Col. H. La Trobe Cambell, wounded.' They were wounded by a Minenwerfer; General Longbourne was badly wounded in the neck. [Lt.-Col. Cambell died of his wounds.] He was made a C.M.G. in 1919. In 1928 he took the name of More-Molyneux [his wife's father was Admiral Sir Robert More-Molyneux], but in 1943 added his own surname of Long-bourne. He died in November, 1963.

---

1 L.G. 18/2/15.   2 PRO WO 95/2967.

Lushington, S. C.B. C.M.G.

C.R.A. 41st Division

Brigadier-General

Wounded: 27 September, 1917

Stephen Lushington was born in January, 1864. He was commissioned into the Royal Artillery in February, 1884, was Adjutant of Militia from 1895 to 1900, and was Inspector-General of Police and Commandant of Militia in British Guiana from 1902 to 1907. He was made a C.M.G. in 1907. His appointment as C.R.A. of the 37th Division was made in April, 1915, and he was wounded whilst commanding the artillery of the 41st Division on 27 September, 1917, when his H.Q. was at Berthen.[1] He returned to command the artillery of the 68th Division in May, 1918. Brigadier-General Lushington retired from the Army in 1919 and died in December, 1940.

---

1 PRO WO 95/2621.

MacBrien, J. H.   C.M.G.   D.S.O.   Brigadier-General
G.O.C. 12th Canadian Brigade   4th Canadian Division   Wounded: 28 September, 1918

James Howden MacBrien was born in Myrtle, Ontario, Canada, in June, 1878, and was educated at the High School, Port Perry, Ontario. He served in the South African War with the South African Constabulary, and also served with the Royal Canadian Dragoons. In 1914 he was a G.S.O.3 at the War Office prior to joining the Canadian Contingent on its arrival in England. He became A.Q.M.G. of the Canadian Corps from September, 1915, until January, 1916, when he became A.A. & Q.M.G. of the 3rd Canadian Division. He was awarded the D.S.O.[1] for his services in the field. In September, 1916, he was appointed to command the 12th Canadian Infantry Brigade, and the brigade's diary[2] contains a 'Report. Bourlon Wood Operations 27 Sept.- 1 Oct., 1918.' The brigade's H.Q. was at the Ferme-des-Lilas. Part of the report reads: 'The 10th Cnd. Inf. Bde. was checked before reaching the Cambrai – Douai Road; their forward troops were disposed in the Marcoing line, X24a and X17b. About 3 pm. on the 28th September the enemy was seen massing for a counter-attack against the 10th Cnd. Inf. Bde. Brig-Gen. J. H. MacBrien, C.M.G. D.S.O., Cmd. 12th Inf. Bde. was shot through the right leg while making a reconnaissance of the situation. He returned to Bde. H.Q. but did not go out until Lt.Col. J. Kirkcalldy, D.S.O., (78th Btn.) had arrived and taken over command.' This was the second time that he had been wounded in the war. He was awarded a Bar[3] to his D.S.O. 'For conspicuous gallantry and fine leadership in an attack. He successfully captured the whole of his first objective, and under heavy machine-gun fire reconnoitred his line and directed further operations, thereby assisting very materially the advance of the flanking units.' He was made a C.M.G. in 1918. In 1919 he was promoted to Major-General, made a C.B. and became Chief of the General Staff Overseas Military Forces of Canada. He was Chief of the General Staff, Canadian Militia in 1920, and Chief of Staff of the Canadian Defence Force in 1923, and Commissioner of the Royal Canadian Mounted Police in 1931. In 1935 he was created a K.C.B. Major-General Sir James Howden MacBrien died in March, 1938.

---

1 L.G. 23/6/15.   2 PRO WO 95/3907.   3 L.G. 2/12/18.

M'Cay, J. W.   Brigadier-General
G.O.C. 2nd Australian Brigade   1st Australian Division   Wounded: 9 May, 1915

James Whiteside M'Cay was born at Ballynure, Ireland, in December, 1864, and was educated at the Scotch College, Melbourne, and at Melbourne University. M'Cay was a lawyer, but since his early days he had been a keen militiaman, and in 1886 he was a Lieutenant in the Victoria

Volunteer Forces. He was a Member of the Federal Parliament and held many ministerial posts including that of Minister of State for Defence from 1904 to 1905. At the outbreak of war, in 1914, he was made a censor, but he gave up that post to command his brigade. Brigadier-General M'Cay [He was a Colonel at the time that he was wounded, but shortly afterwards the Australian Government promoted Brigade Commanders to temporary Brigadier-Generals.] commanded the 2nd Australian Infantry Brigade at Gallipoli and in the 'Struggle for Krithia' on 8 and 9 May, 1915, 'all members of the Brigade Staff whom M'Cay had taken with him in the advance were hit, and at 2 am. his own leg was broken by a bullet'.[1] His Brigade-Major, Major Cass, was seriously wounded. The General's wound healed and he returned to the brigade on 8 June. He was chosen for command of the 2nd Australian Division, but 'on July 11th, the day before he was to leave Anzac, M'Cay was descending a steep and dangerous corner of the communication trench in rear of Scott's Point when his leg, previously wounded at Helles, snapped at the point where the bullet had injured the bone'.[1] In 1915 he was made a C.B. He subsequently commanded the 5th Australian Division in Egypt and France, and became G.O.C. Australian Imperial Forces U.K. He was created a K.C.M.G. in 1918 and a K.B.E in 1919. Lieutenant-General Hon. Sir James Whiteside M'Cay died in October, 1930.

---

1 *Official History of Australia in the War of 1914 – 1918*, Vol. 2.

MacDonell, A. C. C.M.G. D.S.O.   Brigadier-General
G.O.C. 7th Canadian Brigade   3rd Canadian Division   Wounded: 17 February, 1916

Archibald Cameron MacDonell was born at Windsor, Ontario, Canada, in October, 1864, and was educated at Trinity College School, Port Hope, Canada, and the R.M.C., Kingston, Canada. He was commissioned into the Royal Artillery, but resigned without actually joining (for family reasons). In June, 1886, he became a Lieutenant in the Canadian Militia, and two years later he joined the Canadian Army. In 1889 he exchanged into the Royal North-West Mounted Police. He volunteered to join the 2nd Battalion Canadian Mounted Rifles for service in the South African War and at Diamond Hill on 12 June, 1900, he was dangerously wounded and invalided home to Canada. For his services he was awarded the D.S.O.[1] He returned to South Africa in 1902 in command of the 5th Regiment of Canadian Mounted Rifles, but the war had just been concluded. He served with the Royal North-West Mounted Police until 1907 when he was appointed Major and 2nd in command of the Canadian Mounted Rifles, (Lord Strathcona's Horse). He commanded his regiment from 1912 until December, 1915, and took part in many of the early battles of the Great War. He was appointed Brigadier-General Commanding the

7th Canadian Infantry Brigade when it was formed in France in December, 1915, and was made a C.M.G. in January, 1916. On 17 February, 1916, he was wounded when, as the brigade diary[2] records: 'Kemmel Trenches. Brigadier-General A. C. MacDonell was wounded while out in front of the trenches in the vicinity of the Bull Ring.' 'He had his left arm broken by a bullet near the shoulder and had another through the top of the shoulder, when caught in the open by a sniper'.[3] Three months later, in May, 1916, he returned to command his brigade. In June, 1917, he was made a C.B. and was promoted to Major-General Commanding the 1st Canadian Division, which he commanded until May, 1919. One of his sons, in the Royal Flying Corps, was killed in action on the Somme on 2 July, 1916. After the war he was created a K.C.B., in January, 1919, and became Commandant of the R.M.C., Kingston, Ontario. Lieutenant-General Sir Archibald Cameron MacDonell died in December, 1941.

1 L.G. 19/4/01. 2 PRO WO 95/3864. 3 Creagh & Humphries. *The V.C. and D.S.O.*

Mackenzie, C. J. C.B.
G.O.C. 61st Division

Major-General
Wounded: 27 April, 1918

Colin John Mackenzie was born in November, 1861, and was educated at the Edinburgh Academy and the R.M.C., Sandhurst. He was commissioned into the 16th Foot in January, 1881, in May he transferred to the 78th Foot, and in July, 1881, he was a Lieutenant in the Seaforth Highlanders. He saw much foreign service with the Egyptian Expedition of 1882, when he was present at the Battle of Tel-el-Kebir, with the Burmese Expedition of 1887 and the Hazara Expedition of 1888. In 1891 and 1892 he was with the Hunza-Nagar Expedition, and in 1894 and 1895 was in the Waziristan Expedition. He was at the Battle of Khartoum in the Nile Expedition of 1898, and from 1899 to 1902 he served in the South African War and for his services he was made a C.B. Between the wars he was a Staff officer with the 5th Division from 1902 to 1905, and then a Brigadier-General with the 4th and 6th Brigades, Aldershot Command until October, 1910, when he was promoted to Major-General. When the Great War started he was Divisional Commander of the 3rd Division until March, 1915, when he was transferred to Staff Duties at the War Office, but in May, 1916, he returned to France to command the 61st Division. It was whilst serving with this division that he was wounded on 27 April, 1918. The divisional headquarters was at Molinghem [between Liliers and Aire] when the divisional diary[1] recorded: 'The G.O.C. was wounded by enemy snipers (flesh wound in face) whilst visiting the line of the 183rd Bde. south of St. Floris. 20th May: The G.O.C. was taken to the C.C.S. near Moulin de Comte for a few days, owing to his wound, received on the 27th April, not progressing favourably. 31 May: Major-General Colin

Mackenzie was evacuated sick this afternoon to England as a result of his wound.' Colonel C. H. Howkins (who had been A.M.S. of the 61st Division), writing[2] in December, 1933, said: 'Major-General Colin Mackenzie was shot through the cheek and parotid gland [in front of the ear] soon after we arrived; an injury which did not respond to treatment.' He was made a K.C.B. in 1918 and retired from the Army in 1920. Major-General Sir Colin John Mackenzie died in July, 1956.

1 PRO WO 95/3035.   2 PRO CAB 45/123.

Malcolm, N. D.S.O.   **Major-General**
G.O.C. 66th Division   **Wounded: 29 March, 1918**

Neill Malcolm was born in October, 1869, and was educated at St. Peter's School, York, Eton and the R.M.C., Sandhurst. He was commissioned into the Argyll and Sutherland Highlanders in 1889. He saw service on the north-west frontier of India and in Uganda in 1897 and 1898, and for his services in Uganda he was awarded the D.S.O.[1] He served in the South African War from 1899 to 1900, where he was severely wounded at Paardeburg. From 1912 to 1914 he was a G.S.O.2 at the Staff College, but when war broke out he went to France as a Staff officer with the 1st Army and in November, 1914, he became a G.S.O.1 with the 1st Corps, then served as a G.S.O.1 with the 11th Division in Gallipoli and with the Salonika Army. He was promoted to Brigadier-General and then to Major-General with the General Staff of Reserve Corps and Divisions until, in December, 1917, he took command of the 66th Division in France. On 29 March, 1918, the 'Narrative of Operations' in the divisional diary[2] records: 'At 1.15 pm. General Malcolm was wounded by shrapnel in Domart and General Hunter assumed command of the Division.' He returned in September, 1918, to command the 39th Division until the end of the war. After the war he commanded the 30th Division and then, in April, 1919, he became Chief of the British Military Mission to Berlin. In 1919 he was made a C.B. and in 1924 he was created a K.C.B. He retired from the Army in 1924 and served on the High Commission for German refugees from the Nazi Regime from 1936 to 1938. He was a F.R.G.S. Major-General Sir Neill Malcolm died in December, 1953.

1 L.G. 24/1/99.   2 PRO WO 95/3121.

Marshall, W. R.   **Brigadier-General**
G.O.C. 87th Brigade   29th Division   **Wounded: 25 April, 1915**

William Raine Marshall was born in October, 1865, and was educated at Repton and the R.M.C., Sandhurst He was commissioned into the Derbyshire Regiment in January, 1886. From 1887 to 1888 he was in various actions on the north-west frontier of India including Malakand, Landakai and Mohmand, and was with the Tirah Expedition. In the South African War, in which he served from 1899 to 1902, he was twice wounded. In 1914 he commanded the 1st Battalion Sherwood Foresters in France, and in January, 1915, he was appointed Brigadier-General Commanding the 87th Infantry Brigade. He took the brigade to Gallipoli and at the 'X' Beach landings on 25 April, 1915, 'Brigadier-General Marshall received a slight flesh wound in the leg at about 10 am., but continued in command.' He was shot in the leg above the knee[1] . [The Brigade-Major, Major Lucas, who recorded this event in the brigade diary[2], the pages of which have been torn and repaired, expressed his 'regret [that] these pages have been damaged by a shell which fell in Bde. Hd. Qrs.] This was the second time that Marshall had been wounded during the war. Subsequently he commanded the 42nd, 29th and 53rd Divisions in the Mediterranean Expeditionary Force and then, in 1916, commanded the 27th Division at Salonika. He was made a C.B. in 1916. In Mesopotamia, from 1916 to 1917, he commanded the 3rd Indian Army Corps and then became the G.O.C. in C. of the Mesopotamian Expeditionary Force from 1917 to 1919. He was created a K.C.B. in 1917, a K.C.S.I in 1918 and a G.C.M.G. in 1919. After the war he was G.O.C. Southern Command, India, until 1923 and he retired from the Army in 1924. He wrote a book, *Memories of Four Fronts*, which was published in 1929. Lieutenant-General Sir William Marshall died in May, 1939.

---

1 *The Story of the 29th Division.*   2 PRO WO 95/4311.

Matheson, T. G.   **Major-General**
G.O.C. 20th Division   **Gassed: 7 August, 1917**

Torquhil George Matheson was born in February, 1871, and was educated at Eton. He served in the Herts. Militia and in the 4th Battalion Bedfordshire Regiment from 1890 to 1894, and was then commissioned into the Coldstream Guards in June, 1894, and served in the South African War from 1899 to 1902. He was Lieutenant-Colonel commanding the 3rd Battalion Coldstream Guards in 1915 and in July of that year he was appointed to command of the 46th Infantry Brigade. In March, 1917, he was promoted to Major-General Commanding the 20th Division and it was whilst holding this command that he was gassed on 7 August, 1917. The divisional diary[1] records: 'Dragon Camp. Major-General T. G. Matheson admitted to hospital suffering from Gas poisoning.' His division was about to go into action and from his hospital bed he sent the following message, 'Sudden illness, caused by the fumes of gas shells, has compelled me to relinquish the command of the 20th Division. At any time this would be a very heavy blow to me; at the present moment I cannot express the bitterness of my disappointment.' He returned in September to command the 4th Division until September, 1918, when he took command of the Guards Division until September, 1919. He was made a C.B in 1918 and a C.M.G. in 1919. After the war he commanded the 2nd Guards Brigade and the 7th Division, Northern Command. He was created a K.C.B. in 1921, promoted to General in 1934 and retired from the Army in 1935. In 1944 he succeeded his brother and became the 5th Bt. of Lochalsh. General Sir Torquhil George Matheson died in November, 1963.

---

1 PRO WO 95/2097.

McCracken, F. W. N. C.B. D.S.O.
G.O.C. 7th Brigade 3rd Division

Brigadier-General
Wounded: 26 August, 1914

Frederick William Nicholas McCracken was born in August, 1859. He was educated at the R.M.C., Sandhurst and entered the Army, as a Second-Lieutenant in the 49th Foot, in August, 1859, and he became a Lieutenant in the Royal Berkshire Regiment in July, 1880. He saw service in the Egyptian Campaign of 1882, and in the Sudan in 1885 and 1886; he was in the Suakin Campaign and with the Frontier Field Force in the action at Giniss. From 1892 to 1897 he was D.A.A.G. in Barbados. He served in the South African War from 1899 to 1902, in which he commanded the 2nd Battalion Royal Berkshire Regiment during 1901 and 1902. He was awarded the D.S.O.[1] for his services. He was made a C.B. in 1910. From 1911 to 1912 he was a Brigadier-General of the General Staff, Irish Command. When the Great War started he commanded the 7th Infantry Brigade, a command that he had held since 1912. He was put out of action very early in the war. McCracken was stunned by a shell, probably the first General Officer casualty of the war. He was promoted to Major-General in October, 1914, for distinguished service in the field. He returned in 1915 to command the 15th Division and from 1917 as a Lieutenant-General he commanded XIII Corps. He was created a K.C.B. in 1917. After the war he was C. in C. Scottish Command. Lieutenant-General Sir Frederick McCracken retired from the Army in 1922 and he died in August, 1949.

---

1 L.G. 31/10/02.

McCulloch, A. J. D.S.O. D.C.M.
G.O.C. 64th Brigade 21th Division

Brigadier-General
Wounded: 24 August, 1918

Andrew Jameson was born in July 1876, the son of A. Jameson, Lord Ardwall, a Scottish Judge. He assumed the surname of McCulloch in 1892. He was educated at Edinburgh Academy, St. Andrews University and

167

New College, Oxford. He obtained his B.A. and became a Barrister at Law. In the South African War he served in the ranks of the City Imperial Volunteers for nearly eight months, during which time he was awarded the D.C.M., and was commissioned from their ranks into the Highland Light Infantry in August, 1900. Later he transferred to the 7th Dragoon Guards and then to the 14th Hussars. As a Lieut.-Colonel he commanded the 9th Battalion Yorkshire Light Infantry from October, 1917, until July, 1918, when he was appointed to command the 64th Infantry Brigade. He was awarded the D.S.O.[1]for conspicuous gallantry and devotion to duty throughout many days of severe fighting. 'His courage, energy and unfailing cheerfulness contributed in a most marked manner to the various successful withdrawals of the battalion, and were a magnificent example to his men, whose confidence he gained in the highest degree. Later, in command of a mixed force, his skill and coolness in difficult operations were worthy of the highest praise.' He was awarded a Bar[2] to the D.S.O. for conspicuous gallantry and devotion to duty. 'At a most critical time he handled his battalion with great skill and gallantry, and blocked the enemy's advance. While making a valuable reconnaissance he was gassed and wounded, but continued his command of the battalion for another two days until the situation was righted. He showed fine leadership and determination.' When the 64th Infantry Brigade took Grandcourt, Brigadier-General McCulloch was wounded. The brigade diary[3] contains an account of the operations of 19–27 August, 1918, which includes the following: 'August 23rd. It was decided that the 64th Inf. Bde., supported by the 110th Inf. Bde. should cross the River Ancre and form up on the southern side in R.13.c. and should advance straight on to the high ground south of Miraumont in R.11.b. [At 11.30 pm.] the advance started. Bde. H.Q. followed the reserve companies. Some opposition was encountered in Battery Valley, but after that Grandcourt Road (the first objective) was reached without difficulty. August 24th. At 3.30 am. the advance to the second objective was commenced. The B-G.C. who had been with the foremost troops was unfortunately wounded just as the Brigade reached the objective.' The diary also contains Brigadier-General McCulloch's report of the operations which includes the following: 'A night attack to seize an objective 3 miles distant. It was fought against the 68th R. I. Regiment and the 30th R. I. Regiment of the 16th Res. Div. The Brigade Reserve who were ordered to concentrate at 3.15 pm. did not come on and as I could not wait for them I sent back to tell them to follow on to the first objective. By this time I was wounded. The 15/D.L.I. were attacked on the right while crossing Boom Valley Ravine and so were delayed. I then went south for a few hundred yards to see if I could find the 15/D.L.I. Just as I found them I was hit in the thigh by a German Machine Gunner. As I was bleeding a lot and unable to walk I considered that if I stayed I would be more hindrance than help.' Brigadier-General

McCulloch was carried back by Germans captured by his division. From 10 B.R.C. Hospital, Le Treport, Brigadier-General McCulloch wired to 'know how the fight ended' and to ask that the ground between St. Pierre Divion and Miraumont 'be searched for my wounded'. He received a reply that the objectives had been secured and all wounded were collected. He was awarded a second Bar[4] to his D.S.O. for conspicuous gallantry and ability to command. 'On a pitch dark night he penetrated 4,500 yards into the enemy lines, occupied his objective, and captured between 300 and 400 prisoners and two guns, as well as a village. The advance was over the worst country, and the right flank of his brigade was entirely uncovered throughout. Success was entirely due to his magnificent leadership, moving at the head of his brigade.' He was wounded three times during the war. At the end of the war he commanded the 62nd Infantry Brigade and then went to India to become Commandant of the Staff College at Quetta. From 1926 he was Brigadier of the 2nd Infantry Brigade at Aldershot and in 1930 was Commandant of the Senior Officers School, Sheerness. He was made a C.B. in 1934 and was created a K.B.E. in 1937. Major-General Sir Andrew Jameson McCulloch retired from the Army in 1938 and died in April, 1960.

---

1 L.G. 26/7/18.   2 L.G. 16/9/18.   3 PRO WO 95/2160.   4 L.G.11/1/19.

McNicoll, W. R. D.S.O.   Brigadier-General
G.O.C. 10th Australian Brigade   3rd Australian Division   Gassed: 6 June, 1917

Walter Ramsay McNicoll was born in South Melbourne, Victoria, Australia, in May, 1877, and was educated at the Training College, Melbourne, and Melbourne University, where he obtained a B.A. and a Diploma of Education. He was commissioned in the Australian Cadet Forces in March, 1895, and transferred to the 5th Australian Infantry Regiment in November, 1905. In civilian life he was a schoolmaster; from 1905 until 1911 he was Senior Master at Melbourne High School, and from 1911 until the outbreak of war in 1914 he was Headmaster of Geelong High School. Major McNicoll joined the A.I.F. on 15 August, 1914, as 2nd i/c the 7th Battalion. He served in Gallipoli, and in April, 1915, he was promoted Lieutenant-Colonel commanding the 6th Battalion. On 8 May, 1915, he was wounded in the attack on Krithia and he returned to Australia in December of that year. He was awarded the D.S.O.[1] for gallantry and devotion to duty in connection with operations at the Dardanelles. In February, 1916, he was appointed Brigadier-General and was sent to France in November to command the 10th Australian Infantry Brigade. The official history[2] records that 'Major E. W. Connelly of the 10th, with his brigadier, McNicoll (who was hampered by an old leg wound), were badly gassed on the night of the 6th.' He returned to command his brigade in many more actions until the end of the war, when he became Director of Education for the A.I.F. He was made a C.M.G. in 1918 and a C.B. in 1919. After the war he was A.D.C. to the Governor General and Member of the House of Representatives for Werriwa, N.S.W., from 1931 to 1934. He was Administrator of New Guinea from 1934 to 1943, and was created a K.B.E. in 1937. Brigadier-General Sir Walter McNicoll died in December, 1947.

---

1 L.G. 3/6/15.   2 *Official History of Australia in the War of 1914 – 1918*, Vol. 4.

Melliss, Sir Charles J.   V.C.   K.C.B.
G.O.C. 30th Brigade   6th Indian Division

Major-General

P.O.W.: 29 April, 1916

Charles John Melliss was born in September, 1862, and was educated at Wellington College and the R.M.C., Sandhurst. He was commissioned into the East Yorkshire Regiment in September, 1882, and transferred to the Indian Staff Corps in January, 1884. He served in East Africa on operations in Somaliland in 1896, and on the north-west frontier of India, in the Tirah Campaign of 1897 and 1898. He was awarded the Bronze Medal of the Royal Humane Society in 1898. From 1898 to 1902 he was with the Northern Nigeria Regiment of the West African Frontier Force and during the Ashanti Campaign of 1900 he earned the award of the Victoria Cross. The *London Gazette* of 15 January, 1901, announced the award:

'On the 30th Sept. 1900, at Obassa, Major Melliss, seeing that the enemy were very numerous, and intended to make a firm stand, hastily collected all stray men and any that he could get together, and charged at their head into the dense bush where the enemy were thick. His action carried all along with him; but the enemy were determined to have a hand-to-hand fight. One fired at Major Melliss, who put his sword through the man, and they rolled over together. Another Ashanti shot him through the foot, the wound paralysing the limb. His wild rush had, however, caused a regular panic among the enemy, who were at the same time charged by the Sikhs, and killed in numbers. Major Melliss also behaved with great gallantry on three previous occasions.'

He was wounded four times during the operations in Ashanti. From 1902 to 1904 he was on operations in Somaliland. He was made a C.B. in 1911, and held Brigade Command in India from 1910 to 1914. In the Great War he commanded the 30th Brigade of the Indian Expeditionary Force in Mesopotamia. He was at the Battle of Shaiba, near Basra, in April, 1915, and took part in the prolonged operations before Nasariyeh. He was in the retreat on Kut-el-Amara and in its defence from December, 1915, to April, 1916. He was created a K.C.B. in 1915. After the fall of Kut he was a prisoner of the Turks for two and a half years. In November, 1918, he was repatriated and was created a K.C.M.G. in the same year. Major-

170

General Sir Charles John Melliss retired from the Army in February, 1920, and died in June, 1936.

Minshull-Ford, J. R. M. D.S.O. M.C. **Brigadier-General**
G.O.C. 115th Brigade 38th Division **Wounded: 3 June, 1917**

John Randle Minshull Minshull-Ford was born in May, 1881, and was educated at Twyford School, Winchester; Haileybury and the R.M.C., Sandhurst. He was commissioned into the Royal Welsh Fusiliers in August, 1900, and was Adjutant of the 4th Battalion from 1912 until he joined the 1st Battalion of his Regiment in France in November, 1914. In 1915 he commanded the battalion until wounded in the arm at Neuve Chapelle in June, 1915. He was awarded the M.C. In February, 1916, he was appointed Brigadier-General Commanding the 91st Infantry Brigade, and from November, 1916, until March, 1917, commanded 11th Reserve Brigade of the Home Forces, but he returned to France to take command of the 115th Brigade in March, 1917. He was awarded the D.S.O.[1] for distinguished service in the field. The diary[2] of the 115th Brigade for 3 June, 1917, records that 'at 5 am. enemy plane was again over our lines and at 5.30 am. enemy barraged the road from White Hope Corner to Cabaret Bleu, Bridge Street, X Line from the tramway to Cabaret Bleu and the right of the Belgian C Line, chiefly with long range 77 mms. This barrage continued till 9.30 am. From 2 pm. to 2.30 pm. enemy shelled Boesinghe Wood with 10.5 cm. howitzers, blocking Bridge Street in two places between the Château and village street. After registration about noon, Elverdinghe Château grounds and the junction of Poperinge Road with the Woesten Road were heavily shelled with 15 cms. from 2 pm. to 3pm. and from 4 pm. to 5pm. Some damage was done to the Blockhouse at the corner of the road and to dugouts in the Château grounds, and Brigadier-General J. R. Minshull-Ford, D.S.O. M.C., and 1 O.R. were wounded. Brigadier-General Minshull-Ford removed to C.C.S.' He recovered from his wound, his third in the war, and returned to France to command the 1st Brigade in 1917 and then the 97th Brigade in 1918. After the war he commanded the 151st Brigade and the 2nd Brigade in B.A.O.R. He was promoted to the rank of Major-General in 1932 and was made a C.B. in 1933. In 1938 he retired from the Army and died in April, 1948.

---

1 L.G. 1/1/17. 2 PRO WO 95/2560.

Morant, H. H. S. D.S.O.* **Brigadier-General**
G.O.C. 3rd Brigade 1st Division **Wounded: 21 May, 1918**

Hubert Horatio Shirley Morant was born in December, 1870, and was educated at Charterhouse and the R.M.C., Sandhurst. He was commissioned into the Durham Light Infantry in October, 1889, served with the Egyptian Army from 1898 to 1908, and was with the the Nile Expedition of 1898. He raised the 10th Battalion Durham Light Infantry in 1914 and commanded the battalion until January, 1918. He was awarded the D.S.O.[1] and Bar[2] for distinguished services in the field. In January, 1918, he was appointed to command the 3rd Infantry Brigade and was wounded, for the fourth time in the war, on 21 May, 1918. The brigade diary[3] records that the brigade headquarters was at Annequin, Fosse No.9, when Brigadier-General Morant was wounded. On 23 May Brigadier-General Sir William Kay (q.v.) assumed command of the brigade. Brigadier-General Morant returned to France to command the 147th Infantry Brigade in the last few month of the war and remained in command until March, 1919. After the war he commanded the 1st Battalion Durham Light Infantry until 1923, then commanded the Northumberland Infantry Brigade (T.A.) until 1927. Brigadier-General Morant retired from the Army in 1927 and died in September, 1946.

---

1 L.G. 1/1/17.   2 L.G. 1/1/18.   3 PRO WO 95/1277.

Mullens, R. L.
G.O.C. 2nd Cavalry Brigade   1st Cavalry Division

Brigadier-General
Gassed: 24 May, 1915

Richard Lucas Mullens was born in February, 1871. He was educated at Eton and commissioned into the 16th Lancers in October, 1890, and transferred to the 2nd Dragoon Guards in February, 1896. He served in the South African War as Adjutant of the Queen's Bays, and was severely wounded. He was Brigade-Major of the 4th Cavalry Brigade from 1905 to 1909, and then commanded the 4th Dragoon Guards from 1911. He took his Regiment to France in August, 1914, and in October of the same year was appointed to the command of the 2nd Cavalry Brigade. During the Second Battle of Ypres the headquarters of the 2nd Cavalry Brigade was in a dug-out west of Bellewaarde Lake when, on 24 May, 1915, as the brigade diary[1] records: 'Owing to the falling back of our infantry on our left, which exposed our dug-out to rifle fire and to the overpowering effects of the gas fumes, it was found impossible to remain in our present position, so it was decided to withdraw Bde. Hd. Qrs. to the neighbourhood of the G.H.Q. Line further to the west. The Brigadier went to Hd. Qrs., 9th Cavalry Brigade and thence to the Menin Gate, where the 4th D.G's. were, where he reorganised all troops he could lay hands on, but about 4.30 am. he was overcome by gas fumes and had to be evacuated.' Captain Paget, his Brigade-Major, was also badly gassed. In October, 1915, he returned to command the 1st Cavalry Division and he was made a C.B. in 1917. Major-General Mullens retired from the Army in 1920 and died in May, 1952.

---

1 PRO WO 95/1110.

Musgrave, A. D. D.S.O.
C.R.A. 52nd Division

Brigadier-General
Wounded: 2 August, 1918

Arthur David Musgrave was born in March, 1874. He was educated at Harrow and was commissioned into the Royal Artillery in October, 1893. He served in France from October, 1914, and commanded the 40th Brigade Royal Artillery from October to December, 1915. He was then sent to join the Indian Expeditionary Force 'D' and served as C.R.A. of the 7th Indian Division with the Mesopotamian Expeditionary Force from April, 1917, until April, 1918, and was awarded the D.S.O.[1] for distinguished services rendered in connection with military operations in Mesopotamia. He returned to France in June, 1918, to become C.R.A. of the 52nd Division. He was wounded on 2 August[2] , but returned to his division on 4 August and continued in his appointment until October, 1918. Brigadier-General Musgrave died in September, 1931.

1 L.G. 7/2/18.   2 Becke. *Order of Battle Part 2A.*

Northey, E.
G.O.C. 15th Brigade   5th Division

Brigadier-General
Wounded: 22 June, 1915

Edward Northey was born in May, 1868. He was educated at Eton and the R.M.C., Sandhurst, and was commissioned into the King's Royal Rifle Corps in March, 1888. He served with the Hazara and the Miranzai Expeditions of 1891; Isazai Expedition of 1892 and in the South African War, from 1899 to 1902. He commanded the 1st Battalion K.R.R.C. from 1914 to March, 1915, when he was appointed Brigadier-General Commanding the 15th Infantry Brigade, but a few months later, at Ypres, as the brigade diary[1] records: '22nd June, 1915. 7.10 pm. the Brigadier (General Northey) wounded in the thigh near Verbrandenmolen when discussing digging of new communication trench with the Brigade-Major (Capt. W. H. Johnston, V.C. R.E.).' When he had recovered from his wound Northey commanded the Nyasa-Rhodesia Field Force in German East Africa from 1916 to 1918. He was made a C.B. in 1917 and was promoted to Major-General in 1918 for distinguished services in the field. From 1918 to 1922 he was Governor and C. in C. of Kenya Colony, and H.M.'s High Commissioner for the Zanzibar Protectorate. He was created a K.C.M.G in 1918 and a G.C.M.G. in 1922. He was G.O.C. 43rd Division (T.A.) and S.W. Area from 1924 to 1926. In 1926 Major-General Sir Edward Northey retired from the Army and died in December, 1953.

1 PRO WO 95/1566.

Odlum, V. W. C.M.G. D.S.O.*   **Brigadier-General**
G.O.C. 11th Canadian Brigade 4th Canadian Division   **Wounded: 5 September, 1918**

Victor Wentworth Odlum was born at Cobourg, Ontario, Canada, in October, 1880. He was educated at Toronto University, and became Editor of the Vancouver *Daily World*. He was associated continuously for 22 years with the Canadian Militia, becoming Major and 2nd i/c of the 11th Irish Fusiliers of Canada. During the South African War he served with the 1st Canadian Contingent (2nd R.C.R.) and afterwards with the 3rd Canadian Mounted Rifles. In the Great War he served in France with the 7th Canadian Infantry Battalion (1st British Columbia Regiment) and from April, 1915, to July, 1916, he was in command of the battalion. It was during this period that he was awarded the D.S.O.[1] for conspicuous ability and energy. 'He personally superintended all arrangements for a bombing attack made by his battalion on the night 16–17 November, 1915, near Messines, and by his coolness and determination was largely instrumental in bringing about the success of the exploit.' In July, 1916, he was appointed to command the 11th Canadian Infantry Brigade of the 4th Canadian Division. He was made a C.M.G. in 1917. On 5 September, 1918, when brigade headquarters was just south-west of Saudemont, on the north side of the Arras – Cambrai road, the brigade diary[2] records that, 'about 5.00 pm. General Odlum, while reconnoitring forward positions, was wounded by an enemy sniper. The General went out to have his wound dressed.' This was his third wound of the war, but on 7 September he returned to his command. In December, 1918, he was awarded a Bar[3] to his D.S.O. for conspicuous gallantry and ability during an advance. 'He personally superintended and carried out a difficult operation under heavy shell fire, inspiring his battalions by his continued resource and intrepid leadership. When his advance was temporarily held up, he organized the details of the final attack. He has always shown marked gallantry and initiative.' He was made a C.B. in 1918. After the war he was the Publisher of the Vancouver *Daily Star* from 1924 to 1932, and during this period he was also Liberal Member for Vancouver City in the provincial Legislature. In the following years he was Governor of the Canadian Broadcasting Corporation and Governor of the University of British Columbia. During the Second World War he commanded the 2nd Division of the Canadian Active Service Force until 1941 when he became the Canadian High Commissioner to Australia. From 1942 to 1952 he was Canadian Ambassador to China and then to Turkey. Major-General Odlum died in April, 1971.

---

1 L.G. 23/12/15.   2 PRO WO 95/3901   3 L.G. 2/12/18.

Oldfield, L. C. L.   D.S.O.
C.R.A. 51st Division

Brigadier-General
Wounded: 28 April, 1918

Leopold Charles Louis Oldfield was born in February, 1872, and was educated at Clifton College. He was commissioned into the Royal Artillery in April, 1892. As a Major with the 33rd Battery Royal Field Artillery he was awarded the D.S.O.[1] 'for conspicuous gallantry at Neuve Chapelle on 10th March, 1915, in command of his battery in action, and for successful service in cutting wire entanglements. He took one of his guns to within 700 yards of the enemy, and so greatly facilitated the advance of our infantry.' In July, 1916, he was appointed C.R.A. of the 51st Division, and on 28 April, 1918, when his headquarters was at Molinghem, he was wounded. The C.R.A's. diary[2] briefly records the event: 'C.R.A. 51 D.A. wounded by a shell which wrecked the motor car near Hamet Billot.' He returned to his post as divisional C.R.A. in July, 1918. He was made a C.B. in 1918, and a C.M.G. in 1919. After the war he commanded the Royal Artillery of the London Division of the British Army of the Rhine. He became Chief Instructor at the School of Artillery from 1924 to 1925, and then commanded the 47th Division (T.A.) from 1927 to 1930. From 1931 until he retired from the Army he was G.O.C. Malaya. In 1934 he was created a K.B.E. Major-General Sir Louis Oldfield died in January, 1949.

1 L.G. 28/4/15.   2 PRO WO 95/2850.

Oldman, R. D. F.   C.M.G.   D.S.O.
G.O.C. 15th Brigade   5th Division

Brigadier-General
Wounded: 11 May, 1918
Gassed: 25 June, 1918

Richard Deare Furley Oldman was born in June, 1877, and was commissioned into the Norfolk Regiment in February, 1897. He served in West Africa (Northern Nigeria) from 1903 to 1906, and as Captain Oldman he was awarded the D.S.O.[1] for services during operations in Northern Nigeria. At the beginning of the Great War he served as D.A.A.G. at G.H.Q., B.E.F. and from September, 1915, he commanded the 1st Battalion Cheshire Regiment until appointed to command the 117th Infantry Brigade. In 1917 he was made a C.M.G. and he became Brigade Commander in the Home Forces until, in November of that year, he took command of the 15th Infantry Brigade. The brigade diary[2] records that on 11 May, when his headquarters was at L'Epinette: '5 pm. Brigadier-General R. D. F. Oldman, C.M.G. D.S.O., who had been wounded in the foot, went down to C.C.S. at Aire for a few days.' He returned to command his brigade on 20 May. In July the same diary records: 'Night 24/25th June, 1918. Heavy gas shelling of Croix Marraise and Amont Wood, including Bde. H.Q. 25th June. Brigadier-General Oldman went to C.C.S. – gassed.'

On 7 July he went to England for three weeks sick leave, but he was back again on 25 July to assume command of his brigade. This was the third time that he was wounded in the Great War. After the war he became Inspector General, West African Frontier Force from 1924 to 1926, and then commanded the 6th Infantry Brigade from 1926 to 1930. He was made a C.B. in 1923. Major-General Oldman retired from the Army in 1935 and died in November, 1943.

1 L.G. 25/8/05.   2 PRO WO 95/1569.

Osborn, W. L.   C.M.G.   D.S.O.
G.O.C. 5th Brigade   2nd Division

Brigadier-General
Wounded: 5 October, 1918

William Lushington Osborn was born in July, 1871, and was educated at the United Services College, Westward Ho! and the R.M.C., Sandhurst. He was commissioned into the Royal Sussex Regiment in November, 1890. In 1897 and 1898 he served on the north-west frontier of India and took part in the Tirah Campaign. He was Brigade-Major of the Sirhind Brigade in the Punjab, India, from 1905 to 1909, and then commanded the 1st Battalion Royal Sussex Regiment in India until 1912. He commanded the 7th Battalion Royal Sussex Regiment from August, 1914, to July, 1916, when he was awarded the D.S.O.[1] for gallantry on 3 March, 1916, at the Hohenzollern Redoubt. He was promoted to command the 16th Infantry Brigade in 1916, and in 1917 commanded the 192nd Infantry Brigade. He was made a C.M.G. in 1917. In April, 1918, he was appointed to command the 5th Infantry Brigade and it was with this brigade that he was wounded on 5 October, 1918. The brigade diary[2] describes what happened: 'Brigadier-General W. L. Osborn, C.M.G. D.S.O., was wounded this morning by an H.E. shell which exploded close to him as he was inspecting the billets of the 24th Royal Fusiliers in Noyelles.' After the war he was made a C.B. and he commanded the Depôt of the Machine Gun Corps. He retired from the Army in 1921 and died in April, 1951.

1 L.G. 15/4/16   2 PRO WO 95/1346.

Ouseley, R. G.   C.M.G.   D.S.O.
C.R.A. 17th Division

Brigadier-General
Wounded: 21 July, 1916

Ralph Glyn Ousel was born in May, 1866, and was commissioned into the Royal Artillery in February 1886. His service in the South African War, from 1899 to 1902 , included the Defence of Ladysmith. He was a Major when he was awarded the D.S.O.[1] in recognition of his services. After the war he was a Magistrate in Transvaal. In the Great War he commanded the 18th Brigade Royal Field Artillery from September, 1914, to January,

1916. He was made a C.M.G. in 1915. He then commanded the artillery of the 17th Division until 21 July, 1916, when he was wounded near Dernancourt. He was made a C.B. in 1916 and he returned as C.R.A 59th Division and, from April, 1917, became C.R.A. of the 61st Division. Brigadier-General Ousley retired from the Army in 1920 and died in Switzerland in September, 1931.

---

1 L.G. 19/4/01.

Paris, A. C.B. — Major-General
G.O.C. 63rd (RN) Division — Wounded: 12 October, 1916

Archibald Paris was born in November, 1861. He was educated at the Royal Naval College, Greenwich, and entered the Royal Marine Artillery in September, 1879. He served with Naval Intelligence from 1899 to 1900, and then with the Rhodesian Field Force until 1902. From 1903 to 1906 he was a Professor and then Chief Instructor at the Royal Military Academy. In 1907 he was made a C.B. From 1913 to the outbreak of war he was Inspector of Marine Recruiting. In October, 1914, he was promoted to Major-General and appointed to command the Royal Naval Division. He served with the division at Antwerp and at Gallipoli. The division returned to serve in France and on 12 October, 1916, when the divisional head-quarters was at Léalvillers, Major-General Paris was wounded. The divisional diary[1] records that 'at about 1.55 pm. when the G.O.C. 63rd Division accompanied by Major Sketchley, D.S.O., (G.S.O.2) and Lt. Nicolson (A.D.C.) were proceeding to the trenches in the REDAN Sector, a German shell exploded in the trench (about 400 yards along 6th Avenue) killing Major Sketchley, D.S.O., and seriously wounding the G.O.C. Lt. Nicolson was unhurt. The G.O.C. was transferred to 3rd Casualty Clearing Station, Puchevillers, suffering from a compound fracture of the leg and several wounds on the leg and arm.' The General's leg had to be amputated. He was created a K.C.B. in 1916. As a result of his severe wound Major-General Sir Archibald Paris went on the retired list in 1917, and died in Switzerland in October, 1937.

---

1 PRO WO 95/3093.

Paton, J. C.B. — Brigadier-General
G.O.C. 7th Australian Brigade 2nd Australian Division — Wounded: 7 November, 1916

John Paton was born in Newcastle, N. S. W., Australia, in November, 1867. He was educated at the High School, Newcastle, and was trained in a mercantile house and eventually became the Managing Director of a general merchants in Sydney and Newcastle. He was a keen Militia man and served for 30 years in the N. S. W. Citizen Forces. At the outbreak of the Great War he went with the Naval and Military Expeditionary Force which captured the German islands in the Western Pacific. He commanded the mixed force of 600 men at the capture of Rabaul, the capital of German New Guinea, and commanded the garrison there for five months. He also commanded the party which captured the German gun boat, *Komet*. He joined the 7th Brigade of the Australian Imperial Forces and served in Gallipoli, where he was in command of the rear party at the evacuation. He served in France from March, 1916. On 5 November, 1916, his brigade was about to attack 'The Maze', a small salient in the German line south-east of Le Sars. The brigade diary[1] recorded: 'G.O.C. wounded in the back when reconnoitring line.' The official history[2] describes what happened: 'While Paton was standing with Walker (Colonel) of the 25th Btn. on the parapet – the trenches being too muddy – arranging the necessary movement, a German sniper wounded him.' He was not indifferent to the conditions under which his men had to fight. During the Battle of Passchendaele in October, 1917, 'General Paton of the 6th Infantry Brigade had been warned by several of his battalions that their men were unfit for the operation on the 9th. General Smyth (2nd Division) accordingly went forward with him to inspect the conditions. The two generals themselves had great difficulty in getting through the mud. Smyth warned Birdwood of the troops' condition.'[2] He was made a C.B. in 1916 and a C.M.G. in 1918. After the war he became President of the Newcastle Chamber of Commerce from 1920 to 1923, and in 1926 he commanded the 2nd Division of the N. S. W. Commonwealth Military Forces. He retired as Hon. Major-General in 1926 and he died in November, 1943.

1 PRO WO 95/3337. 2 *Official History of Australia in the War of 1914 – 1918*, Vol. 3.

Paynter, G. C. B. D.S.O.   **Brigadier-General**
G.O.C. 172nd Brigade 57th Division   **Wounded: 4 October, 1918**

George Cambourne Beauclerk Paynter was born at Eaton Square, London, in August, 1880. He was educated at Eton, and commissioned into the Scots Guards from the Militia in October, 1899. He served in the South African War from 1899 to 1902. In 1914 he went to France as a Captain with the 2nd Battalion Scots Guards and was awarded the D.S.O.[1] for his action 'on the night of the 24th October while in command of the battalion, fought his trenches all night against repeated attacks from front and rear.' He commanded his battalion from October, 1914, to March, 1915. He was promoted to Brigadier-General in August, 1916, and took command of the 172nd Infantry Brigade. A Bar[2] to his D.S.O. was awarded 'for fine leadership and gallantry while commanding his brigade in an attack, which involved a wheel to the right, to cover the flank of the direct

178

attack of another division. Under heavy fire he personally reconnoitred the position of his troops during the operation, and reported the result when his final objective was attained. Throughout he displayed great courage and initiative.' On 4 October, 1918, he was wounded near Cambrai when a shell burst in a concrete pill-box. The brigade diary[3] records that 'at 2.5 pm. a 4.2 High Velocity shell burst in the entrance of Brigade H.Q. dugout. The G.O.C., Brigadier-General G. C. B. Paynter D.S.O., and the Brigade-Major, Capt. C. V. Fisher-Rowe, M.C., were wounded. 5 O.R's. killed, 2 wounded.' He recovered from his injuries, his second wound of the war, and returned to command the brigade on 12 December. He was made a C.M.G. in 1919, and he commanded the South Lancs. and Cheshire Infantry Brigade from June, 1920, and retired from the Army in 1929. He was an Equerry-in-Ordinary to The King from 1927 to 1930, and then a Groom-in-Waiting to The King. In 1939 he became a King's Messenger, and Lord Lieutenant of Sutherland in 1945. He was made a C.V.O. in 1930, and was created a K.C.V.O. in 1950. Brigadier-General Sir George Paynter died in August, 1950.

1 L.G. 1/12/14.   2 L.G. 2/12/18.   3 PRO WO 95/2984.

Pereira, C. E.
G.O.C. 85th Brigade 28th Division

Brigadier-General
Wounded: 26 May, 1915
Wounded: 27 September, 1915

Cecil Edward Pereira was born in July, 1869. He was educated at the Oratory School, Edgbaston, and was gazetted a Second-Lieutenant in the Coldstream Guards in January, 1890. He was employed in the Uganda Protectorate from 1897 to 1898, and served in the South African War from 1899 to 1902. In 1914 he commanded the 2nd Battalion Coldstream Guards from August, and in May, 1915, was appointed to command the 85th Brigade. Within three weeks of taking command he was wounded when visiting his brigade in the trenches near Vermelles on 26 May. He returned from hospital on 10 June and resumed his command. On 27 September, during the Battle of Loos, he was wounded for a second time. The brigade diary[1] records: '1.15 pm. Information was received that the line had been lost. The Bde. will move at once and hold the Hohenzollern Redoubt. General Pereira and Staff lead the way. Colonel Roberts, 3rd Royal Fusiliers, to go up and report on the situation. [When Roberts returned] to bring up the 3rd Royal Fusiliers he found General Pereira had been wounded. The Brigade-Major, Captain J. Flower, was missing and it was afterwards discovered that he had been wounded.' He returned to command the 1st Guards Brigade in 1916 until he was promoted to Major-General and appointed to command the 2nd Division. He was made a C.M.G. in 1917, a C.B. in 1918 and was created a K.C.B. in 1919. Major-

General Sir Cecil Pereira retired from the Army in 1923 and died in October, 1942.

1 PRO WO 95/2278.

Pilcher, T. D. C.B.   Major-General
G.O.C. 17th Division   Wounded: 26 July, 1915

Thomas David Pilcher was born in July, 1858. He was educated at Harrow, and joined the 22nd Foot from the Militia in June, 1879, transferring to the 5th Foot in the following month. In January, 1881, he was a Lieutenant in the Northumberland Fusiliers. He served in West Africa from 1897 to 1900 and then commanded mounted infantry in the South African War from 1900 to 1902, being made a C.B. in 1901. From 1902 to 1907 he held Brigade Command of the 3rd and 5th Infantry Brigades, Aldershot Command. From 1907 to 1914 he held brigade command and then divisional command in India. In January, 1915, he returned to command the 17th Division in England and France, and it was whilst his divisional headquarters was at Reninghelst that he was slightly wounded by shell splinters whilst visiting the trenches[1]. He continued in command of the division until July, 1916, and then became commander of the Reserve Centre. He retired from the Army in January, 1919, and died in December, 1928.

1 PRO WO 95/1986.

Pollard, J. H.-W. C.M.G.   Brigadier-General
G.O.C. 2nd Brigade 1st Division   Wounded: 1 October, 1915

James Hawkins-Whitshed Pollard was born in May, 1866, and was educated at Repton and the R.M.C., Sandhurst. He was commissioned into the Manchester Regiment in August, 1886, but transferred to the Royal Scots Fusiliers in the following month. He served with the Burmese Expedition from 1887 to 1889; Chin-Lushi Expedition of 1890; the Isazai Expedition of 1892; the Waziristan Expedition from 1894 to 1895, and was with the Chitral Relief Force in 1895. From 1899 to 1902 he served in the South African War, and afterwards was in East Africa on operations in Somaliland from 1902 to 1904. In the years leading up to the Great War he was a Brigade-Major with the 4th and 6th Infantry Brigades of the Aldershot Army Corps, and at the outbreak of war was a G.S.O.1 with the Coastal Defence, Eastern Command. In the Great War he commanded the 2nd Battalion Royal Scots Fusiliers from January to August, 1915. He was appointed to command the 2nd Infantry Brigade in August, 1915, and held the command for just over a month before he was wounded. The brigade diary[1] records that at Loos on 1 October, 1915, there was 'Heavy Shelling. Brigade to be relieved about 10 pm. by 1st and 3rd Battalions of the 114th French Infantry Regiment. 9 pm. Shell struck brigade head-quarters and killed Brigade-Major (Major R. J. Terry, M.V.O. D.S.O.) and French Brigadier-General and wounded Brigadier-General J. H. W. Pollard, C.M.G., (Cmd. 2nd Inf. Bde.) and 2nd i/c French Regiment.' He was made a C.M.G. in 1915 and when he had recovered from his wounds he returned to France in April, 1916, to take command of the 24th Infantry Brigade until January, 1917. In May, 1917, he took command of the 106th Infantry Brigade and later he commanded the 178th Infantry Brigade until September, 1919. He was made a C.B. in 1918 and was awarded the D.S.O.[2] in 1919. After the war he continued to hold brigade command until he retired from the Army in 1925. Major-General Pollard died in February, 1942.

---

1 PRO WO 95/1267.   2 L.G. 3/6/19.

Potter, H. C.
G.O.C. 9th Brigade   3rd Division

Brigadier-General
Wounded: 23 July, 1916

Herbert Cecil Potter was born in October, 1875. He was educated at Bedford Modern School, and was commissioned into the King's (Liverpool) Regiment in February, 1896. He served in the South African War from 1901 to 1902 and was then employed with the Egyptian Army from 1903 to 1913. In the Great War he commanded the 1st Battalion King's (Liverpool) Regiment from October, 1915, until he was appointed to command the 9th Infantry Brigade in March, 1916. The brigade diary[1] contains a copy of the Operations Orders dated 22 July, 1916, which includes the following: 'At 3.40 am. on 23 July the 9th Brigade with 8/King's Own and 17/West Yorks attached will attack and clear Longueval village and Delville Wood.' On the 23rd the diary records: 'Montauban. 3 pm. Brigadier-General slightly wounded.' As he had received no news of the progress of the attack he went forward to see for himself and heard from Major Sir G. Dunbar (12/West Yorks) that the attack had failed. As he was giving orders to Major Dunbar he was wounded by a shell which burst overhead.[2] He was wounded in 'Pont Street' which was a trench which ran along the road from Longueval to High Wood. On 25 July Brigadier-General Potter was evacuated, but he returned to the brigade on 5 August, 1916. He was wounded three times during the war, and was awarded the D.S.O.[3] for distinguished service in the field. After the war he commanded a brigade in the British Army on the Rhine until November, 1919. He was made a C.M.G. in 1918. In 1927 he was made a C.B. and retired from the Army. He died in June, 1964.

---

1 PRO WO 95/1426.   2 PRO CAB 45/136   3 L.G. 1/1/17.

Prescott-Decie, C.   **Brigadier-General**
C.R.A. 4th Division   **Wounded: 24 January, 1917**

Cecil Prescott-Decie was born in August, 1865, and was educated at Clifton College and the R.M.A., Woolwich. He was commissioned into the Royal Artillery in April, 1885, and served in the South African War from 1899 to 1900. He was C.R.A. of the 1st Indian Division at Peshawar from February, 1915, to February, 1916, and during this time was on operations against the Mohmands and Swatis in the vicinity of Hafiz Kor and Shabkadar. In April, 1916, he was appointed to command the Royal Artillery of the 4th Division in France. On 24 January of the following year he was severely wounded and evacuated to the 48th Casualty Clearing Station.[1] He was awarded the D.S.O.[2] in recognition of his services, and in August, 1918 was appointed as B.G.R.A., Irish Command. Brigadier-General Prescott-Decie retired from the Army in April 1920 and he died in September, 1953.

---

1 PRO WO 95/1459. 2 L.G. 4/6/17.

Ravenshaw, H. S. L. C.M.G.   **Major-General**
         P.O.W.: December, 1916

Hurdis Secundus Lalande Ravenshaw was born in June, 1869, and was commissioned from the Militia into the East Yorkshire Regiment in December, 1888. In August, 1890, he transferred to the Devonshire Regiment, served on operations in Chitral in 1895, and on the north-west frontier of India in the Malakand and Tirah Expeditions of 1897 and 1898. He served in the South African War from 1899 to 1902 as Adjutant of the 1st Battalion Devonshire Regiment, and became Adjutant of the R.M.C. from 1903 to 1907. In 1914 he was Lieutenant-Colonel commanding the 1st Battalion Connaught Rangers until April when he was appointed A.A. & Q.M.G. 1st Division. A month later he was a Brigadier-General commanding the 83rd Brigade which he commanded in France and with the Mediterranean Expeditionary Force, and from September until November of 1916 he was a Major-General commanding the 27th Division of the British Salonika Force. He took over command of the division from Major-General Marshall on 1 October, 1916, but two months later the A & Q.M.G. diary[1] records that he left for Base, accompanied by his A.D.C., Captain Vickerman, on vacating command. In his book[2], General Marshall writes: 'Ravenshaw was appointed to command of the 27th Division in my place – he was captured very shortly afterwards by an Austrian submarine, when on his way home, and remained a prisoner for the rest of the war.' His end seems to have been a tragic one as the Probate Register of 1920 states that he was last seen alive on 6 June, 1920, and that he was found dead in Addo Bush near Port Elizabeth, South Africa, two days later.

---

1 PRO WO 95/4880. 2. Marshall. *Memories of Four Fronts.*

Rees, H. C. D.S.O.   **Brigadier-General**
G.O.C. 150th Brigade 50th Division   **P.O.W.: 27 May, 1918**

Hubert Conway Rees was born at Conway, North Wales, in March, 1882. He was educated at Charterhouse, and was commissioned into the 3rd (Militia) Battalion East Surrey Regiment in December, 1900. He served in the South African War from 1901 to 1902, and was gazetted to the Welsh Regiment, as a Second-Lieutenant, in January, 1903. He was a Captain with the 2nd Battalion Welsh Regiment when it went to France in August, 1914, and it was with this battalion that he won his D.S.O.[1] in October, 1914. 'In the course of the action on the 21 Oct. by his particularly skilful reconnaissance and by gallant leading, successfully supported the advance line with a company under a heavy fire, relieving the pressure on the South Wales Borderers.' He commanded the battalion during the latter half of the First Battle of Ypres. He was an Officer of the Company of Gentleman Cadets at the R.M.C. for a while in 1915 before becoming G.S.O.2 of the 43rd and then the 38th Divisions in France from April, 1915, until June, 1916. He was then appointed to command the 94th Infantry Brigade and in July, 1916, when Brigadier-General Prowse (q.v.) died of wounds, he succeeded to command of the 11th Infantry Brigade. This was followed by a short spell at home where he commanded the 13th Reserve Brigade until, in March, 1917, he took command of the 149th Infantry Brigade until September, 1917. In February, 1918, he was appointed to command the 150th Infantry Brigade and in May, during the German advance, the brigade diary[2] records: '26th May. The 150th Brigade was occupying the Plateau de Californie (or Craonne Plateau). 27th May. The Brigadier-General decided in view of the general advance being made by the enemy along the whole front that no counter-attack carried out by the 4th Yorks. could be expected to meet with success. He intended therefore to hold the Intermediate Line with this battalion moving his headquarters back to P. C. Terrasse (600 yards S. of Craonelle). About 7 am. the Brigade H.Q. left La Hutte with the intention of re-establishing at P. C. Terrasse. On arrival there, however, it was discovered that the 4th Yorks. had been overwhelmed on the Mt. Hermal – Tr. Behart line and that the enemy were already approaching P. C. Terrasse from the west. An attempt to organise into defence at this point had therefore to be abandoned. The Brigade H.Q. had now become dispersed as a result of hostile shelling. The Staff-Captain and Intelligence Officer had been wounded and the Brigade-Major was wounded whilst withdrawing towards the Aisne. Brigadier-

General Rees, it is believed, became too exhausted to continue and was captured.' In a letter[3] written after the war, Captain J. G. Garrard of the 6/Northumberland Fusiliers, who was a P. O. W., said that a German gave him a photograph of the Kaiser interrogating Brigadier-General Rees. He was repatriated in December, 1918, and was made a C.M.G. He retired from the Army in 1922 and died in January, 1948.

1 L.G. 9/11/14.   2 PRO WO 95/2883.   3 PRO CAB 45/114

Riddell, E. P. A.   D.S.O.*   **Brigadier-General**
G.O.C. 149th Brigade   50th Division   **Wounded: 27 May, 1918**

Edward Pius Arthur Riddell was born in May, 1875. He was commissioned into the Northumberland Fusiliers from the Militia in February, 1900, and transferred to the Rifle Brigade in June, 1908. He served in the South African War from 1901 to 1902. At the outbreak of the Great War he was at Sandhurst in command of a Company of Gentlemen Cadets, but in June, 1916, he went to France in command of the 1/1st Cambridgeshire Regiment (T.F.) and it was whilst commanding this battalion that he was awarded the D.S.O.[1] for conspicuous gallantry in action. 'He showed the greatest skill and foresight in assembling his Btn. and subsequently launching them to the attack without a casualty, in broad daylight, on ground observed by the enemy. His personal bravery, energy and example exercised great influence over all ranks.' In 1917 he was awarded a Bar[2] to his D.S.O., 'for conspicuous gallantry and devotion to duty when in command of a battalion in reserve during an attack. He threw in a counter-attack at a counter-stroke by the enemy and held on to an eminence of the highest tactical importance throughout the afternoon. His dispositions not only allowed the brigade to fall back in order before superior numbers, but materially reduced the enemy's strength as he held off three counter-attacks and inflicted crushing casualties on the enemy. He eventually assumed command and reorganised two other units of the brigade, and passed four times through a heavy hostile barrage to his brigade head-quarters to report on the situation. He handled a most difficult situation with consummate skill, and his utter disregard of danger not only encouraged the men to further effort but was a magnificent example of courage and determination.' In October, 1917, he was appointed to command the 149th Brigade. He was the second Riddell to command the brigade; the first, J. F. Riddell (q.v.) was killed in action on 26 April, 1915. The brigade diary[3] for May, 1918, records: 'Pontavert Sector. 27/5/18. 7.30 am, Enemy reached Brigade H.Q. Brigade H.Q. moved to Chaudardes. General Riddell wounded just outside Beaurepaire Wood.' Brigadier-General Martin (q.v.) of the 151st Brigade was with Riddell when a German shell burst overhead killing Martin and wounding Riddell. The brigade diary contains a letter written to General Riddell in October, 1918, by his Brigade-Major in the 149th Brigade, Captain H. W. Jackson, in which the Captain describes the events after the General had left for treatment and enquires about his health as, 'I knew you had lost an awful lot of blood when we parted on the bridge near Concevreux.' Brigadier-General Riddell wrote[4] his own account of events in October, 1918: 'My Brigade headquarters were at Centre d'Evreux about 300 yards N.E. of the 151st Brigade headquarters. I decided to leave my own headquarters and join General Martin with a view to holding the trenches about our own headquarters as a last ditch. --- "It was all hands to the pumps." Martin and I with Leathart of the gunners ran towards the 5th Northumberland Fusiliers. We had only gone a few yards when a shell burst on our left. I felt a terrific blow in my face and saw Martin roll over. I went to him. He was quite dead. I walked on half dazed, with a great hole in my face into which I could put my hand, but I did not feel much pain. I could not have my wound bound up as the bandage would have prevented me from giving orders.' This was the third time that Riddell was wounded during the war. He was awarded a second Bar[5] to his D.S.O. 'for conspicuous gallantry and devotion to duty during several days of severe fighting in rearguard actions, when he repeatedly organised counter-attacks, and personally led two of them. After the whole of his staff had become casualties and two of his C.O.'s had been hit, his magnificent example, and total disregard of danger had the greatest effect in steadying his command.' After the war he was made a C.M.G. in 1919, commanded the Northumberland Infantry Brigade, Northern Command in 1920, and retired from the Army in 1925. Brigadier-General Sir Edward Riddell was created a K.C.M.G. in 1945 and died in August, 1957.

---

1 L.G. 11/12/16.   2 L.G. 26/9/17.   3 PRO WO 95/2827.   4 PRO CAB 45/114.
5 L.G. 26/7/18.

Ritchie, A. B. C.M.G.   Major-General
G.O.C. 11th Division   Wounded: 9 May, 1917

Archibald Buchanan Ritchie was born in May, 1869. He was educated at the United Services College, Westward Ho! and the R.M.C., Sandhurst, and was commissioned into the Seaforth Highlanders in September, 1889. He served with the Nile Expedition of 1898, being present at the Battle of Khartoum, and in the South African War from 1899 to 1902. At the outbreak of the Great War he commanded the 1st Battalion Seaforth Highlanders from October, 1914, until he was appointed to command the 26th Brigade in May, 1915. In December, 1916, he was appointed to command the 11th Division and in May, 1917, when his divisional headquarters was just to the north-west of Beaulencourt he was wounded, as the division's diary[1] records: 'N.11 Central, Sheet 57c. 9 May, 1917. About 4 pm. the G.O.C., Major-General A. B. Ritchie, C.M.G., and his A.D.C. [Lieutenant R. C. D. Hargreaves], were both hit by shell fire while riding in the left sector, both horses were killed and the G.O.C. and his A.D.C. severely wounded.' He recovered from his wounds and returned to France in May, 1918, to command the 16th Division. He was made a C.B. in 1919 and as G.O.C. 51st (Highland) Division (T.A.) was created a K.B.E. in 1927. Major-General Sir Archibald Ritchie retired from the Army in 1928 and died in July, 1955.

---

1 PRO WO 95/1788.

Rosenthal, C. C.B. C.M.G. D.S.O.
G.O.C. 2nd Australian Division

Major-General

Wounded: 19 July, 1918

Charles Rosenthal was born at Berrima, N. S. W., Australia, in February, 1875. He was an architect by profession and he joined the Militia Forces in Australia in 1903. He left Australia with the Expeditionary Force in September, 1914, and he served in the Gallipoli Campaign as commander of the 3rd Australian Field Artillery Brigade of the 1st Australian Division, and was wounded on 5 May, 1915, when a shell burst in the headquarters dugout.[1] He served in France as C.R.A. of the 4th Australian Division and then as G.O.C. of the 9th Australian Brigade until May, 1918. On 15 October, 1917, when the brigade was somewhere east of Ypres, the brigade headquarters came under a barrage of 5.9 H.E and 77 mm. gas shells, and all the brigade headquarters personnel were affected by gas. He was made a C.B. in 1915, C.M.G. in 1917 and he was awarded the D.S.O.[2] for distinguished service. In 1918 he commanded the 2nd Australian Division at Villers Bretonneux and in the final advance. The Australian history[3] records how he was wounded: 'on visiting the Mound [the Mound was on the Somme, east of Villers Bretonneux] on the morning of the 19 [July, 1918], resplendent in red staff cap and gorget patches, and accompanied by an equally conspicuous figure – the new commander of the 6th [Australian] Brigade, Brigadier-General Campbell Robertson – (who felt he could not don his steel helmet unless the divisional commander did likewise) – attracted the attention of a German sniper, who, with a single shot, severely wounded him. The bullet hit Rosenthal in the thumb and forearm, severing an artery. The general was exercising, for him, particular caution – he had been warned against the deadly sniping at the east end of the Mound, and consequently was viewing the landscape from the western end. He tried to have his injuries dealt with locally, but General Howse (D.M.S. A.I.F.) packed him off to England.' The divisional diary[4] records that he was shot at 6 am. and that he was evacuated to No.3 A.G.H., Abbeville, at 10.30 am. He commanded A.I.F. Depôts in the U.K. until September, 1919, and was created a K.C.B. in that year. He was G.O.C. 2nd Division Australian Military Forces in N. S. W. from 1921 to 1926 and from 1932 to 1937. Major-General Sir Charles Rosenthal died in May, 1954.

1 & 3 *Official History of Australia in the War of 1914 – 1918*, Vol. 2 & 6.   2 L.G. 3/6/18.
4 PRO WO 95/3258.

Ross, J. M. D.S.O.*   **Brigadier-General**
G.O.C. 5th Canadian Brigade 2nd Canadian Division   **Wounded: 9 August, 1918**

John Munro Ross was born in 1887. He served in the South African War where he was slightly wounded at Houtnek (Thoba Mountain). In the Great War, as a Major in the Canadian Infantry, he was awarded the D.S.O.[1] for distinguished service in the field. In July, 1917, he was appointed to command the 5th Canadian Infantry Brigade, and was awarded a Bar[2] to his D.S.O. for further distinguished service. On 8 August, 1918, the Canadian Corps, in conjunction with the First French Army on the right and the Australian Corps on the left, attacked the enemy's position east of Amiens. The brigade diary[3] records the events of 9 August, 'Near Snipe Copse, south of Wiencourt l'Equipée. The brigade was ordered to attack through 2nd Canadian Infantry. Zero hour to be 11 am. [The G.O.C. and Brigade H.Q. moved to a point of observation in the old Amiens Defence Line about 800 yds. south-east of Caix at 2.30 pm.] At about 3 pm. a shell wounded Brigadier-General Ross, killed Major A. L. Walker, the Brigade-Major, and wounded Captain Campbell, Staff-Captain (I).' The same shell also killed Major Burnham, G.S.O.3 of the 2nd Canadian Division. Brigadier-General Ross returned to command the 6th Canadian Brigade in October, 1918. He was made a C.M.G. in 1919 and died in January, 1959.

1 L.G. 1/1/17.   2 L.G.. 1/1/18   3 PRO WO 95/3821.

Ruggles-Brise, H. G. M.V.O.   **Brigadier-General**
G.O.C. 20th Brigade 7th Division   **Wounded: 2 November, 1914**

Harold Goodeve Ruggles-Brise was born in March, 1864, and was educated at Winchester and Balliol College, Oxford. He entered the Army, as a Lieutenant in the Grenadier Guards, in May, 1885. He was a Brigade-Major at Gibraltar when the South African War broke out and he went to serve in South Africa from 1899 to 1900. He was the Staff officer sent by Lieutenant-General Colvile to tell Brigadier-General Broadwood (q.v.) to report to Colvile in the middle of the action at Sannah's Post. He held various posts as Brigade-Major and was made a M.V.O. in 1910. At the outbreak of the Great War he was Commandant of the School of

Musketry. In September, 1914, he was appointed to command the 20th Brigade and on 2 November he was wounded near Ypres. The brigade diary[1] records: 'Château Heronthage [near Gheluvelt]. 2 November, 1914. During a heavy shelling on our reserves, Brigadier-General H. Ruggles-Brise was wounded in both arms and the shoulder blade.' Brigadier-General F. Heyworth (q.v.) took command. Ruggles-Brise survived and was made a C.B. in 1915, and promoted to Major-General Commanding the 40th Division from September, 1915, to August, 1917. He served as Military Secretary G.H.Q., France, in 1918, and was created a K.C.M.G. in 1919. Major-General Sir Harold Ruggles-Brise retired from the Army in March, 1920, and died in June, 1927.

1 PRO WO 95/1650.

Ryrie, G. de L.   Brigadier-General
G.O.C. 2nd Australian L.H. Brigade   1st Australian Division   Wounded: 29 September, 1915
Wounded: 10 December, 1915

Granville de Laune Ryrie was born at Michelago, N. S. W., Australia, in July, 1865, and was educated at King's School, Parramatta, Australia. He served in the South African War from 1900 to 1901 and was severely wounded. The 2nd Light Horse Brigade, commanded by Colonel G. de L. Ryrie, was offered for service to the British Government on 3 September, 1914. The Australian official history[1] described him as 'an officer of the citizen forces, an Australian pastoralist coming of an old "squatting" family – Colonel Granville Ryrie, who for many years had been a member of the Commonwealth Parliament.' The brigade arrived in Egypt in June, 1915, and in May was dismounted and sent to Gallipoli, where it was attached to the 1st Australian Division. The brigade diary[2] for 29 September, 1915, records: 'Anzac. position shelled at 5 pm. from direction of Olive Groves. Brigadier-General Ryrie wounded by shrapnel pellets in neck and evacuated to hospital ship.' The Orderly Officer's diary[2] for the same day describes his wound in greater detail: 'Brigadier-General Ryrie wounded in neck by shrapnel bullet which penetrated 2 inches and rested on sheath of carotid artery.' In November he returned to his command and was again wounded on 10 December, 1915, but this time he was not evacuated. He commanded the Australian Light Horse Division in Syria and was G.O.C. A.I.F. in Egypt in 1919. He remained a member of the Commonwealth Parliament of Australia until 1927, and during that time was Assistant Minister for Defence from 1919 to 1922. From 1923 to 1927 he was Major-General Commanding 1st Cavalry Division, New South Wales, and from 1927 to 1932 he was the High Commissioner for Australia in Great Britain. He was made a C.M.G. in 1916, a C.B. in 1918 and was created a K.C.M.G. in 1919. Major-General Hon. Sir Granville Ryrie died in October, 1937.

1 *Official History of Australia in the War of 1914 – 1918*, Vol. 1   2 PRO WO 95/4286.

Sackville-West, The Hon. C. J.   C.M.G.   Brigadier-General
G.O.C. 21th Brigade   30th Division   Wounded: 30 July, 1916
G.O.C. 190th Brigade   63rd Division   Wounded: 29 October, 1916

Charles John Sackville-West was born in August, 1870, and was educated at Winchester and the R.M.C., Sandhurst. He was commissioned into the K.R.R.C. in December, 1889, and served with the Expeditions to Manipur in 1891, and to Burma from 1891 to 1892. This was followed by service in many staff posts at home and overseas, including serving in the South African War from 1899 to 1900, until he became a G.S.O.2 at the Staff College in December, 1906. In 1914 he was a G.S.O.2 at the War Office, but from September, 1914, until January, 1915, he was G.S.O.1 to the Indian Army Corps in France. He was made a C.M.G. in 1915 and was appointed to command the 21st Infantry Brigade in December of that year. At the Battle of the Somme he was wounded. The brigade diary[1] records the event: 'Happy Valley. 30 July, 1916. The remainder of the 21st Brigade including Bde. H.Q. remained in Happy Valley. This morning the Brigadier was wounded by bomb dropped from enemy aeroplane, wounds were not serious.' He recovered from his wounds and returned to France and on 24 October took command of the 190th Brigade. Five days later the diary[2] of his new brigade contained the following entry: 'Varennes. 29 October, 1916. Orders issued to take over the Hamel Sector now occupied by the 188th and 189th Inf. Bdes. The Brigadier and Brigade-Major together with the Brigadier of the 189th Inf. Bde. [Brigadier-General L. F. Philips] went up to the trenches to inspect the sector with a view to taking over. Whilst standing in a trench an enemy H.E. shell exploded amongst and partially buried the party. Brigadier-General Sackville-West was wounded in the jaw, but was able to walk to the dressing station, whence he was evacuated.' In March, 1917, he again returned to France to command the 182nd Brigade until November when he was promoted to Major-General General Staff and became the British Military Representative on the Supreme War Council at Versailles, and was created a K.B.E. He was made a C.B. in 1921 and was Military Attaché in Paris from 1920 to 1924. From 1925 he was Lieutenant Governor of Guernsey until he retired from the Army in 1929. He succeeded his brother as the 4th Baron Sackville in 1928 and died in May, 1962.

1 PRO WO 95/2327.   2 PRO WO 95/2042

Sadleir-Jackson, L. W. de V. C.M.G. D.S.O.*

G.O.C. 54th Brigade 18th Division

Brigadier-General

Wounded: 22 August, 1918

Lionel Warren de Vere Sadleir-Jackson was born in December, 1876. He entered the Army from the Militia, as a Second-Lieutenant in the 9th Lancers, in May, 1898. He served in the South African War from 1899 to 1902, was slightly wounded, and was awarded the D.S.O.[1] in recognition of his services in South Africa. In 1909 he resigned from the Army, but was reinstated in the same year. He joined the Army Signals Service in September, 1912, and served with this branch until May, 1917. He was made a C.M.G. in 1915. From May to October, 1917, he commanded the 10th Battalion London Regiment, and was then appointed to command the 54th Brigade of the 18th Division. The divisional history[2] in describing the capture of Albert in 1918 says that 'during the attack, Brigadier-General Sadleir-Jackson, G.O.C. 54th Brigade, having gone forward to secure a better control of the situation, was wounded in the knee by a bullet from a machine gun firing over the crest towards Bellevue Farm [just south-east of Albert, where a supermarket now stands]. General Jackson was actually trying to get some Lewis gunners on to this gun when he was hit. He managed to walk back a considerable part of the way, but had to give in at last; this piece of hard fortune kept him away from the brigade until after the Armistice.' This was the second time that he had been wounded during the war. He was awarded a Bar[3] to his D.S.O. for conspicuous gallantry and devotion to duty. 'Throughout recent operations he proved himself a bold leader of men, and under all conditions full of energy and fine fighting spirit. He personally organized and led most successful counter-attacks, in one of which he captured a village and took 150 prisoners and eleven machine guns. He did splendid work under very difficult conditions.' In 1919 he was made a C.B., and in May of that year was appointed to command the North Russian Relief Force in Archangel until 1920, when he took command of the Yorks and Notts Mounted Brigade. He was Inspector of Levies in the Middle East from 1921 to 1923, and in 1925 he retired from the Army. Fourteen years after he was wounded on the Somme, he died on the Somme, in a motor accident. On Sunday 22 May, 1932, he was killed when the car that he was driving overturned near Peronne. 'In trying to avoid a farm cart in front of him, General Sadleir-Jackson wrenched the steering wheel over too far and the car left the road and dashed into an electric pylon. The off fore-wheel of the car was torn off and the machine capsized, fracturing his skull[4]' He died at Estrées-en-Chaussees[5] , near Peronne, 11 miles from where he was wounded in 1918.

---

1 L.G. 27/9/01. 2 *The 18th Division in the Great War.* 3 L.G. 17/9/18. 4 *The Times.* 23 May 1932. 5 Probate Register 1932.

Sandys, W. B. R.   C.M.G.

B.G.R.A. XIX Corps

Brigadier-General

Wounded: 8 September, 1917

William Bain Richardson Sandys was born in May, 1868, and was educated at Marlborough College and the R.M.A., Woolwich. He was commissioned into the Royal Artillery in July, 1887, and served on the north-west frontier of India and was with the Tirah Expeditionary Force of 1897 and 1898. In the Great War he commanded the 28th Brigade R.F.A. until September, 1915, when he was appointed C.R.A. of the 14th Division, and was made a C.M.G. He was appointed B.G.R.A. of XIX Corps in February, 1917, and later that year he was wounded on 8 September. The diaries for this time are missing so there is no record of how he was wounded, but he later returned to the Corps until the end of the war and was made a C.B. in 1918. From 1920 he was C.R.A. of the 5th Division until he retired in 1922. He died in December, 1946.

Scott-Kerr, R.   M.V.O.   D.S.O.

G.O.C. 4th Guards Brigade   2nd Division

Brigadier-General

Wounded: 1 September, 1914

Robert Scott-Kerr was born in November, 1859. He entered the Army from the Militia, as a Second-Lieutenant in the 24th Foot, in March, 1879, and transferred to the Grenadier Guards in November, 1879. He served in the Zulu Campaign of 1879, being present at the Battle of Ulundi. In 1885 he was with the Sudan Expedition, served in the South African War from 1900 to 1902, and was awarded the D.S.O.[1] for his services in South Africa. He was made a M.V.O. in 1908. At the outbreak of the Great War Scott-Kerr, who was appointed to command the 4th Guards Brigade of the 2nd Division, was wounded in the retreat from Mons. The divisional history[2] records that, 'South of Villers-Cotterêts, in the Forêt Domanial de Retz, the Guards Brigade, before proceeding towards Thury, halted and called the roll. The day's fighting had been costly – 20 officers and 471 other ranks killed, wounded or missing. The Brigadier, General Scott-Kerr, was badly wounded in the thigh.' The official history[3] describes the event: 'Rear Guard at Villers-Cotterêts. Brigadier-General Scott-Kerr was severely wounded while leaving the Rond de la Reine. The Germans having brought up a machine gun which raked the broad main ride.' He was made a C.B. in 1914. He did not serve overseas again, but continued to command brigades of the Home Forces until 1918 when he went on half pay. In 1919 he was made a C.M.G. and retired from the Army. He died in November, 1942.

---

1 L.G. 27/9/01.   2 Wyrall. *History of the Second Division* Vol. 1.   3 Edmonds. *Military Operations France & Belgium 1914.*

Sergison-Brooke, B. N. D.S.O.   **Brigadier-General**
G.O.C. 2nd Guards Brigade Guards Division   **Gassed: 22 March, 1918**

Bertram Norman Sergison-Brooke was born in July, 1880. He was educated at Eton, and was commissioned into the Grenadier Guards in
August, 1899. He served in the South African War from 1899 to 1902, and
was employed with the Egyptian Army from 1908 to 1910. At the outbreak
of the Great War he was an Assistant Embarkation Officer at South-
ampton, but in September, 1914, he went to France as Staff-Captain of the
20th Infantry Brigade, and in November he became Brigade-Major of the
1st Guards Brigade. In 1915 he was awarded the D.S.O.[1] for his services in
the field, and in November he became G.S.O.2 of the 5th Army Corps.
From January, 1916, he commanded the 3rd Battalion Grenadier Guards
until he was wounded in September of that year at Lesboefs. He returned
to France in August, 1917, as Brigadier-General Commanding the 2nd
Guards Brigade and it was whilst holding this command that he was
wounded (gassed) on 22 March, 1918. The brigade was billeted in huts on
the Beaurains – Mercatel Road when the brigade diary[2] recorded that
'about this time [2.45 pm.] the Brigadier was forced to go to hospital
through gas poisoning. The effects of a gas shelling which took place a
week beforehand began to make themselves felt.' However, the diary also
records that he resumed command of the brigade on 25 April and
commanded it until March, 1919. He was made a C.M.G. in 1919. After
the war he commanded the 1st Guards Brigade at Aldershot until 1931
and then became Brigadier-General General Staff, Eastern Command,
India from 1931 to 1934. From 1934 to 1938 he was G.O.C. London
District. He was made a C.B. in 1935 and created a K.C.V.O. in 1937. He
retired from the Army in 1939, but was re-employed at the outbreak of
the Second World War. He served as G.O.C. London District from 1939
to 1942 and was with the British Red Cross Commission until 1945. He
was created a K.C.B. in 1942. Lieutenant-General Sir Bertram Sergison-
Brooke died in March, 1967.

---

1 L.G. 18/2/15.   2 PRO WO 95/1218.

Shaw, F. C. C.B.   **Brigadier-General**
G.O.C. 9th Brigade 3rd Division   **Wounded: 12 November, 1914**

Frederick Charles Shaw was born in July, 1861, and was educated at
Repton. He entered the Army from the Militia as a Lieutenant in the
Derbyshire Regiment (Sherwood Foresters), in January, 1882. He served
in the Egyptian War of 1882, and was in the South African War from 1892
to 1902. He held various Staff appointments with the 6th Division and
with Scottish Command between the wars. In 1913 he was made a C.B.

and appointed Commander of the 9th Brigade, Scottish Command. At the outbreak of the Great War he was promoted to Brigadier-General Commanding the 9th Brigade of the 3rd Division, and in November, 1914, when brigade headquarters was in an estaminet just to the east of Hooge, the brigade diary[1] records: '12 November, 1914. Brigadier-General Shaw, his Staff-Captain, Lt. Harter and Signalling Officer, Lt. Deakin, were wounded by a shell about 10 am.' He recovered from his wound in time to serve as G.O.C. 13th Division in Gallipoli from May to October, 1915. Promoted to the rank of Major-General for distinguished conduct in the field, for the remainder of the war he was Director Home Defence and then Chief of Staff Home Forces. He was created a K.C.B. in 1917, and from 1918 to 1920 he was G.O.C. in Chief of Forces in Ireland, and became a Privy Councillor (Ireland) in 1918. Lieutenant-General Rt. Hon. Sir Frederick Charles Shaw retired from the Army in 1920 and died in January, 1942.

---

1 PRO WO 95/1452.

Stevenson, E. H. D.S.O. — Brigadier-General
C. R. A. 29th Division — Wounded: 30 November, 1917

Edward Hall Stevenson was born in July, 1872, and was commissioned into the Royal Artillery in January, 1893. He served in the South African War from 1899 to 1902, was severely wounded in 1900 and was awarded the D.S.O.[1] From 1907 to 1910 he was Adjutant R.A. and then became Garrison Adjutant, Eastern Command. In October, 1915, he was a Lieutenant-Colonel R.A. until June, 1917, when he was appointed C.R.A. of the 30th Division then, in August, 1917, he became C.R.A. of the 29th Division. During the Battle of Cambrai, when the headquarters of 29th Division's Artillery was at Quentin Mill [south-west of Gonnelieu], the C.R.A's. diary[2] contains a 'Report on Operations of 30th November, 1917' which includes the following: 'On November 30th the enemy attacked on the front and the flanks of the 29th Division. During this action D.A.H.Q. was captured. Brigadier-General Stevenson (C.R.A. 29th Div.) who had been wounded [hit in the knee] by shell fire about 8 am. could not be moved from D.A.H.Q. and had to be left behind with a wounded orderly. As a result of a counter-attack by another division, General Stevenson and the orderly were rescued early on the morning of December 1st.' He was made a C.M.G. in 1918 and retired from the Army in October 1919. He became a Justice of the Peace in Wiltshire from 1920 to 1934, and died in January, 1964.

---

1 L.G. 27/9/01.   2 PRO WO 95/2287.

Stewart, A. E. D.S.O.   **Brigadier-General**

G.O.C. 3rd N.Z.(Rifle) Brigade   New Zealand Division   **Wounded: 17 July, 1918**

Alexander Edward Stewart was born in January, 1867. He commanded the 2nd Battalion New Zealand Rifles in Gallipoli and in France, and was awarded the D.S.O.[1] for his services in the field. As a Colonel, he took temporary command of the 2nd New Zealand Brigade in February, 1918, when Brigadier-General Hart (q.v.) was gassed. When Brigadier-General Fulton (q.v.) was mortally wounded in March, 1918, Stewart was appointed to command the 3rd New Zealand Brigade. On 17 July, 1918, the brigade diary[2] records that the brigade headquarters was at Sailly-au-Bois [on the Somme] when, 'Brigadier-General Stewart, D.S.O., was wounded by a sniper's bullet in the arm and thigh while going round the brigade front with an officer from the incoming brigade.' He was made a C.M.G. in 1919, retired from the Army in 1932 and died in May, 1940.

---

1 L.G. 1/1/17.   2 PRO WO 95/3707.

Stewart, D. B. D.S.O.   **Brigadier-General**

C.R.A. 66th Division   **Wounded: 28 August, 1917**

Davison Bruce Stewart was born in November, 1871, and was commissioned into the Royal Artillery in July, 1890. He was a Major in 1908, a Lieutenant-Colonel in 1915 and was awarded the D.S.O.[1] for distinguished service in the field. He was appointed C.R.A. of the 66th Division in June, 1917, and two months later, on 28 August, at St. Idesbalde the C.R.A.'s diary[2] of the division, records: '11.00 am. C.R.A. Brigadier-General D. B. Stewart, D.S.O., wounded in the forearm by shrapnel. Removed to C.C.S. 24.' He was replaced by Lt. Colonel A. C. Lowe, D.S.O., and three months later Brigadier-General Lowe (q.v.) was killed in action. Brigadier-General Stewart returned to active service in November, 1917, when he became C.R.A. of the 54th Division of the Egyptian Expeditionary Force, and served with this division until the end of the war. He retired from the Army in 1920 and died in August, 1958.

---

1 L.G. 3/6/16.   2 PRO WO 95/3123.

Stewart, J. S. D.S.O.   **Brigadier-General**

G.O.C. 3rd Canadian Division Artillery   **Wounded: 10 July, 1918**

John Smith Stewart was born at Brampton, Ontario, Canada, in May, 1877, and was educated at Brampton Public and High Schools, and was an Honours Graduate of Trinity University, Toronto, Canada. In the South African War, from 1900 to 1901, he served as a Private in Strathcona's Horse. From 1902 he practised dentistry at Lethbridge City, Alberta,

Canada, and raised and commanded the 25th Battery C.F.A. (Militia) in 1908. At the outbreak of the Great War he raised the 20th Battery C.F.A. for overseas service in November, 1914. He was appointed to command the 7th Brigade C.F.A. in March, 1915, and went to France in January, 1916, and was twice wounded. As O.C. 4th Brigade C.F.A. he was awarded the D.S.O.[1] for distinguished service in the field. In December, 1917, he was appointed Brigadier-General Commanding the Artillery of the 3rd Canadian Division. The Artillery diary[2] of the division records on 10 July, 1918: 'Basseux. Enemy artillery was more active than usual on our forward area. Some shells also fell in our rear area and a fragment from one of these wounded Brigadier-General J. S. Stewart, D.S.O., fortunately, his injury was not serious and he was able to continue his duties.' He was made a C.M.G. in 1918 and returned to Canada where he was an elected member of the Legislative Assembly for Lethbridge City. In 1957 he was made an LL.D h.c. by Alberta University. He died in August, 1970.

1 L.G. 1/1/17.   2 PRO WO 95/3847.

Stone, P. V. P. D.S.O.   **Brigadier-General**
G.O.C. 17th Brigade   24th Division   **Wounded: 11 April, 1917**

Percy Vere Powys Stone was born in September, 1883, and was educated at Blundell's and the R.M.C., Sandhurst. Commissioned into the Norfolk Regiment in January, 1902, he went straight to the South African War and joined the 2nd Battalion of his Regiment. He was seconded for service with the 2nd Northern Nigerian Regiment of the W.A.F.F. from 1905 to 1910, and served with the Munshi and Hadeija Expeditions. In 1914 he joined the 1st Battalion Norfolk Regiment in France and was wounded at Hill 60. He returned to command the battalion and was wounded near Arras in March, 1916. He was appointed Brigadier-General Commanding the 17th Infantry Brigade in February, 1917, and two months later his name appears on the Casualty List of the A & Q diary[1] of X Corps as wounded by a shell, but remaining at duty. This, his third wound, was received at the Battle of Arras. He continued to command the brigade until June, 1918, the year in which he was awarded the C.M.G. Brigadier-General Stone retired from the Army in 1920 and died in October, 1959.

1 PRO WO 95/608.

Sweny, W. F.   **Brigadier-General**
G.O.C. 61st Brigade   20th Division   **Wounded: 2 June, 1916**

William Frederick Sweny was born in June, 1873, and was educated at Wellington College, Trinity College School and the R.M.C., Kingston,

Canada. He was commissioned into the Royal Fusiliers in September, 1893. From 1902 to 1906 he served with the Egyptian Army, and from 1911 to 1913 he commanded the 2nd Battalion Mounted Infantry in South Africa. In 1914 he was attached to the Canadian Militia and was A.A.G. of the 1st Canadian Contingent at Valcartier, the camp 16 miles north-west of Quebec City, which was the place of mobilization of the Canadian Expeditionary Force. At the beginning of the Great War he commanded, successively, the 2nd Battalion South Lancs. Regiment, the 2nd East Yorks. Regiment and the 4th Battalion Royal Fusiliers. His appointment to command the 61st Infantry Brigade was effective from 13 November, 1915. On 2 June, 1916, his headquarters was at Poperinghe when the brigade diary[1] recorded: 'Brigadier-General Sweny, the Brigade-Major (Capt. Dashwood) and Capt. Beddington (acting Staff-Capt.) were all wounded by one shell in Ypres.' He rejoined his brigade six weeks later, on 18 July, but was evacuated on 24 July. This was the third time that he had been wounded during the war. He was awarded the D.S.O.[2] for distinguished service in the field. In March, 1917, he was appointed to command the 72nd Infantry Brigade, with which he served until December of that year when he returned to England on a six months exchange with Brigadier-General Morgan. In September, 1918, he commanded the 41st Infantry Brigade. He was made a C.M.G. and retired from the Army in August, 1920.

1 PRO WO 95/2123.   2 L.G. 1/1/17.

Thomson, N. A. C.M.G. D.S.O.

Brigadier-General

G.O.C. 44th Brigade 15th Division

Gassed: 2 August, 1918

Noel Arbuthnot Thomson was born in April, 1872, and was educated at Wellington College. He entered the Army from the Militia, as a Second Lieutenant in the Seaforth Highlanders, in April, 1892, and served in the Nile Expedition of 1898, being present at the Battle of Atbara, where he was wounded, and at the Battle of Khartoum. He served in the South African War from 1899 to 1902, where he commanded a mounted infantry brigade. In the Great War he commanded the 8th Battalion Seaforth Highlanders and was awarded the D.S.O.[1] He was appointed to command the 102nd Brigade in April, 1917, and held the command until May, 1918, when he was appointed to the 44th Brigade of the 15th Division. The 44th Brigade Operation Order of 1/8/18, issued at Oulchy-le-Château, stated that 'the 15th Division will attack on the north of the Bois d'Hartennes.' The brigade diary[2] records that the brigade attacked at 9 am. on 1 August and that on 2 August it was in position across the ridge between Chacrise and Ambrief. On 3 August they were 'relieved at 2 am by French 74th Regiment. Marched to Domiers, arriving at 4 pm.

Brigadier-General N. A. Thomson, C.M.G. D.S.O. [and others of his staff] admitted to hospital – Gas casualties.' The divisional history[3] states that, 'whilst retiring the Germans drenched the woods and cornfields, as well as the dug-outs and caves, for which they had no further use, with gas, from the effects of which many suffered before its presence was discovered. The officers commanding both the 44th and 45th Brigades and most of the staff of the latter suffered from this but managed to carry on until the Division was relieved that night.' Brigadier-General Thomson recovered from this, his second wound in the war, and returned to command his brigade until May, 1919. He was made a C.M.G. in 1918, retired from the Army in 1923 and died in October, 1959.

1 L.G. 3/6/16.　2 PRO WO 95/1936.　3 Stewart & Buchan. *The Fifteenth (Scottish) Division*

Thorpe, E. I. de S. D.S.O.

Brigadier-General

G.O.C. 107th Brigade   36th Division

Wounded: 13 September, 1918

Edward Ivan de Sausmarez Thorpe was born in September, 1871. He was commissioned into the Bedfordshire Regiment in February, 1892, and in 1897 served on operations in the Niger, including the Expedition to Egbon and Bida. In the Great War he commanded a battalion of the Border Regiment from June, 1915, to October, 1917, and then commanded a battalion of his own regiment, the Bedfordshire and Hertfordshire, until, in April, 1918, he was appointed to command the 152nd Brigade, but within a few weeks he was transferred to command the 107th Brigade. He was awarded the D.S.O.[1] as a Lieutenant-Colonel of the Bedfordshire Regiment for distinguished service in the field. In September, 1918, the 107th Brigade held a sector around Ploegsteert Wood. The brigade diary[2] for 13 September records that, 'Brigadier-General E. I. de S. Thorpe was wounded in the front line about 11 pm.' What it doesn't say is that he was shot by one of his own men! The divisional history[3] describes the event: 'General Thorpe, commanding the 107th Brigade, had gone up with General Brock (Div. B.G.R.A., who took command of 107th Brigade on 23 September.) on the night of the 13th to visit Hill 63 and the sentry posts north of it. Moving along Winter Trench he was suddenly fired at from point-blank range by one of his own men and severely wounded in the arm, his elbow being shot away. ----- He was able to return to the command of his regiment after the war, but with an arm well-nigh useless for life.' Brigadier-General Thorpe was made a C.M.G. in 1922, retired from the Army in 1922 and died in January, 1942.

1 L.G. 1/1/17.　2 PRO WO 95/2502.　3 *History of the 36th (Ulster) Division.*

Thwaites, W.   **Brigadier-General**
G.O.C. 141st Brigade   47th Division   **Wounded: 23 May, 1916**

William Thwaites was born in June, 1868, and was educated at Wellington College and the R.M.A., Woolwich. He was commissioned into the Royal Artillery in February, 1887, and served in the South African War from 1899 to 1900. In the Great War he served first as G.S.O.1 with the 47th Division from 1914 to 1915. In July, 1915, he was appointed to command the 141st Brigade, and on 23 May, 1916, when the brigade headquarters was at Cabaret Rouge [south-west of Lens], the brigade diary[1] records that Brigadier-General Thwaites was wounded at 11.30 pm. It also reported that he was wounded at 7.47 am. on the following day, but as command of the brigade had passed to Lieutenant-Colonel Tredennick at 12.30 am on the 24th he must have been wounded on 23 May. He returned to France with the rank of Major-General to command the 46th Division until September, 1918. At the end of the war he was Director of Military Intelligence at the War Office and was created a K.C.M.G. From 1927, when he was created a K.C.B., to 1929 he was G.O.C. in C. of the British Army of the Rhine. In 1931 he was promoted to the rank of General and he retired from the Army in 1933. General Sir William Thwaites died in June, 1947.

1 PRO WO 95/2734.

Tivey, E.   C.B.   D.S.O.   V.D.   **Brigadier-General**
G.O.C. 8th Australian Brigade   5th Australian Division   **Wounded: 22 October, 1917**

Edwin Tivey was born at Inglewood, Victoria, Australia, in September, 1866. He was a stockbroker of Toorak, Victoria, and he served in the South African War from 1900 to 1902. He was awarded the D.S.O.[1] in 1901, when he was a Captain with the Victorian Imperial Bushmen, 'for prompt action and brave defence, which prevented occupation of Phillipstown, Cape Colony.' From 1915 to 1918 he commanded the 8th Australian Infantry Brigade and was wounded on 22 October, 1917. The brigade had its headquarters on Westhoek Ridge when, as the brigade diary[2] records, 'The Brigade commander was wounded in the right arm at 11.30 am. whilst in the O. P., on the top of the Brigade H.Qrs. Pill Box. He walked to the dressing station. Lt. Col. Clark (30th Btn.) arrived at Brigade H.Qrs. before the General left, and took over temporary command of the brigade.' He was made a C.B. in 1917. From 1918 to 1919 he commanded the 5th Australian Division, and was made a C.M.G. His only son died in 1943 of wounds received at El Alamein. Major-General Tivey died in May, 1947.

1 L.G. 25/3/01.   2 PRO WO 95/3612.

Townshend, Sir C. V. F.   K.C.B.   D.S.O.   **Major-General**
G.O.C. 6th Indian Division   **P.O.W.: 29 April, 1916**

Charles Vere Ferrers Townshend was born in February, 1861, and entered the Royal Marines, as a Lieutenant in the Royal Marines Light Infantry, in February, 1881. He served in the Sudan Expedition of 1884 and 1885, and the Hunzar-Nagar Expedition of 1891 and 1892. In 1895 he commanded the garrison of Chitral during the siege of the fort, and was made a C.B. In 1896 he was with the Expedition to Dongola, and with the Nile Expeditions of 1897 and 1898. He was present at the Battles of Atbara and Khartoum and was awarded the D.S.O.[1] in recognition of services during the operations. He served in the South African War from 1899 to 1900. In 1900 he transferred to the Royal Fusiliers and in 1906 he again transferred to the King's Shropshire Light Infantry. He held brigade command in India from 1913 until April, 1915, when he took command of the 6th Division of the Indian Expeditionary Force 'D'. He commanded the division in Mesopotamia at the Battles of Kurna, Kut-el-Amara, Ctesiphon and at the Defence of Kut-el-Amara, where he was taken prisoner by the Turks. He was created a K.C.B. in 1916. Major-General Sir Charles Townshend resigned from the Army in 1920 and died in May, 1924.

---

1 L.G. 15/11/98.

Vincent, B.   C.M.G.   **Brigadier-General**
G.O.C. 35th Brigade   12th Division   **Gassed: 9 August, 1918**

Berkeley Vincent was born in December, 1871, and was educated at Wellington College and the R.M.A., Woolwich. He was commissioned into the Royal Artillery in July, 1891. During the Russo – Japanese War he was attached to the Japanese Army in Manchuria from 1904 to 1905. He held various Staff appointments until the outbreak of the Great War when he was a G.S.O.2 in India. He became G.S.O.2 with the Indian Army Corps of the B. E. F. until December, 1914, then became G.S.O.1 with the 37th Division until January, 1917, when he was appointed to command the 35th Infantry Brigade. He was made a C.M.G. in 1916. The divisional history[1] records that 'during the night of the 7th August [1918] the enemy carried out a heavy bombardment with gas shells, greatly interfering with the movements of the 35th Brigade to its assembly positions and causing several casualties, amongst whom, unfortunately, was the commander, Brigadier-General Vincent, who had to be removed to a field ambulance.' The diary of his own brigade makes no reference to what happened to him. However, he recovered and returned to his brigade on 19 September, 1918, and remained in command until April, 1919. He was made a C.B. in 1919. In 1922 he was Colonel Commandant of the

Military Forces in Iraq and took part in the operations in Kurdistan in 1923. In 1924 he was created a K.B.E. and took retired pay. Brigadier-General Sir Berkeley Vincent died in January, 1963.

1 Scott & Brumwell. *The History of the 12th Division in the Great War.*

Walker, H. A. C.M.G. D.S.O.

Brigadier-General

G.O.C. 16th Brigade 6th Division

Wounded: 16 October, 1918

Henry Alexander Walker was born in October, 1874, and entered the Army from the Militia, as a Second-Lieutenant in the Royal Fusiliers, in December, 1894. He saw service in East Africa from 1902 to 1904, in Nandi from 1905 to 1906, and again in East Africa from 1908 to 1910. He was a Brigade-Major in India when the Great War started and went to France as Brigade-Major of the Dehra Dun Brigade. He was awarded the D.S.O.[1] for distinguished service in the field. From June, 1915, to October, 1917, he was a G.S.O. with the 8th Division, then the 40th Division and finally the 65th Division (Home Forces). In October, 1917, he was appointed to command the 16th Brigade in France. He was made a C.M.G. in 1918. The brigade diary[2] records that on 16 October, 1918, the brigade headquarters was at Becquigny [S.W. of Le Cateau] when, 'shortly after dark the village of Becquigny was shelled and while standing behind the house occupied by Brigade H.Q. the B-G.C. – Brigadier-General H. A. Walker, C.M.G. D.S.O. – was unfortunately seriously wounded and lost his left arm.' After the war he served in Mesopotamia during the insurrection of 1920 and was made a C.B. From 1927 he was Inspector General of the King's African Rifles until he retired from the Army in 1931. He died in May, 1953.

1 L.G. 23/6/15.   2 PRO WO 95/1607.

Walker, H. B. C.B. D.S.O.

Major-General

G.O.C. 1st Australian Division

Wounded: 13 October, 1915

Harold Bridgwood Walker was born at Dilhorne, North Staffordshire, in April 1862, and was educated at Shrewsbury and Jesus College, Cambridge. He entered the Army from the Militia, as a Lieutenant in the D.C.L.I., in May, 1884, and transferred to the Border Regiment in July, 1904. He served with the Nile Expedition in 1884 and 1885 and was in the Sudan in 1885 and 1886 with the mounted infantry of the Frontier Force, being in action at Giniss. In operation on the north-west frontier of India in 1897 and 1898 he saw action with the Tirah Expeditionary Force. He served in the South African War from 1899 to 1902 and was awarded the D.S.O.[1] in recognition of his services during operations. At the outbreak of the Great War he was a G.S.O.1 in India until November, 1914, when he became a B.G.G.S. He commanded the New Zealand Brigade at the landing in Gallipoli and then took command of the 1st Australian Infantry Brigade until May, 1915, when he became commander of the 1st Australian Division. The Australian official history[2] records that 'on September 29 [1915], [he was] half-buried by a shell which burst in his dugout, and a fortnight later was severely wounded by a machine gun when visiting a loop-holed gallery in the cliff at the southern end of Silt Spur.' This second incident is recorded in the divisional diary[3] on 13 October, when the division's headquarters was at White Valley, Anzac: 'Major-General Walker was wounded in the morning whilst inspecting the trenches, and command of the Division devolved upon Brigadier-General J. T. Hobbs, Commanding Divisional Artillery.' He was made C.B. in 1915. Major-General Walker returned to command the division until July, 1918, when he was transferred to command the 48th Division in Italy, and in March, 1919, became G.O.C. in C. British Forces in Italy. He was created a K.C.B. in 1918 and a K.C.M.G. in 1919. After the war he commanded the South Midland Division, Southern Command, and from 1924 he was G.O.C. in C. Southern Command, India. Lieutenant-General Sir Harold Walker retired from the Army in 1928 and died in November, 1934.

1 L.G. 31/10/02. 2 *Official History of Australia in the War of 1914 – 1918*, Vol. 2.
3 PRO WO 95/4330.

Walshe, F. W. H. D.S.O.   **Brigadier-General**
C.R.A. 42nd Division   **Wounded: 26 September, 1917**

Frederick William Henry Walshe was born in July, 1872, and was educated at Bedford and the R.M.A., Woolwich. He was commissioned into the Royal Artillery in July, 1892. From 1908 to 1912 he held staff appointments in India, and at the outbreak of war in 1914 he was G.S.O.2 of the Lowland Division, Scottish Command. He then became G.S.O.1 of the 52nd Division and went with it to join the Mediterranean Expeditionary Force. He served in Gallipoli before returning, in October, 1916, to join the 42nd Division in France as C.R.A. He was awarded the D.S.O.[1] for his services. The C.R.A's. diary of the 42nd Division does not record the fact that he was wounded, but it does record his return from hospital on 12 October. However, the A. & Q.M.G. diary[2] of the 3rd Division lists Brigadier-General Walshe in its casualty list as wounded on 26 September, 1917. The divisional history[3] records that after the action on Frezenburg Ridge: 'When relieved on the 29 September batteries could barely muster more than 100 N.C.O's. and men. ------ Brigadier-General Walshe and Major Highet severely wounded.' Walshe served with the North Russian Expeditionary Force and with the British Military Mission to South Russia in 1919. He was made a C.M.G. in 1919. In 1928 he was made a C.B. and retired from the Army. He died in January, 1931.

1 L.G. 1/1/17.   2 PRO WO 95/1385.   3 Gibbon. *The 42nd Division 1914–18.*

Watson, C. F.   C.M.G.   D.S.O.   **Brigadier-General**
G.O.C. 180th Brigade   60th Division   **Wounded: 5 November, 1917**

Charles Frederic Watson was born in June, 1877, and was educated at Wellington College. He entered the Army from the Militia, as a Second-Lieutenant in the Royal West Surrey Regiment, in June, 1898. He served in the South African War from 1899 to 1902 and was awarded the D.S.O.[1] in recognition of his services. From the outbreak of the Great War until January, 1917, he was in France as a G.S.O. with the 2nd Division and then the 23rd Division, and was made a C.M.G. in 1916. He commanded a Service Battalion of his Regiment in April and May of 1917, and in July, 1917, went to join the Egyptian Expeditionary Force as a G.S.O.1 at G.H.Q. In September of that year he was appointed to command the 180th Brigade. In November, 1917, his H.Q. was south of Beersheba, Palestine, when, as the A & Q.M.G. diary[2] of the 60th Division records: 'November 5 1917. Brigadier-General Watson, Commanding 180th Infantry Brigade, slightly wounded by hostile bombs, (at duty).' He continued to command his brigade until December, 1920. He commanded the Rangoon Brigade from 1927, retired from the Army in 1931, and died in July, 1948.

1 L.G. 27/9/01.   2 PRO WO 95/4667.

Webb-Bowen, W. I.   D.S.O.   **Brigadier-General**
G.O.C. 8th Brigade   3rd Division   **Wounded: 2 April, 1918**

William Ince Webb-Bowen was born in July, 1882, and joined the Army from the Militia, as a Second-Lieutenant in the Middlesex Regiment, in July, 1901. He served in the South African War from 1899 to 1902. In Uganda, in 1911, he commanded troops in operations against tribes in the Northern Province. He was with the King's African Rifles and the West African Frontier Force until August, 1916, when he went to France as a Lieutenant-Colonel commanding various battalions, and was awarded the D.S.O.[1] In April, 1918, he was appointed to command the 8th Infantry Brigade, and the brigade diary[2] records his arrival and departure on the same day: 'Auchel. 2 April, 1918. Lt. Col. W. I. Webb-Bowen [he was a temporary Brigadier-General], D.S.O., Lincolnshire Regiment, arrived and assumed command of 8th Inf. Bde. During the afternoon he proceeded on a tour of the forward area accompanied by the Brigade-Major. He was wounded by hostile shell fire and evacuated to C.C.S.' This was the second time that he was wounded in the war. He returned to command the 11th Infantry Brigade in September, 1918. Brigadier-General Webb-Bowen retired from the Army in March, 1922.

1 L.G. 4/6/17.   2 PRO WO 95/1419.

White, The Hon. R. C.M.G. D.S.O.   Brigadier-General
G.O.C. 184th Brigade 61st Division   Wounded: 22 March, 1918

The Hon. Robert White, the fourth son of the 2nd Baron Annaly, was born in October, 1861, and was educated at Eton and Trinity College, Cambridge. He was commissioned into the Derbyshire Regiment in May, 1882, but transferred to the Royal Welsh Fusiliers in July, 1882. He served in the Nile Campaign from 1884 to 1885, and was a Magistrate in Bechuanaland in 1894. He retired in 1896, but was reinstated on half pay in 1898, and served on the Staff of the 6th Division in the South African War in 1900. In August, 1914, he raised and commanded the 10th Battalion Royal Fusiliers from the staff of the Stock Exchange. He was made a C.M.G. in 1916 and appointed to command the 184th Brigade. His D.S.O.[1] was awarded in 1918. On 22 March, 1918, his brigade headquarters was at Beauvois [west of St Quentin] when the brigade diary[2] records: 'The enemy attacked at 7 am. under a very heavy barrage and broke through at Vaux. The 2/5 Glosters repulsed the enemy attack and held the position east of Beauvois till 2 am. on the morning of the 23rd inst. During the attack Brigadier-General The Hon. R. White, C.M.G. D.S.O., was wounded at 10 pm. A general withdrawal to the line of the Somme Canal through Ham, Voyennes and Bethencourt was ordered. Billancourt. 23/3/18. Lt. Col. H. de R. Wetherall, D.S.O. M.C., took over command of the Brigade.' Three days later Wetherall was wounded. This was the second time that Brigadier-General White was wounded in the war. He was made a C.B. in 1919 and died in November, 1936.

1 L.G. 1/1/18.   2 PRO WO 95/3064.

Wigan, J. T. D.S.O.   Brigadier-General
G.O.C. 7th Mtd. Brigade Desert Mounted Corps   Wounded: 28 November, 1917

John Tyson Wigan was born at West Hartlepool in July, 1877, and was educated at Rugby. He entered the Army from the Militia, as a Second-Lieutenant in the 13th Hussars, in May, 1897. He served in the South African War with his regiment and was severely wounded. He transferred to the Territorial Forces in 1909. At Gallipoli where he commanded the Berkshire Yeomanry he was wounded at Suvla Bay. In 1916 he was awarded the D.S.O.[1] for distinguished service in the field. He was wounded again at Gaza in April, 1917. He was appointed Brigadier-General Commanding the 7th Mounted Brigade in July, 1917, and in November he was wounded for the third time in the war. His brigade's diary[2] reads: 'Tahata [Sinai]. Nov. 28th 1917. 0.800 hrs. Every available man of the 7th Mtd. Bde. pushed into the firing line. G.O.C. wounded.' The Australian official history[3] says: 'The struggle was still running strongly about Suffa, which, after twice changing hands, became No-Man's Land. The 7th Brigade at once became hotly engaged, and General Wigan was wounded.' He was made a C.M.G. in 1918 and a C.B. in 1919. He was Member of Parliament for the Abingdon Division of Berkshire from 1918 to 1921, High Sheriff of Essex in 1930, and died in November, 1952.

1 L.G. 3/6/16. 2 PRO WO 95/4475. 3 *Official History of Australia in the War of 1914 – 1918*, Vol. VII

Wiggin, E. A.   Brigadier-General
G.O.C. 1st Comp. Mtd. Brigade   2nd Mtd. Division   Wounded: 18 September, 1915

Edgar Askin Wiggin, the fourth son of Sir Henry Wiggin, 1st Bart. of Metchley Grange, Harborne, near Birmingham, was born in November, 1867. He was educated at Clifton College and the R.M.C., Sandhurst, and was commissioned into the 13th Hussars in August, 1885. He served in the South African War from 1899 to 1902, and was in command of a mounted infantry battalion from April, 1901. He retired from the his Regiment in 1907, but served with the Staffordshire Yeomanry from 1908 to 1914. At the outbreak of war he was appointed to command the 1st South Midland Mounted Brigade in Gallipoli and Egypt, and it was at Gallipoli that he was wounded. The brigade diary[1] records: 'Gallipoli, Nicholl Warren. 18/9/15. General, Brigade-Major and Staff-Captain visit trenches. Turks suddenly start "Straff" and General E. A. Wiggin gets wounded in the chest and is taken away to the clearing hospital. rifle bullet wound, but not dangerous.' In 1917 he served in Sinai and Palestine and was awarded the D.S.O.[2] He retired from the Army in April, 1919. In 1930 he was High Sheriff of Warwickshire. He died in November, 1939.

1 PRO WO 95/4293. 2 L.G. 1/1/17.

Williams, V. A. S.   Brigadier-General
G.O.C. 8th Canadian Brigade   3rd Canadian Division   Wounded and P.O.W.: 2 June, 1916

Victor Arthur Seymour Williams joined the North-West Mounted Police in 1886, but transferred to the School of Mounted Infantry, as a Lieutenant, in 1889. He served in the South African War with the 1st Canadian Mounted Infantry. From 1912 he held the post of Adjutant General, but when the Great War started Colonel Williams, as he then was, became Camp Commandant of Valcartier Camp, where the Canadian Contingents were formed. He commanded the first contingent to sail from Canada in September, 1914, and he led a detachment of 350 Canadians at the Lord Mayor's Show in London in November, 1914. In December, 1915, he was appointed Brigadier-General commanding the 8th Canadian Infantry Brigade. On the morning of 2 June, 1916, Brigadier-General Williams went from his headquarters, which was on the western edge of Zillebeke lake, with Major-General Mercer (q.v.) to the front line near Mount Sorrel. Whilst they were there the trenches were suddenly subjected to a tremendous bombardment. Williams was badly wounded in the face and was senseless when the enemy attacked at about 1 pm. He was captured and removed to hospital in Menin, a prisoner.[1] Brigadier-General Williams died in December, 1949.

1 Harwood Steele. *The Canadians in France 1915–1918*

Wilkinson, P. S. C.B. C.M.G.   **Major-General**
G.O.C. 50th Division   **Wounded: 13 April, 1917**

Percival Spearman Wilkinson was born in July, 1865, and was educated at Uppingham. He entered the Army from the Militia, as a Lieutenant in the Northumberland Fusiliers, in April, 1886. In 1897 and 1898 he served in West Africa on operations on the Niger, and in 1900 on operations in Ashanti, where he was wounded. He was Inspector General of the West African Frontier Force from 1909 to 1913 and then a Brigade Commander in India until October, 1914. He returned home and was made a C.B. and a C.M.G. He became G.O.C. Troops at Shorncliffe in June, 1915, and was appointed to command the 50th Division in France in August. Near Arras in 1917, he was wounded on Friday, 13 April. The divisional diary[1] records that: 'Major-General P. S. Wilkinson, C.B. C.M.G., while up in the line visiting Brigade H.Q. was hit with a piece of shell in the leg; causing considerable contusion.' He remained at duty and continued to command the division until March, 1918, when he left to become Inspector of Musketry. He was created a K.C.M.G. in 1917. After the war he commanded the 50th (Northumberland) Division, Northern Command. Major-General Sir Percival Wilkinson retired from the Army in 1923 and died in November, 1953.

1 PRO WO 95/2810.

Young, R. C.M.G. D.S.O.   **Brigadier-General**

G.O.C. 3rd N.Z. (Rifles) Brigade   New Zealand Division   Wounded: 9 August, 1917

Robert Young was born at Sunderland in January, 1877. He served in the Great War with the Wellington Battalion of the New Zealand Forces, taking part in the operations in Gallipoli. He was awarded the D.S.O.[1] for distinguished services in the field during the operations in the Dardanelles. In 1916 he was made a C.M.G. When Brigadier-General Johnston (q.v.) was killed in action on 7 August, 1917, Lieut. Colonel Young was appointed Brigadier-General Commanding 3rd N. Z. Brigade. The brigade diary[2] records his arrival: 'English Farm (Sht.36. T.27.b.4.9) 8 Aug., 1917. Lt. Col. R. Young, C.M.G. D.S.O., reported for duty and assumed command of the Brigade.' On the next day the diary reads: 'Brigade H.Q. shelled and shell blew up the cook house. Lt. Col. R. Young was dangerously wounded by a bullet when visiting the 3rd Battalion front.' He was made a C.B. in 1919. After the war he commanded the Canterbury Military District from 1919 to 1921, and then became Colonel Commandant of the New Zealand Staff Corps. In 1925 he was promoted to Major-General and became G.O.C. New Zealand Forces until 1931. From 1940 he commanded the New Zealand Home Guard. Major-General Young died in February, 1953.

---

1 L.G. 8/11/15.   2 PRO WO 95/3706.

APPENDIX 1

Cemeteries Where The Generals Are Buried or Commemorated

The map references refer to Michelin Maps 51, 52 or 53 overprinted 'Commonwealth War Cemeteries and Memorials.'

AUSTRALIA

Duntroon.
Near the Military College.
Bridges, Sir William Throsby. K.C.B. C.M.G. Major-General. G.O.C. 1st Australian Division.

BELGIUM

Brandhoek Military Cemetery. Vlamertinghe.
Map 51, Section Number 5, Reference Number 42.
Heyworth, Frederic James. C.B. D.S.O. Brigadier-General. G.O.C. 3rd Guards Brigade. Plot II, Row C, Grave 2.

Huts Cemetery, Dikkebus.
Map 51, Section Number 5, Reference Number 53.
Rawling, Cecil Godfrey. C.M.G, C.I.E. Brigadier-General. G.O.C. 62nd Brigade. Plot XII, Row C, Grave 20.

Lijssenthoek Military Cemetery, Poperinghe.
Map 51, Section Number 5, Reference Number 40.
Fitton, Hugh Gregory. C.B. D.S.O. Brigadier-General. G.O.C. 101st Brigade. Plot II, Row A, Grave 27.
Gordon, Alister Fraser. C.M.G. D.S.O. Brigadier-General. G.O.C. 153rd Brigade. Plot XIV, Row A, Grave 13.

Gore, Robert Clements. C.B. C.M.G. Brigadier-General. G.O.C. 101st Brigade. Plot XXVI, Row FF, Grave 1.

Mercer, Malcolm Smith. C.B. Major-General. G.O.C. 3rd Canadian Division. Plot VI, Row A, Grave 38.

Locre (Loker) Hospice Cemetery.
Map 51, Section Number 5, Reference Number 74.

Maclachlan, Ronald Campbell. D.S.O. Brigadier-General. G.O.C. 112th Brigade. Plot II, Row C, Grave 9.

Menin Gate Memorial to the Missing (Ypres).
Map 51, Section Number 5, Reference Number 32.

FitzClarence, Charles. V.C. Brigadier-General. G.O.C. 1st Guards Brigade.

Ploegsteert Memorial to the Missing.
Map 51, Section Number 5, Reference Number 96.

McMahon, Norman Reginald. D.S.O. Brigadier-General. O.C. 4th Royal Fusiliers.

Reninghelst New Military Cemetery.
Map 51, Section Number 5, Reference Number 51.

Gordon, Charles William Eric. Brigadier-General. G.O.C. 123rd Brigade. Plot III, Row D, Grave 16.

Tyne Cot Cemetery, Passchendaele.
Map 51, Section Number 6, Reference Number 4.

Riddell, James Foster. Brigadier-General. G.O.C. 149th Brigade. Plot XXXIV, Row H, Grave 14.

White House Cemetery, St Jan.
Map 51, Section Number 5, Reference Number 31.

Hasler, Julian. Brigadier-General. G.O.C. 11th Brigade. Plot III, Row A, Grave 5.

Ypres Reservoir Cemetery.
Map 51, Section Number 5, Reference Number 29.

Lowe, Arthur Cecil. C.M.G. D.S.O. Brigadier-General. C.R.A. 66th Division. Plot I, Row C, Grave 7.

Maxwell, Francis Aylmer. V.C. C.S.I. D.S.O. Brigadier-General. G.O.C. 27th Brigade. Plot I, Row A, Grave 37.

FRANCE

Albert Communal Cemetery Extension.
Map 53, Section Number 12, Reference Number 50.
Barnett-Barker [listed as Barker in Chapter 1], Randle. D.S.O.* Brigadier-General. G.O.C. 99th Brigade. Special Memorial Number 4.
Clifford, Henry Frederick Hugh. D.S.O. Brigadier-General. G.O.C. 149th Brigade. Plot I, Row L, Grave 1.

Anzac Cemetery, Sailly-sur-la-Lys.
Map 51, Section Number 15, Reference Number 14.
Broadwood, Robert George. C.B. Lieutenant-General. G.O.C. 57th Division. Plot II, Row 1, Grave 6.

Bailleul Communal Cemetery and Extension.
Map 51, Section Number 5, Reference Number 89.
Brown, Charles Henry Jeffries. D.S.O. Brigadier-General. G.O.C. 1st New Zealand Infantry Brigade. Plot III, Row C, Grave 265.
Johnston, Francis Earl. C.B. Brigadier-General. G.O.C. 3rd New Zealand (Rifle) Brigade. Plot III, Row C, Grave 260.

Beaumetz Cross Roads Cemetery, Beaumetz-les-Cambrai.
Map 53, Section Number 3, Reference Number 59.
Follett, Gilbert Burrell Spencer. D.S.O. M.V.O. Brigadier-General. G.O.C. 3rd Guards Brigade. Row F, Grave 24.

Berles New Military Cemetery, Berles-au-Bois.
Map 53, Section Number 2, Reference Number 108.
Lumsden, Frederick William. V.C. C.B. D.S.O.*** Brigadier-General. G.O.C. 14th Brigade. Plot III, Row D, Grave 1.

Béthune Town Cemetery.
Map 51, Section Number 14, Reference Number 19.
Matthews, Godfrey Estcourt. C.B. C.M.G. Brigadier-General. G.O.C. 198th Brigade. Plot III, Row K, Grave 56.
Nugent, George Colborne. M.V.O. Brigadier-General. G.O.C. 141st Brigade. Plot II, Row J, Grave 1.

Bucquoy Road Cemetery, Ficheux.
Map 53, Section Number 2, Reference Number 100.
Tanner, John Arthur. C.B. C.M.G. D.S.O. Brigadier-General. Chief Engineer VII Corps. Plot 1. Separate grave behind rows L and M.

Citadel New Military Cemetery, Fricourt.
Map 53, Section Number 12, Reference Number 58.
Phillpotts, Louis Murray. C.M.G. D.S.O. Brigadier-General. C.R.A. 24th Division. Plot II, Row A, Grave 1.

Cité Bonjean Military Cemetery, Armentières.
Map 51, Section Number 15, Reference Number 3.
Stewart, Charles Edward. C.M.G. Brigadier-General. G.O.C. 154th Brigade. Plot II, Row F, Grave 2.

Couin British Cemetery.
Map 53, Section Number 1, Reference Number 14.
Long, Walter. C.M.G. D.S.O. Brigadier-General. G.O.C. 56th Brigade. Plot VI, Row C, Grave 19.

Doullens Communal Cemetery Extension No.1.
Map 53, Section Number 1, Reference Number 11.
Fulton, Harry Townsend. C.M.G. D.S.O. Brigadier-General. G.O.C. 3rd New Zealand Brigade. Plot VI, Row A, Grave 4.

Duisans British Cemetery, Etrun.
Map 51, Section Number 14, Reference Number 37.
Lumsden, Alfred Forbes. D.S.O. Brigadier-General. G.O.C. 46th Brigade. Plot VI, Row G, Grave 33.

Estaires Communal Cemetery and Extension.
Map 51, Section Number 15, Reference Number 19.
Gough, John Edmond. V.C. K.C.B. C.M.G. Brigadier-General. C.O.S. 1st Army. Plot II, Row A, Grave 7.

Etaples Military Cemetery.
Map 51, Section Number 11, Reference Number 2.
Cox, Edgar William. D.S.O. Brigadier-General. B.G.G.S. (Intelligence). G.H.Q. France. Plot XXVIII, Row O, Grave 4.
MacInnes, Duncan, Sayre. C.M.G. D.S.O. Brigadier-General. Inspector of Mines G.H.Q. France. Plot XXVIII, Row L, Grave 2.

Five Points Cemetery, Lechelle.
Map 53, Section Number 13, Reference Number 2.
Sanders, Arthur Richard Careless. C.M.G. D.S.O.* Brigadier-General. G.O.C. 50th Brigade. Row D, Grave 6.

Gouy-en-Artois Communal Cemetery Extension.
Map 53, Section Number 1, Reference Number 8.
Bulkeley-Johnson, Charles Bulkeley. C.B. Brigadier-General. G.O.C. 8th Cavalry Brigade. Row A, Grave 30.

Guards' Cemetery, Windy Corner, Cuinchy.
Map 51, Section Number 15, Reference Number 45.
Hepburn-Stuart-Forbes-Trefusis, The Hon. John Frederick. D.S.O. Brigadier-General. G.O.C. 20th Brigade. Plot III, Row J, Grave 4.

Heilly Station Cemetery, Méricourt-l'Abbé
Map 53, Section Number 11, Reference Number 21.
Glasfurd, Duncan John. Brigadier-General. G.O.C. 12th Australian Brigade. Plot V, Row A, Grave 17.

Hermies British Cemetery.
Map 53, Section Number 3, Reference Number 70.
Bradford, Roland Boys, V.C. M.C. Brigadier-General. G.O.C. 186th Brigade. Row F, Grave 10.

Hervin Farm British Cemetery, St. Laurent-Blangy.
Map 51, Section Number 15, Reference Number 98.
Gosling, Charles. C.M.G. Brigadier-General. G.O.C. 10th Brigade. Row C, Grave 6.

La Kreule Military Cemetery, Hazebrouck.
Map 51, Section Number 4, Reference Number 28.
Taylor, Stuart Campbell. D.S.O. Brigadier-General. G.O.C. 93rd Brigade. Plot IV, Row C, Grave 1.

Lapugnoy Military Cemetery.
Map 51, Section Number 14, Reference Number 20.
East, Lionel William Pellew. C.M.G. D.S.O. Brigadier-General. C.H.A. XIII Corps. Plot X, Row D, Grave 1.
Shephard, Gordon Strachey. D.S.O. M.C. Brigadier-General. G.O.C. 1st R.F.C. Brigade. Plot VI, Row B, Grave 15.

Le Trou Aid Post Cemetery, Fleurbaix.
Map 51, Section Number 15, Reference Number 28.
Lowry-Cole, [listed as Cole in Chapter 1.] Arthur Willoughby George. C.B. D.S.O. Brigadier-General. G.O.C. 25th Brigade. Row E, Grave 22.

Lillers Communal Cemetery and Extension.
Map 51, Section Number 14, Reference Number 14.
Capper, Sir Thompson. K.C.M.G. C.B. D.S.O. Major-General. G.O.C. 7th
   Division. Grave in front of Plot II, Row A.

Loos Memorial to the Missing.
Map 51, Section Number 15, Reference Number 59.
Nickalls, Norman Tom. Brigadier-General. G.O.C. 63rd Brigade.
Thesiger, George Handcock. C.B. C.M.G. Major-General. G.O.C. 9th
   Division.

Louvencourt Military Cemetery.
Map 53, Section Number 1, Reference Number 20.
Prowse, Charles Bertie. D.S.O. Brigadier-General. G.O.C. 11th Brigade.
   Plot I, Row E, Grave 9.

Nedonchel Churchyard.
*Map 51, Section Number 14. No Reference Number. Nedonchel is N.W. of
   Bruay.*
Wormald, Frank. C.B. Brigadier-General. G.O.C. 5th Cavalry Brigade.
   His grave is at the west-end of the church.

Noeux-Les-Mines Communal Cemetery and Extension.
Map 53, Section Number 2, Reference Number 1.
Peake, Malcolm. C.M.G. Brigadier-General. B.G.R.A. I Corps. Plot I,
   Row U, Grave 2.
Wing, Frederick Drummond Vincent. C.B. Major-General. G.O.C. 12th
   Division. Plot I, Row K, Grave 15.

Péronne Communal Cemetery and Extension.
Map 53, Section Number 13, Reference Number 26.
Cape, George Augustus Stewart. C.M.G. Brigadier-General. C.R.A.,
   Acting G.O.C. 39th Division. Plot I, Row C, Grave 40.

Picquigny British Cemetery.
Map 52, Section Number 7, Reference Number 7.
Feetham, Edward. C.B. C.M.G. Major-General. G.O.C. 39th Division.
   Row F, Grave 10.

Pozières Memorial to the Missing.
Map 53, Section Number 12, Reference Number 25.
Forster, George Norman Bowes. C.M.G. D.S.O. Brigadier-General.
   G.O.C. 42nd Brigade.

Quéant Communal Cemetery, British Extension.
Map 53, Section Number 3, Reference Number 23.
Lipsett, Louis James. C.B. C.M.G. Major-General. G.O.C. 4th Division.
 Row F, Grave 1.

Soissons Memorial to the Missing.
Department of the Aisne.
Martin, Cuthbert Thomas. D.S.O. Brigadier-General. G.O.C. 151st
 Brigade.

Trois-Arbres Cemetery, Steenwerck.
Map 51, Section Number 5, Reference Number 102.
Holmes, William. C.M.G. D.S.O. V.D. Major-General. G.O.C. 4th Aus-
 tralian Division. Plot I, Row X, Grave 42.

Vadencourt British Cemetery, Maissemy.
Map 53, Section Number 13, Reference Number 35.
Kay, Sir William Algernon Ireland. C.M.G. D.S.O. Brigadier-General.
 G.O.C. 3rd Brigade. Plot III, Row B, Grave 4.

Vailly British Cemetery.
Department of the Aisne.
Findlay, Neil Douglas. C.B. Brigadier-General. C.R.A. 1st Division. Plot
 IV, Row A, Grave 53.

Varennes Military Cemetery.
Map 53, Section Number 11, Reference Number 4.
Bull, George. D.S.O. Brigadier-General. G.O.C. 8th Brigade. Plot I, Row
 C, Grave 31.
Howell, Philip. C.M.G. Brigadier-General. B.G.G.S. II Corps. Plot I, Row
 B, Grave 37.

Vendresse British Cemetery.
Department of the Aisne.
Husey, Ralph Hamer. D.S.O.* M.C. Brigadier-General. G.O.C. 25th
 Brigade. Plot II, Row G, Grave 1.

Villers-Faucon Communal Cemetery & Extension.
Map 53, Section Number 13, Reference Number19.
Ormsby, Vincent Alexander. C.B. Brigadier-General. G.O.C. 127th Brig-
 ade. Row D, Grave 41.

Warloy-Baillon Communal Cemetery & Extension.
Map 53, Section Number 11, Reference Number 8.
Ingouville-Williams, Edward Charles. C.B. D.S.O. Major-General. G.O.C.
  34th Division. Plot III, Row D, Grave 13.

GALLIPOLI

Green Hill Cemetery, Suvla.
Longford, Thomas, 5th Earl of. K.P. M.V.O. Brigadier-General. G.O.C.
  2nd Mounted Brigade. Special Memorial E. 3.

Helles Memorial.
Baldwin, Anthony Hugh. Brigadier-General. G.O.C. 38th Brigade.
Napier, Henry Edward. Brigadier-General. G.O.C. 88th Brigade.

Lala Baba Cemetery, Suvla.
Kenna, Paul Aloysius. V.C. D.S.O. Brigadier-General. G.O.C. 3rd
  Mounted Brigade. Plot II, Row A, Grave 1.

Twelve Tree Copse Cemetery, Helles.
Scott-Moncrieff, William. Brigadier-General. G.O.C. 156th Brigade.
  Special Memorial C. 132.

IRAQ

Amara War Cemetery.
Harvey, William James St.John. Brigadier-General. G.O.C. 19th Brigade.
  Plot I, Row C, Grave 21.

Baghdad (North Gate) War Cemetery.
Maude, Sir Frederick Stanley. K.C.B. C.M.G. D.S.O. Lieutenant-General.
  C. in C. Mesopotamian Expeditionary Force

Kut War Cemetery.
Hoghton, Frederick Aubrey. Brigadier-General. G.O.C. 17th Brigade.
  Row D, Grave 4.

MALTA

Pieta Military Cemetery.
Hodson, George Benjamin. C.B. D.S.O. Brigadier-General. G.O.C. 33rd
  Indian Army Brigade. Plot C, Row XII, Grave 1.

Lee, Noel. V.D. Brigadier-General. G.O.C. 127th Brigade. Row XXV, Grave 4.

SWITZERLAND

Berne (Schosshalde) Cemetery.
Granet, Edward John. C.B. Brigadier-General. C.R.A. 11th Division.

UNITED KINGDOM

Aldershot Military Cemetery, Hampshire
Lomax, Samuel Holt. C.B. Lieutenant-General. G.O.C. 1st Division.

Cheriton (St. Martin's) Churchyard, Kent.
Hamilton, Hubert Ion Wetherall. C.V.O. C.B. D.S.O. Major-General. G.O.C. 3rd Division.

Hollybrook Memorial. Hollybrook Cemetery, Chilworth Road, Shirley, Hampshire.
Ellershaw, Wilfrid. Brigadier-General.
Kitchener, Rt. Hon. Horatio Herbert. Earl of Khartoum. K.G. K.P. P.C. G.C.B. O.M. G.C.S.I. G.C.M.G. G.C.I.E. Field Marshal. Secretary of State for War.

APPENDIX 2

Abbreviations

A. & Q.M.G.	Adjutant & Quartermaster-General
A.A. & Q.M.G.	Assistant Adjutant & Quartermaster-General
A.A.G.	Assistant Adjutant-General
A.C. of O.	Assistant Commissary of Ordnance
A.D.C.	Aide-de-camp
A.D.M.S.	Assistant Director of Medical Services
A.D.S.	Assistant Director of Signals
A.D.V.S.	Assistant Director of Veterinary Services
A.G.H.	Australian General Hospital
A.I.F.	Australian Imperial Forces
A.M.	Albert Medal
A.M.S.	Army Medical Services
A.N.Z.A.C.	Australian and New Zealand Army Corps
A.O.D.	Army Ordnance Department
A.P.M.	Assistant Provost Marshal
A.Q.M.G.	Assistant Quarter Master General
B.A.	Bachelor of Arts
B.A.O.R.	British Army on (later of) the Rhine
B.E.F.	British Expeditionary Force
B.G.C.	Brigadier-General Commanding
B.G.G.S.	Brigadier-General General Staff
B.G.R.A.	Brigadier-General Commanding Royal Artillery
B-M	Brigade-Major
B.R.C.	British Red Cross
B.R.C.S.	British Red Cross Society
B.S.	Bachelor of Surgery
Bde.	Brigade
C.in C.	Commander in Chief
C.B.	Companion of the Order of the Bath
C.B.E.	Companion of the Order of the British Empire
C.C.S.	Casualty Clearing Station
C.E.	Chief Engineer

C.F.A.	Canadian Field Artillery
C.H.A.	Commander of Corps Heavy Artillery
C.I.E.	Commander Order of the Indian Empire
C.M.	Master of Surgery
C.M.G.	Companion of the Order of St. Michael & St. George
C.M.G.O.	Chief Machine-Gun Officer
C.O.	Commanding Officer
C.O.S.	Chief of Staff
C.R.A.	Commanding Royal Artillery
C.R.E.	Commanding Royal Engineers
C.S.I.	Companion of the Order of the Star of India
C.V.O.	Commander Royal Victorian Order
C.W.G.C.	Commonwealth War Graves Commission
Ch.B.	Bachelor of Surgery
Cmdr.	Commander
Cmnd.	Commanding
Comp.	Composite
D.A. & Q.M.G.	Deputy Adjutant & Quartermaster-General
D.A.A. & Q.M.G.	Deputy Assistant Adjutant & Quartermaster-General
D.A.A.G.	Deputy Assistant Adjutant-General
D.A.D.	Deputy Assistant Director
D.A.D.M.S.	Deputy Assistant Director of Medical Services
D.A.D.O.S.	Deputy Assistant Director of Ordnance Services
D.A.Q.M.G.	Deputy Assistant Quartermaster-General
D.C.L.	Doctor of Civil Law
D.C.L.I.	Duke of Cornwall's Light Infantry
D.C.M.	Distinguished Conduct Medal
D.D.M.S.	Deputy Director of Medical Services
D.H.	Douglas Haig
D.H.Q.	Divisional Headquarters
D.M.S.	Director of Medical Services
D.P.H.	Diploma in Public Health
D.S.O.	Distinguished Service Order
D.Sc.	Doctor of Science
E.A.	Enemy Aircraft
F.A.	Field Ambulance
F.R.C.P.	Fellow Royal College of Physicians
F.R.C.S.	Fellow Royal College of Surgeons
F.R.C.V.S.	Fellow Royal College of Veterinary Surgeons
F.R.G.S.	Fellow of the Royal Geographical Society
G.C.B.	Knight Grand Cross of the Order of the Bath
G.C.I.E.	Knight Grand Commander of the Indian Empire

G.C.M.G.	Knight Grand Cross of St. Michael & St. George
G.C.S.I.	Knight Grand Commander of the Star of India
G.H.Q.	General Headquarters
G.O.C.	General Officer Commanding
G.S.O.	General Staff Officer
G.S.O.1	General Staff Officer 1st Grade
G.S.O.2	General Staff Officer 2nd Grade
G.S.O.3	General Staff Officer 3rd Grade
H.A.	Heavy Artillery
h.c.	honoris causa
H.E.	High Explosive
H.L.I.	Highland Light Infantry
H.M.	His Majesty's
H.Q.	Headquarters
i/c	in command
Ind.	Indian
Inf.	Infantry
K.B.E.	Knight Commander Order of the British Empire
K.C.B.	Knight Commander Order of the Bath
K.C.I.E.	Knight Commander of the Indian Empire
K.C.M.G.	Knight Commander Order of St. Michael & St. George
K.C.S.I.	Knight Commander of the Star of India
K.C.V.O.	Knight Commander Royal Victorian Order
K.G.	Knight of the Order of the Garter
K.O.S.B.	King's Own Scottish Borderers
K.O.Y.L.I.	King's Own Yorkshire Light Infantry
K.P.	Knight of the Order of St. Patrick
K.R.R.C.	King's Royal Rifle Corps
K.S.L.I.	King's Shropshire Light Infantry
L.G.	Lieutenant-General
L-G.O.C.	Lieutenant-General Officer Commanding
L.H.	Light Horse
L.R.C.P.	Licentiate Royal College of Physicians
LL.D	Doctor of Laws
Lt. Col.	Lieutenant Colonel
M.A.	Master of Arts
M.B.	Bachelor of Medicine
M.C.	Military Cross
M.D.S.	Main Dressing Station
M.G.	Machine Gun
M.G.O.	Machine-Gun Officer
M.O.	Medical Officer
M.P.	Member of Parliament

M.R.C.S.	Member Royal College of Surgeons
M.V.O.	Member Royal Victorian Order
Mtd.	Mounted
N.C.O.	Non-Commissioned Officer
N.S.W.	New South Wales
N.Z.	New Zealand
O.B.E.	Officer Order of the British Empire
O.M.	Order of Merit
O.P.	Observation Post
O.R.	Other Rank
O.T.C.	Officers' Training Corps
P.C.	Privy Councillor
P.O.W.	Prisoner of War
PRO	Public Record Office
q.v.	quod vide (which see)
Q.V.O.	Queen Victoria's Own
R.A.	Royal Regiment of Artillery
R.A.F.	Royal Air Force
R.A.M.C.	Royal Army Medical Corps
R.A.P.	Regimental Aid Post
R.B.	Rifle Brigade
R.C.R.	Royal Canadian Regiment
R.E.	Corps of Royal Engineers
R.F.A.	Royal Field Artillery
R.G.A.	Royal Garrison Artillery
R.H.A.	Royal Horse Artillery
R.I.Rgt.	Royal Irish Regiment
R.M.A.	Royal Military Academy
R.M.C.	Royal Military College
R.M.L.I.	Royal Marine Light Infantry
R.N.	Royal Navy
R.N.V.R.	Royal Naval Volunteer Reserve
R.W.K.	Royal West Kent Regiment
R.War.R.	Royal Warwickshire Regiment
S.S.O.	Special Service Officer
S.W.B.	South Wales Borderers
T.D.	Territorial Decoration
T.A.	Territorial Army
T.F.	Territorial Force
T.M.	Trench Mortar
V.C.	Victoria Cross
V.D.	Volunteer Officers Decoration
W.A.F.F.	West African Frontier Force
W.W.	Walking Wounded

Bibliography

National War Histories

Aspinall-Oglander, C.F., *Official History. Military Operations in Gallipoli 1915 Vols. 1 & 2.* Heinemann 1929/32.

Bean, C.W. *Official History of Australia in the War of 1914–1918.* Angus & Robertson. Sydney. 1921–1932.

Becke, Major A.F. *Order of Battle.* H.M.S.O. 1935–1945.

Duguid, Colonel Fortescue. *Official History of the Canadian Forces in the Great War 1914–1919. Vol.1.* Pub. by the authority of the Minister of National Defence 1938.

Edmonds, Brigadier General Sir James E. *Official History. Military Operations in France and Belgium. 1914-1918.* Macmillan.

Moberley, Brigadier General. F.J. *Official History of the War, Military Operations Mesopotamia Campaign 1914–1918.* H.M.S.O. 1927.

Nicholson, Colonel G.W.L. *Canadian Expeditionary Force 1914–1919.* Roger Duhamel, Queen's Printer & Controller of Stationery, Ottawa 1962.

Steele, Captain Harwood. *The Canadians in France 1915–1918.* Fisher Unwin 1920.

Stewart, Colonel H. *Official History of New Zealand's Effort in the Great War, Vol.3. France.* Whitcombe & Tombs. N.Z. 1921.

Various Authorities. *Canada in the Great World War.* United Publishers of Canada Ltd., Toronto 1919.

Newspapers, Journals and Reference Documents

AIR 1. Air Historical Branch Records Series 1. 1862–1959. Public Record Office, Kew..

Army Lists and Supplements, Quarterly & Monthly.

CAB 45. Cabinet Office Historical Section Official War Histories: Correspondence and Papers. Public Record Office, Kew.

Cemetery Registers. Commonwealth War Graves Commission. Maidenhead.

Gun Fire. A. J. Peacock (Editor). A journal of the Northern Branch of the Western Front Association. Issued from 126 Holgate Road, York.

Harrow Memorials of the Great War, Vols. I to V. Harrow School Publication. Printed by Philip Lee Warner.

Journal of the Royal United Services Institute 1933.

List of Etonians who fought in the Great War 1914–1919. Eton College.

Liverpool Daily Post & Mercury.

Officers Died in the Great War 1914–1919. Hayward & Son, Polstead, Suffolk. 1988.

Our Heroes. Supplement to Irish Life 1914–16. Reprinted by London Stamp Exchange.

Probate Registers 1914–1920.

Royal Artillery Commemoration Book. Pub. G. Bell & Sons 1920.

Stand To! The Journal of the Western Front Association.

The Army Quarterly October 1939.

The Bond of Sacrifice , Vol. 1 & 2. Colonel L. A. Clutterbuck, (Military Editor.) The Anglo-African Publishing Contractors.

The Crosby Herald.

The Liddle Collection , Brotherton Library, Leeds University.

The Liverpool Echo.

The London Gazette .

The Roll of Honour Vol.1. The Marquis de Ruvigny. The Standard Art Book Co., Ltd.

The Times.

The War Illustrated. J. A. Hammerton (Editor).

The V.C. and D.S.O. Sir O'Moore Creagh & E.M. Humphries. The Standard Art Book Co. Ltd, London.

WO 95. War Diaries 1914–1922. Public Record Office, Kew.

WO 105. The Roberts Papers. Public Record Office, Kew.

WO 329. The Medal Rolls for the First World War. Public Record Office, Kew.

Books

Anon. *The 54th Infantry Brigade 1914–1918.* Gale & Polden, Aldershot.

Atkinson, C.T. *The Seventh Division.* 1914–1918. John Murray 1927.

Atkinson, C.T. *The Devonshire Regiment 1914–18* . Eland Bros, Exeter, 1926.

Atteridge, A.H. *The History of the 17th Division.* Robert Maclehose & Co. 1929.

Ballard, Brig-Gen. C. *Smith-Dorrien.* Constable & Co. Ltd. 1931.

Barnes, B.S. *This Righteous War* Richard Netherwood Ltd. Fulston Barn, New Mill, Huddersfield 1990.

Barrow, General Sir George. *The Life of General Sir Charles Carmichael Munro.* Hutchinson & Co. 1931.

Berkley, R. *The Rifle Brigade in The War of 1914–1918.* Pub. The Rifle Brigade Club 1927.

Birdwood. *Khaki and Gown.* Ward Locke 1941.

Blaxland, Gregory. *Amiens 1918.* Frederick Muller 1968.

Blumberg, General Sir H. E. *Britain's Sea Soldiers.*

Bond, Brian. Editor. *Staff Officer. The Diaries of Lord Moyne 1914–1918.* Leo Cooper 1987.

Bourne, J.M. *Britain and the Great War.* Edward Arnold 1989.

Braddon, R. *The Siege.* Jonathan Cape, London 1969.

Brewsher, Major F.W. *History of the 51st (Highland) Division.* William Blackwood & Sons. 1929.

Brice, Beatrix. *The Battle Book of Ypres.* John Murray 1927.

Bridges, Lieutenant General Sir Tom. *Alarms and Excursions.* Longmans Green & Co. 1938.

Buckley, Francis. *Q.6.A. & Other Places.* Spotiswood, Blantyre & Co. 1920.

Callwell, Major General Sir C.E. *Life of Sir Stanley Maude.* Constable 1920.

Carton de Wiart, Lt-Gen. Sir Adrian. *Happy Odyssey.* Jonathan Cape 1950.

Chapman, Guy. *A Passionate Prodigality.* Ivor Nicholson & Watson 1933.

Charlton, Peter. *Pozières 1916.* Leo Cooper/Secker & Warburg 1986.

Charteris, Brigadier General John. *At G.H.Q.* Cassell 1931.

Clark, Alan *The Donkeys.* Hutchinson, London 1961.

Cooper, Bryan. *The 10th (Irish) Division in Gallipoli.* Herbert Jenkins Ltd. 1918.

Cooper, Duff. *Haig.* Faber & Faber. 1936.

Craster, J.M. *Fifteen Rounds A Minute. The Grenadier Guards At War 1914.*

Croft, W. D. *Three Years with the 9th Division.*

Cutlack, F.M. Editor. *War Letters of General Monash.* Angus & Robertson Ltd., Sydney, 1935.

Davson, H.M. Lt.Col. *Memoirs of the Great War.* Gale & Polden, Aldershot, 1964.

Denton, Kit. *Australians at War. Gallipoli–One Long Grave.* Time Life Books. Sydney 1986.

Douglas, Sholto. *Years of Combat.* Collins 1963.

Doyle, Sir A.C. *The British Campaign in France and Flanders. Vols. 1 to 6.* Hodder & Stoughton 1916–1920.

Doyle, Sir A.C. *The British Campaigns in Europe.* J. Bles, London 1928.

Ewing, J. *History of the 9th (Scottish) Division.* John Murry 1921.

Falls, C. *History of the 36th (Ulster) Division.* M'Caw Stevenson & Orr 1922.

Farndale, General Sir Martin, *History of the Royal Regiment of Artillery, Western Front 1914–18.*

Farrar-Hockley, Anthony. *Death of An Army.* Arthur Baker Ltd. 1967.

Farrell, *51st (Highland) Division War Sketches .* Jack, Edinburgh, 1970.

G.S.O. *G.H.Q.* Philip Allan & Co. 1920.

Gibbons. *The 42nd Division 1914–18.* Country Life 1920.

Gillon, S. *The Story of the 29th Division.* Nelson 1925.

Gliddon, Gerald. *When the Barrage Lifts.* Gliddon Books 1987.

Gough, General. *The Fifth Army.* Hodder & Stoughton 1931.

Griffiths, Wyn. *Up To Mametz.* Gliddon Books 1988.

Hamilton, Lord Ernest. *The First Seven Divisions.* Hurst & Blackett Ltd. 1916.

Hamilton, Lt.Col. The Hon. Ralph. *The War Diary of the Master of Belhaven.* John Murray 1924.

Hammerton, Sir John. Editor. *The Great War. I Was There! Vols. 1 to.3.* Amalgamated Press 1938–39.

Head, Lt. Col. C.O., *A Glance at Gallipoli .* Eyre & Spotiswood, London 1931.

Headlam, C. *The Guards Division in the Great War.* John Murray 1924.

Holmes, Richard. *The Little Field Marshal* Jonathan Cape, London 1981.

James, Robert Rhodes. *Gallipoli.* Batsford 1965.

Jerrold, Douglas. *The Royal Naval Division.* Hutchinson 1923.

Liddell Hart, B.H. *The Real War 1914–1918* Faber & Faber, London 1930.

Lloyd George, D. *War Memoirs* Odhams Press, London 1935.

Lumley, L.R. *The Eleventh Hussars .* The Royal United Services Institution 1936.

Macmunn. *Behind the Scenes in Many Wars.* John Murray London 1930.

Magnus, Philip. *Kitchener. Portrait of an Imperialist.* John Murray 1958.

Marden, Major General T.O. *A Short History of the 6th Division.* Hugh Rees 1920.

Marshall, Lieutenant General Sir William. *Memories of Four Fronts.* Ernest Benn 1929.

Montgomery, B.L. *The Memoirs of Field Marshal The Viscount Montgomery* Collins, London 1958.

Maude, A.H. Editor. *The History of the 47th Division.* Amalgamated Press 1922.

Mitchell, F. *Tank Warfare .* Nelson, London 1933.

Mockler-Ferryman, Lt. Col. A.F. (Editor) *The Oxfordshire & Buckinghamshire Light Infantry Chronicle.* Eyre & Spottiswoode.

Murphy, C.C.R. *History of the Suffolk Regiment.* Hutchinson 1928.

Nevinson, Henry W. *The Dardanelles Campaign.* Nisbet & Co. Ltd. 1918.

Nichols, G.H.F. *The 18th Division in the Great War.* Blackwood 1922.

Nicholson, Colonel W.N. *Behind the Lines.* Jonathan Cape 1939.

Nicholls, Jonathan. *Cheerful Sacrifice* . Leo Cooper, London 1990.

O'Neill, H.C. *The Royal Fusiliers in the Great War.* Heinemann 1922.

Priestly, Major R.E. *Breaking the Hindenburg Line. The Story of the 46th Division.* Fisher & Unwin 1919.

Sandes, Major E.W.C. *In Kut and Captivity.* John Murray 1920.

Sandilands, Lt. Col. H. R. *The 23rd Division 1914–1919.* William Blackwood 1925.

Scott & Brumwell. *The History of the 12th Division in the Great War.* Nisbet 1923.

Shakespeare, J. *The Thirty Fourth Division 1915–1919.* Witherby 1921.

Singleton-Gates, Peter. *General Lord Freyberg V.C.* Michael Joseph 1963.

Spender, J.A. & Asquith, Cyril. *The Life of Lord Oxford & Asquith.* Hutchinson 1932.

Spring, Howard. *In the Meantime.* Constable 1942.

Stacke, Capt. H. *The Worcestershire Regiment in the Great War.* Cheshire & Sons. Kidderminster, 1929.

Stewart and Buchan. *The Fifteenth (Scottish) Division 1914–1919.* William Blackwood 1926.

Stewart, Captain P.F. *History of the XII Royal Lancers 1715–1945.* Oxford University Press 1950.

Swinton, Major-General Sir Ernest. *Eyewitness.* Hodder & Stoughton 1932.

Swinton, Major-General Sir Ernest. Editor. *Twenty Years After, 3 Vols.* Newnes 1936–38.

Terraine, John. *The Smoke and the Fire* Sidgwick & Jackson, London 1980.

Thompson, R.A. *The Fifty-Second (Lowland) Division 1914–1918.* Maclehose Jackson & Co. 1923.

Thornton, Lt.Col. L.H. & Fraser, Pamela. *The Congreves, Father and Son.* John Murray 1930.

Travers, Tim. *The Killing Ground.* Unwin Hyman 1987. (paperback)

Walker, R.W. *Officers Died at Gallipoli. To What End Did They Die?* Walker, Worcester, 1985.

Warner, Philip. *Field Marshal Earl Haig.* The Bodley Head 1991.

Wheatley, Dennis. *The Time Has Come.* Hutchinson 1978.

Williams, Jeffery. *Byng of Vimy.* Leo Cooper in Asc. with Secker & Warburg 1983.

Willoughby, Colonel. Editor. *Rifle Brigade Chronicles.* John Bale Sons & Danielsson.

Wilson, H.W. & Hammerton J.A. Editors. *The Great War. 13 Vols.* Amalgamated Press 1914–1918.

Wyrall, E. *History of the 19th Division 1914–1918.* Arnold 1932.

Wyrall, E. *The History of the Second Division.* Thomas Nelson 1921.

Wyrall, E. *The History of the 50th Division.* Lund Humphries 1939.

Wyrall, E. *The Somerset Light Infantry 1914–1919.* Methuen 1927.

Wyrall, E. *The Gloucestershire Regiment in the War 1914–1918.* Methuen 1931.